W9-AHH-764

COLLEGE COOKBOOK

KNACK

COLLEGE COOKBOOK

Dorm Eating and Apartment Feasting

David Poran

Photographs by Viktor Budnik

Guilford, Connecticut
An imprint of Globe Pequot Press

To buy books in quantity for corporate use or incentives, call **(800) 962–0973** or e-mail **premiums@GlobePequot.com.**

KNACK®
MAKE IT EASY

Copyright © 2010 by Morris Book Publishing, LLC

ALL RIGHTS RESERVED. No part of this book may be reproduced or transmitted in any form by any means, electronic or mechanical, including photocopying and recording, or by any information storage and retrieval system, except as may be expressly permitted in writing from the publisher. Requests for permission should be addressed to Globe Pequot Press, Attn: Rights and Permissions Department, P.O. Box 480, Guilford, CT 06437.

Knack is a registered trademark of Morris Book Publishing, LLC, and is used with express permission.

Editorial Director: Cynthia Hughes
Editor: Katie Benoit
Project Editor: Tracee Williams
Cover Design: Paul Beatrice, Bret Kerr
Interior Design: Paul Beatrice
Layout: Joanna Beyer
Cover Photos by: Viktor Budnik
Interior Photos by: Viktor Budnik

Library of Congress Cataloging-in-Publication Data is available on file.

ISBN 978-1-59921- 865-6

The following manufacturers/names appearing in *Knack College Cookbook* are trademarks:
Botox®, Cheez-Whiz®, Chavrie®, Cream of Wheat®, Crock-Pot®, Crystal®, Grape-Nuts®, Hormel®, McCann's Irish Oatmeal™, Nance's®, Nutella®, Robot Coupe®, Skim Plus™, Tabasco®, The Laughing Cow®, Velveeta®, Wheatena®, Wild Rooster®, Wondra Flour®

Printed in China

10 9 8 7 6 5 4 3 2 1

The information in this book is true and complete to the best of our knowledge. All recommendations are made without guarantee on the part of the author or Globe Pequot Press. The author and Globe Pequot Press disclaim any liability in connection with the use of this information.

Dedication

I would like to dedicate this book to my old college crew; memories of your friendship and antics brought many smiles to my face as I wrote this book.

Acknowledgments

Thanks to my incredible wife, Leslie, who encourages me to follow, and who also fulfills my dreams. Thanks to my wonderful family who always believed in me, and gently pushed me into culinary school. And thanks to the many hard working cooks, chefs, dishwashers, waiters, and students who have made my time in kitchens so satisfying. Rock on, all of you.

Photographer Acknowledgments

I would like to say thanks to all at Knack. Thanks to my crew of gifted and talented people—Claire Stancer, a wonderful and talented food stylist who created beautiful food to photograph, Celeste for her perfect shopping and props for all of the recipes and set ups. To Sespe Creek Organics for the wonderful oranges and other items that were prepared for the shoot. Special thanks to the organic farmers markets in Thousand Oaks, CA; Trader Joes (Westlake Village, CA); Whole Foods (Thousand Oaks, CA); and Jimenez Family Organic Farms (Santa Ynez, CA).

Cheers~Viktor Budnik

CONTENTS

INTRODUCTION

Welcome to your new life! You've made it out of high school and are now in the annals of higher learning, college. You are about to have some of the best years of your life, and you should enjoy them. You are here on a mission of knowledge, and learning how to eat well can be an added benefit of your time away at school. Realize that all the choices you make now as a young adult will transfer into your adult life. Many habits that you develop in college will stay with you forever, and your eating habits may be one of the most important. College life can be both incredibly fun and incredibly hectic at the same time. The rigors of dorm rooms, cafeterias, classrooms, and late nights can wreak havoc on your eating habits; many new college students fall victim to the infamous "freshman fifteen," which refers to the average amount of pounds a new student puts on in the first year. These days, it can be more like the freshman thirty, so be careful with your choices.

Learn to Balance

Besides studying, partying, and sleeping, you'll need to do a bit of eating while you're in school, and that, as with everything else, comes with its own set of challenges. You will have to learn how to manage the daily living tasks of college life while also injecting doses of healthy foods to keep yourself primed and ready for your studies.

The great news is that eating in college does not have to be all about late-night snacks, unhealthy fast food, and cafeteria mystery meat, but instead can be an exciting, healthy, and satisfying experience. These days, with the explosion of food television, celebrity chefs, and literally hundreds of cooking schools churning out thousands of wannabe chefs each year, food consciousness has risen to a new level. Never before has there been so much exposure to so many different cuisines and styles of foods. Foods with intense flavors, such as Thai, Vietnamese, and Mexican,

are now commonplace, and this is of great benefit to you, the adventurous college student. The recipes you are about to explore manage to delve into all of these cuisines and many others, while still delivering comfort-food favorites and "Mom-style" classics. There is no lack of flavor or bland foods here, just fun, delicious foods that will leave you satisfied and full of newfound culinary confidence. This book aims to arm you with the tools you need to earn an A+ in college food experiences.

Healthy Choices

Part of your experience in college is learning to make healthy choices, and this book will tell you how to make your everyday foods better for you. The benefits of lean protein, soy, tofu, fiber, and vegetables will hopefully shine through (not to mention that these foods are just plain good to eat!). With the basics explained in this book, you should be able to truly craft excellent meals all by yourself.

We know you're tight on money and you don't have all the time in the world, so many of these recipes rely on wonderfully stocked supermarkets and make use of today's convenience items. This allows you to make intelligent, budget-friendly shortcuts and maximize the small cooking space you have during your dorm years, while preparing you for the more advanced cooking you will experience in apartment living and beyond.

Recipes for the Dorm and the Apartment

The book is divided into three sections: general information and nutrition, dorm room recipes, and apartment recipes. The dorm room section includes recipes tailored specifically to the cooking equipment allowed in most dorm rooms (read: microwaves), while the apartment section includes recipes designed for those students who, as they move forward, wind up in apartments with full kitchens and have more cooking gear to play with.

In the dorm room chapters, you will learn how to be a culinary ace with your "microfridge," and in the apartment section, you will learn how to sauté and roast like a champ. We have also provided recipe variations throughout, regardless of section, that provide in-depth alternate cooking methods so you can utilize the same recipes once you have a full kitchen to work in.

On Your Way to Culinary Honors

Consider this cookbook to be like an extracurricular class, but without the tests! You will learn how to set up your mini–kitchen space for optimum efficiency and make amazing breakfasts in the blink of an eye, allowing for a little more shut-eye. You will be indoctrinated into the world of entree salads and homemade (or dorm-made) salad dressings that are far healthier and more satisfying than the bottled stuff out there. Make desserts, stews, soups, side dishes, and "real deal" entrees that will surprise you and your friends—and will probably make you some new friends along the way. Jazz up favorites like burgers and Caesar salads, drum up fresh pizza dough, and work wonders with leftovers.

We won't try to dissuade you from enjoying the typical rites of passage, such as cold pizza for breakfast and pancakes and bacon at 3 a.m. at the local diner. Heck, you can (and should) enjoy the occasional chili dog for breakfast right before you go to bed after a long night of partying. But you will now be able to temper these choices with some incredible options from this book, including the fantastic Take-Out Revisited chapter, which will show you how to make healthier and cheaper versions of your favorite fast foods and become a hero to your friends in the process. Pizza, Chinese, and Mexican takeout is now only a few steps away in your own kitchen.

You will also learn the history and origin of many foods and recipes, which will provide you not only with knowledge but with an endless supply of cocktail party banter in years to come. So sit down, dig in, and get studying. We promise this will be much more fun than Intro to Biochem!

Cooking 101

Allow this book to be a primer—a "101" of sorts—that serves as a great introduction to the culinary possibilities that are only beginning with your college career. Open the door to a lifelong love affair with food, cooking, and healthy eating that will not only be good for you but will set the stage for years of culinary excitement and continued learning. Hopefully, after mastering the recipes and techniques in this book, you will seek out more culinary knowledge. Search the Web, go to the library and read cookbooks, watch food TV, and maybe even take a class or two when you have the time. And, for goodness sakes, play. Inventions are made by fearless people who are not afraid to mix rosemary with strawberries or chocolate with chili. What's the worse thing that can happen? Follow your culinary instincts as you develop them and have a great time in the kitchen. It really is fun!

One last thing: This should by no means be the last cookbook you read, but it makes a great first one. This book is certainly not limited to the college campus. While it is tailored to college living, it can provide useful information and recipes for years after. Don't forget to dust it off every once in a while long after college has passed, and smile when you think of that crazy night way back when, and that killer breakfast you made for your crew the next morning (or afternoon!). Enjoy, eat well, have fun, and get A's!

APPROVED APPLIANCES
Check your dorm's rules before adding any appliances to your room

For your safety and the safety of your dorm mates, only certain cooking appliances are permitted in your room. Your school undoubtedly has provided you with a list of approved appliances, and it is highly recommended that you abide by this list to avoid any unfortunate events, which could cause you to loose privileges, or even worse, injure yourself or someone else. The key thing to remember is: no open heat sources!

That means no toaster ovens, hot plates, deep-fryers, electric frying pans, or sandwich presses. There are other appliances that also fall into the verboten category, so choose wisely.

Of course the most widely used and popular item in dorm-room cookery is the microwave oven. Many schools have a wattage cap on these ovens, and it is usually about 700 watts. Many recipes in the first chapters of this book assume that

The Nuker

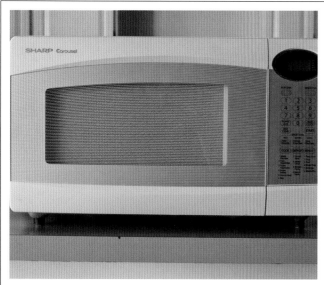

- If you are physics major, you may already understand the principle behind the microwave oven. Microwaves cook food by heating the water molecules in food and, in turn, heating the food.

- This is why dry foods such as pasta and rice will not

- cook without the addition of water.

- Most foods in microwaves heat unevenly, so turning and stirring are recommended throughout the process.

- Beware: Microwaves can burn you just like any oven.

The Microfridge

- Microfridges are the unit of choice at most colleges these days. They can come with or without a built-in freezer unit.

- The freezer option makes the unit more versatile, with ice always at the ready.

- The downside to the microfridge is that if one item breaks down, such as the microwave, you lose the whole unit while it is being serviced.

- Microfridges tend to be very energy efficient, so you can do your part for the environment.

this is the only cooking appliance you have. Your school may also suggest a "microfridge" which is a combination microwave oven and small refrigerator and freezer. Microfridges are compact, energy efficient, multipurpose, and generally dependable.

Remember that microwaves vary greatly in power and size, so some recipes in this book may need to be tweaked, cut in half, or otherwise adjusted to work in your particular environment. You can figure this out. Remember: You are a college student!

The other incredibly important, and some would say indispensible, dorm-room appliance is the coffeemaker. This handy device makes waking up, staying up, and those long study sessions a lot more manageable. Keep in mind there are restrictions on these appliances, as well. Almost all campuses require that your coffeemaker is thermostatically controlled. This is so the heating element has less chance of becoming an open heat source and inadvertently starting a fire.

Must Have Java

- Coffeemakers are also subject to restrictions. Remember: They must be thermostatically controlled.

- Always use the recommended size filter or invest in a "gold" screen filter, which needs to be cleaned but is better for the environment.

- Unplug your coffeemaker when not in use to be on the safe side.

- Coffeemakers can be a versatile tool. You can use them to make instant soups or to get hot water for tea or oatmeal. Coffee water is heated to just under the boiling point.

Getting Away with It

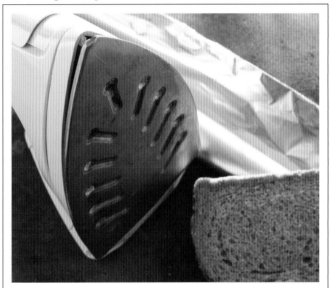

- The clothes iron can be, with some practice, used as a cooking appliance. Check to make sure irons are allowed in your dorm. Most schools allow them.

- The best application for an iron is making grilled or "toasted" sandwiches.

- Buttering the outside of the bread and using heavy aluminum foil will help you achieve your sandwich grilling goals.

- Take a peek at the sandwich in 30-second intervals to make sure you do not burn the bread or butter.

SMALL WARES
Many of these handy little tools share multiple uses and are worth seeking out

Small wares are defined as cooking tools that do not have power and are not knives. The world of kitchen small wares is huge. Wading through this section of the kitchen department of a store can be overwhelming. Do you really need a garlic roaster or a butter curler? Probably not, but I will steer you in the right direction for a few basic items that will make

your life, in the kitchen at least, a lot easier.

Dorm cooking tends to require a fair amount of canned goods, so a good can opener is essential. I tend to shun the electric models, as they take up valuable space and are difficult to clean. These days there are many can openers that have a "safe edge" or branded "safe-cut" can openers that do

Open Cans Safely

- Be sure your can opener and can top are clean before you open the can.

- Always clean your can opener with an abrasive sponge, dish soap, and hot water.

- When using canned foods, always check that cans are

free of rust, are not bloated, and have no dents. Discard any cans that have any of these traits.

- Food in cans has always been cooked to a safe temperature. It is theoretically safe to eat any canned food without heating it.

Strain and Drain

- Your strainer can act as a colander, and draining cans such as beans and tuna becomes a lot easier with one of these handy items.

- Your strainer is a great sieve for straining pureed soups.

- To brew coffee in a pinch, place a coffee filter in your

strainer, fill it with coffee, and pour almost-boiling water over the coffee.

- Look for strainers with sturdy plastic or rubber handles, which are more sanitary than wooden handles.

2

not leave behind a razor-sharp lid or can top for you to cut yourself on. Seek these out.

Many recipes will ask you to drain or strain an item, and a large kitchen colander is way too big to keep in a dorm room. A great substitute for a colander is an 8-inch fine-mesh kitchen strainer with a handle. This tool is very versatile and easy to mount over a bowl to drain or strain.

You will also need to peel the proverbial potato. Now there are peelers and there are *peelers*. You should be eating plenty of veggies to keep healthy. Opt for a European-style peeler,

which has a more comfortable handle, a better peeling blade, and a more ergonomic design.

Garlic is an essential ingredient in so many dishes. Many recipes call for you to mince or grind garlic cloves into a paste. A good garlic press can come in handy, especially if your knife skills are in need of improvement. Buy a sturdy press with a comfortable handle.

Not Just for Carrots

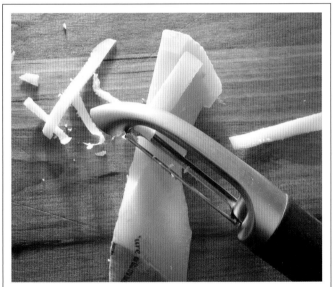

- The vegetable peeler is a very versatile tool and makes peeling veggies a lot easier.

- The peeler makes an excellent cheese "shaver." Try it with Parmesan and peel some nice curls over pasta.

- Your peeler also does an excellent job shaving vegetables into thin strips. Try shaving carrots or apples into a salad.

- Wisps of chocolate over a dessert are such an elegant way to present your sweet creations. Try using your peeler to shave chocolate.

Vampires Beware

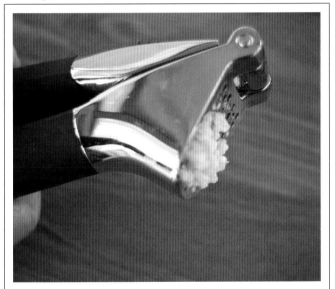

- Always clean your garlic press after use. Use a pin if necessary to poke out the bits.

- Look for presses with reversible heads, which have little cleaning rods built in for ease of cleaning.

- The virtues of using fresh garlic instead of garlic "products" are immeasurable. Try to use freshly pressed garlic whenever fresh garlic is specified.

- Precut or jarred garlic has an inferior flavor, but can be used in a pinch, as mediocre garlic is often better than no garlic.

SUPERMARKET 101

This is not an elective freshman year; it is important to become familiar with basic market layout

Supermarkets have come a long way since their inception decades ago. When shopping, it is important to remember that most supermarkets have been laid out with the refrigerated, most perishable, and essentially healthier items on the perimeter of the store. The best way to navigate the market is to shop first for all your nonperishable items and nongrocery

items (paper towels, toiletries, etc.) in the interior section of the store. Then, after you have procured all your nonperishables, head toward the perimeter. Shop first for fruits and vegetables, then move to prepared items, such as deli meats and prepared meals. After these two categories, move on to the dairy section and then finally to fresh meat, seafood,

Fresh Is Best

- Fresh produce is preferred over canned or frozen items whenever possible.

- Local seasonal vegetables travel shorter distances to reach the market and are in better overall shape. They also have higher nutritional content and are almost always cheaper.

- Choose firm fruits and veggies that are heavy for their size. This usually means they have not spent a lot of time on the shelf evaporating their moisture.

- Prewashed lettuces are a great time and space saver.

Something's Fishy around Here

- Choosing seafood is one of the most intimidating tasks for the average shopper. The main rule is: Let freshness be your guide.

- Whole fish should be very firm and have clear eyes. The fins should be intact, and the gills should be bright red.

- Fillets should be very firm. Ask the seafood associate to actually press into the flesh with a gloved finger. If the dent bounces back, the fish is fresh.

- Many fish and shellfish have been previously frozen; this can adversely affect quality.

and frozen items, in that order. This way your most perishable items spend minimal time out of refrigeration.

These days the amount of prepared foods has grown exponentially. Both hot and cold fully prepared foods are available for the busy professional, family, or college student. While more expensive than unprepared foods, these convenience items are key, especially in the dorm-room environment, where expansive cooking is difficult. Items such as grilled chicken breasts, precooked vegetables, and rotisserie chickens will make your life easier, your meals more varied, and cleanup a snap.

MAKE IT EASY

Rotisserie chickens are one of the most popular prepared foods offered in today's supermarkets. These chickens are very versatile when used as leftovers in recipes calling for pulled or cooked chicken meat. When you get your hot chicken home, cool it quickly if you're not using right away. The best way to do this is to remove the lid and cool the chicken in the fridge before placing the lid back on.

Choosing Fresh Meat

- Do not be afraid to ask your butcher questions.

- Some cuts of meat are better suited for grilling and broiling and others for stewing and braising. It is important to know what you are using.

- The best grade of meat is "prime" and is rarely found in supermarkets. Only the best butchers in big cities will have prime. Next is "choice," which is most common and the best all-around grade. "Select" follows and is generally of much lesser quality. When shopping look for "choice" to fill most of your needs.

Let Someone Else Cook

- Prepared foods are an excellent way to supplement your own kitchen work. They are especially great if you are in a rush.

- Precooked meats and seafood are an excellent way to turn a salad or vegetable soup into a meal.

- Precooked pastas can be quickly heated in sauce or in the microwave to save another pot on the stove.

- Pregrilled chicken breasts are readily available and have myriad uses, including in Caesar salads, in sandwiches, as pasta toss-ins, and in soups.

SETTING UP YOUR SPACE

Here are some easy ways to maximize your cooking abilities in a small space

Space management is important, especially when space is at a premium in places like dorm rooms or college apartments. Most likely you will have a roommate, so it is recommended that the two (or three or more) of you pool your resources and come together with a plan for your kitchen setup. You will probably not all agree on menus, but setting up your space to give everyone a better work environment is a great way to begin your relationship as roommates. Food and cooking have an uncanny way of bringing people together, so capitalize on this opportunity.

Storage options are limitless these days. Shelves in home centers, bed and bath stores, and big box stores are filled with

KNACK COLLEGE COOKBOOK

Measure Twice, Buy Once

- Take accurate measurements of the spaces available to you. Be creative and make the best use of your vertical space.

- Look for stackable plastic drawers that you can pile high to the ceiling. Clear drawers are better than opaque so you can see what is inside from a distance.

- Buy mixing bowls and storage containers that nest and take up minimal space.

- Keep your space clean and organized. Nothing ruins small spaces faster than clutter and messiness.

Pantry Building

- Keep items you go to most often front and center, and place the ones you reach for only occasionally toward the back or out of sight.

- To use space most efficiently, group like items together. Place heavier items on bottom shelves to avoid tipping.

- Items that may spill, such as glass bottles of oil or vinegar, should be kept in spill-proof bins.

- Ziplock bags take up less space than storage boxes for things like open crackers, chips, and cereals.

all manner of plastic tubs, stackable boxes, snap-together shelving, and other options. Before heading out to the store to stock up, layout the space in the dorm room or kitchen and draw a basic diagram with measurements on it. This way, when you go shopping you do not have to guess if items will fit where you hope they will.

Try to design your space with a few distinct sections: a pantry for nonperishable food storage; a section for all your cooking utensils and food-storage containers; and an area for cleaning supplies. Always store any cleaning chemicals or detergents in a place where they cannot spill onto food or food-preparation spaces. You will also need an area for fresh items, such as fruit and bread, which should be stored at room temperature. A well-ventilated basket works well for fruits, and an airtight container keeps bread fresh. Little things like paper towel holders, shelves with hooks for utensils, and large ziplock bags can make a big difference.

Keep 'em Separated

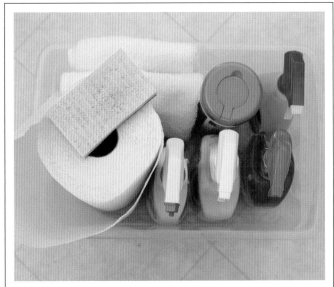

- When setting up your cleaning area, the most important thing is safety. Keep cleansers as far away from and underneath food.

- Many detergents and cleaning supplies are now made to be safe, "green," and biodegradable. Seek them out.

- Household items, such as distilled vinegar and baking soda, also make excellent cleaners and are cheap and safe for food.

- Use paper towels as much as possible to clean instead of dish towels, as paper towels are disposable and pose less of a health hazard.

Fresh but No Fridge

- Certain produce items do not require refrigeration. These include but are not limited to onions, garlic, apples, bananas, potatoes, and unripe fruit.

- Set up a ventilated container or basket system to store these items. There are many space-saving options available.

- Use an airtight container for most breads. If you have sliced bread that you do not use often, store in the freezer and simply snap off slices as you need. Ten seconds in the microwave or 2 minutes on the counter will defrost them.

KEEPING FOOD SAFE
Prevent food-borne illnesses with simple routine habits

The topic of food safety has been in the forefront of the American consciousness in the last few years. With huge recalls of everyday items such as peanut butter and spinach in the headlines, and countless people getting sick, it is important to understand what we can do in our own kitchens to prevent getting sick.

The reason we have refrigeration is to prevent bacteria from growing on our foods. And even food left in the fridge long enough will spoil. The problem with many so-called spoiled foods is that you cannot see or smell anything wrong with them. That is why so many people eat tainted foods each year.

The most basic rules for food safety have to do with time and temperature. Food left out between 40°F and 140°F for

KNACK COLLEGE COOKBOOK

Cold Is Cool

- Cool soups by making an "ice wand." Fill a clean 20-ounce plastic soda bottle with water and freeze. Insert the wand into the soup and place the pot in the fridge uncovered.

- Use a shallow container to get more surface area to help cool things down

quickly, such as soups or sauces.

- Make an "ice bath" by placing ice and cold water in a large bowl and nesting a smaller bowl inside it with the item you are trying to cool.

Know the Zone

- To be sure of temperatures, get a stemmed instant-read thermometer.

- Calibrate the thermometer by placing it in a glass of ice water. It should read 32°F. If it does not, adjust it by using a small wrench to turn the nut under the display.

- You can also calibrate the thermometer in a pot of boiling water. It should read 212°F.

- There is a small dimple about 1 inch up the stem of the thermometer. The dimple must be inside the food to get an accurate reading.

more than 2 hours is in the "danger zone," and care should be taken to be sure food is kept at this temperature for a minimal amount of time. In short, keep hot foods hot and cold foods cold—and cool down hot foods as rapidly as possible.

Defrosting and cooking food is a tricky business. Leaving a Thanksgiving turkey on the counter for a day to defrost is a real gamble. Another no-no is leaving food on the counter for several hours to cool off before putting it in the fridge. On the other hand, putting a covered pot of hot soup or chili

immediately into the fridge is also problematic, as it takes way too long to safely cool. It is better to leave the lid off for an hour or two to allow for quicker cooling.

Buy yourself a stemmed thermometer. It is a handy tool for measuring how hot or cold your foods are and how long it takes them to effectively chill or heat. Four hours is the absolute maximum time cold food should take to heat to 140°F or above and for hot food to chill to 40°F or below.

Keep It Clean

- There is a big difference between clean and sanitized. Something may look, smell, and seem clean and still be dangerous.

- Make a great sanitizing solution with 1 teaspoon bleach per 1 quart cold water. Be sure to use cold water, as hot water will disperse the bleach.

- Or, sanitize using boiling water. If boiling water is used to clean food-handling equipment, the equipment will be rendered safe.

- Don't forget to wash your hands!

Don't Cross-Contaminate

- Always cut raw meat, fish, or poultry last if you are cutting salad fixings or other raw or ready-to-eat items on the same board.

- Buy three separate cutting boards: one for fresh veggies, one for raw meats and poultry, and one for seafood.

- If using the same board for multiple tasks, always sanitize between uses.

- Store raw meat, fish, poultry, and eggs in the bottom of the fridge to avoid spilling juices onto other items.

BEST FRIDGE STORAGE SOLUTIONS

Your fridge is small, so you need to have great solutions to keep food fresh

Storing food even in the largest and most well-equipped refrigerator is challenging enough. Add to the equation a smaller-than-usual fridge, a messy roommate or two, and the rigors of college, and your challenge becomes even greater.

The basics are simple: Know what is in your fridge, when you put it there, and how long it can last. Determining how long food items can last in the fridge has many variables. What is the temperature of your fridge? Has the door been opened excessively? How crowded is your fridge, and is there adequate airflow inside the unit? These are all good things to understand, as many spoiled foods can be traced back to a refrigerator that is running too warm. The optimal

Use Your Office

- Mark perishables in your fridge with the date that you put them in so you don't have to guess.

- Use an indelible marker to write on disposable storage containers such as plastic wrap or bags.

- Use masking tape and a marker to label nondisposable containers such as plastic containers.

- Remind yourself with sticky notes to defrost a food item or that something is cooling in the fridge without a lid.

Like a Doctor's Office

- Ziplock bags with all the air squeezed out as well as vacuum-type bags work great for perishables.

- When storing batches of precooked foods, keep your hands as clean as possible. Wash with hot water and antibacterial soap before handling.

- Certain foods really require your hands. A pair of disposable medical gloves will ensure the food you store is clean and lasts longer.

- A clean paper towel in the bottom of a bag or container will soak up any stray water in foods and greatly increase the food's shelf life.

temperature for your fridge is around 38°F, but anything under 40°F is generally considered safe.

Keep your foods labeled and dated in your fridge. Always keep raw foods on the bottom shelf so they cannot drip onto other foods and contaminate them. Simple tools like masking tape and a magic marker to place dates on foods will save you a lot of trouble as well as money. And always remember: When in doubt, throw it out. If you are not sure about the freshness of a food item, get rid of it.

Now that you understand your refrigerator and its nuances, you will want to pack it and store foods in the most efficient way. There are a few tricks and techniques that will ensure that you do not squander the precious monies you spend on food and that you get the greatest amount of shelf life for your foods. You will be amazed how simple and effective these techniques are and what a huge difference they can make.

Size Matters

- Small square-shaped storage containers are easier to pack in the fridge.

- Ziplock bags take up very little space; look for the ones with the built-in zipper to assure a good closure.

- Pour extra broth or gravy into ice-cube trays and freeze. Then break the cubes into a ziplock bag and keep the small pieces in the freezer. When you need a little broth or sauce, you have a small piece at the ready.

- Buy smaller size condiments.

Use Tools

- Simple tools minimize the amount of contact your hands have with food, which translates into more efficient storage.

- Use tongs instead of your hands. Invest in a heavy gauge set that can lock closed for storage.

- A slotted spoon is a great tool for pulling foods out of cooking liquid and placing into storage containers.

- A ladle is more efficient than pouring from a pot or bowl. Ladle liquids into food-storage containers for minimal mess.

BLENDERS
These machines are good for more than making margaritas and daiquiris

Blenders are excellent tools for the kitchen. They have a multitude of uses, from pureeing soups to making sauces and pesto. There are several types of blenders, including the variable-speed blender that is most common in homes. These blenders have buttons for a wide variety of speeds, from puree to liquefy and everything in between. These are still available in the marketplace but may be a bit cumbersome for smaller spaces, as they take up a lot of countertop space.

A bar blender is a suped-up yet simplified home blender and is the best tool for blending sturdy purees and ice for frozen drinks. Bar blenders have stronger motors and often utilize a stainless steel "pitcher" as opposed to the heavy

Homecoming

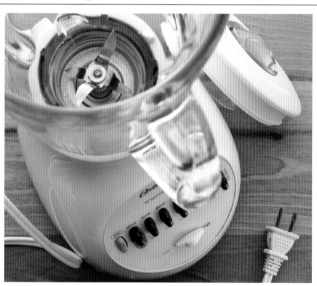

- The home blender definitely has its place in today's kitchens, especially if you have the storage and counter space.

- Many home blenders come with extra attachments, such as juicers, which can make the blender more versatile.

- These blenders have a large variety of speeds, and many people feel comfortable with them, as they have used these blenders since childhood.

- The glass pitcher allows you to clearly see what is going on during the blending process.

Turbocharged

- A bar blender has greatly increased power and sturdier blades.

- These machines are designed to puree ice, so they are incredibly effective tools for kitchen work without all the superfluous bells and whistles of a home blender.

- Pesto is best made in a bar blender, as the blender lets very little air blend into the product and keeps your pesto bright green.

- Dressings, dips, and hummus are all excellent when made in a bar blender.

tempered glass that most home blenders have. Bar blenders are available at restaurant-supply stores and retail shops and come in a variety of sizes and configurations. Look for one that will fit into your storage and cooking needs.

A relative newcomer to the home kitchen is the immersion blender. Professional cooks have been using it for decades. Known as Burr Mixers or burr sticks, immersion blenders are made by many different professional equipment suppliers. The good news is that this simple and effective technology is now available to us at home. The beauty of an immersion blender is that the blender can be immersed into a pot of hot soup or sauce. This minimizes the risk of burns from the splash back that can happen when you place hot liquid in a blender.

Blenders can perform many tasks. Whether you are making a soup, smoothie, or sauce, you can easily find a model to suit your needs.

A Sinking Feeling

- Immersion blenders are best for pureeing hot items, such as soups and sauces, especially if you are going to serve the food right away.

- Immersion blenders can be dangerous; the blades are sharp and exposed. Always be careful when using one.

- Some immersion blenders come with a micro–food processor attachment. This is handy for chopping small items like two or three garlic cloves.

- It is possible to chop ice with some immersion blenders, making that task a snap.

Old School

- Fortunately for the electronically challenged, nonelectric kitchen tools still exist and are easy to use. They just require a bit more work.

- A mortar and pestle is great for preparing pesto and mole sauces.

- Food mills are good for soups, tomato sauces, and mashed potatoes.

- A "ricer" is a food mill, but, instead of a rotating blade and die, it has a chamber with holes that food is pushed through. It is good for preparing mashed potatoes and vegetable purees.

FOOD PROCESSORS

The food processor is perhaps the most revolutionary electric kitchen gadget in history

Many cooks for many centuries have toiled in kitchens, working tirelessly with knives, mills, rolling pins, bare hands, mortars, and graters to process foods. Imagine how revolutionary the food processor would have been a few hundred years ago. It will be grand for you as a novice cook in a college setting to have a machine that does a ton of work for you. Just

make sure you learn how to use the beast properly and keep those sharp blades away from your busy term paper typing fingers.

The first commercial food processor was made in France under the name Robot Coupe. This brand still exists today and is an industry leader in the commercial sector. There are

Who'd a Thunk?

- The food processor is an amazing dough kneader. Many cooks consider themselves blessed after discovering this.

- Make your favorite pizza dough recipe in the food processor. The key is to use the proper water temperature, around 80°F.

- Pasta dough is a snap in the food processor. Egg or eggless pasta dough works equally well.

- Grating cheese has never been easier for those pizzas and nachos.

It Slices It Dices!

- Slicing and dicing is the real "meat and potatoes" of the work these machines can do. You can put your knives away for a while.

- The slicing blades allow you to make perfect thin slices of any vegetable—great for making soups.

- The grater attachment makes short work of grating cheeses for nachos or mac and cheese.

- The julienne blade allows you to cut thin strips (known as matchsticks) in a fraction of the time cutting with a knife would take. It saves fingertips, too!

many others brands for home cooks found in many retail shops. In America, the first domestic food processor was made by the Cuisinart brand, which is still a strong player in the domestic market.

Today's food processors come in myriad shapes, colors, and sizes. Most come with a slew of interchangeable blades and feeder tubes that allow you to perform a huge variety of kitchen tasks, which, in turn, allow you to have more fun or study time.

MAKE IT EASY

These days most of the features of a full-size food processor can be had in a variety of "mini" models. These are ideal if you are mostly working with small batches and meals for one to three people. They take up almost no storage or counter space and really do a great job for almost all tasks. They may not have as many blade options, but they are still a great help.

Smooth Operator

- The beauty of such a fast-moving blade in the bowl of the food processor is the ability to whip sauces and vinaigrettes together (known as emulsifying).

- Make homemade mayonnaise for your sandwiches in the food processor that blows store-bought away.

- Making thick and creamy vinaigrettes just got easier. Be sure to add the oil in a slow and steady stream to avoid separation.

- Dips such as hummus come out silky smooth when made in a food processor, which is great for making a multitude of purees.

Helpful Hints

- When handling the processor blades, remember that they are razor sharp and dangerous.

- Wash all blades with hot soapy water and dry well before placing back in the machine. For apartment dwellers, with a gas oven, one cleaning trick is to place the blades in an off oven for a few hours. The pilot light will dry them.

- Cutting vegetables into manageable sizes before adding them to the machine makes the processor run more efficiently.

THE KNIVES YOU NEED
You don't have to spend a fortune on good knives

The world wants you to believe that you need a block full of expensive knives to be able to cook properly. The truth is, there are a few essentials that will cover almost your entire knife need, and can be purchased at bargain prices if you know where to look.

Never buy knives from an infomercial. Sure it can cut through a tin can and still slice a tomato paper thin, but so can many cheapo knives with superthin blades. Besides, when was the last time you needed to saw through a tin can? In general, new and improved does not really apply to kitchen knives. The basic design for cooking knives has remained unchanged for a long, long time for good reason. In fact, some of the oldest methods for producing blades are still the most sought after, and high-end artisan chef's knives

KNACK COLLEGE COOKBOOK

It's in the Construction

- A quality chef's knife has several hallmarks, which set it apart from an ordinary knife. Learn them and finding bargains becomes easier.

- A good chef's knife has what is known as a "full tang," which means that the metal that the blade is forged from extends fully through the handle.

- The blade should slope toward the handle and the tip. This allows the knife to effectively rock back and forth on a fulcrum.

- Forged blades last longer than stamped blades.

Basic Blades

- There are only a few basic knives you need to be an effective cook, so get the best you can afford.

- One good choice is the chef's knife with a blade length between 6 and 10 inches, depending on your hand size.

- An 8-inch offset serrated knife is great for bread, tomatoes, and tough root vegetables. It's a real workhorse.

- A good 3- to 4-inch pairing knife and a 6-inch flexible utility knife round out your basic kit.

regularly fetch huge dollar amounts. But they are not necessary to cook well.

The most important thing about a knife is that it is comfortable in your hand. If the handle is too thick or too round or the blade is too long or heavy, it will not be an effective tool. Go to the store and actively hold knives in your hand. You can even bring a small cutting board to more realistically test the motions of cutting.

The reason that TV chefs make cutting and chopping look so easy is that they have good technique. A good chef can cut just about as fast and accurately with a cheap blade as with an expensive one.

Different Steels and Sharpening

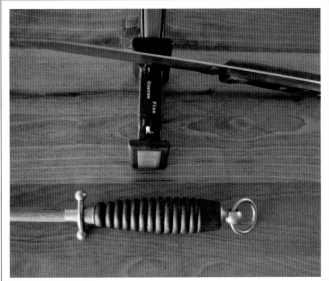

- The steel that a knife is made of makes a huge difference in how well the knife sharpens and holds an edge.

- Stainless steel knives do not rust. The downside is they are difficult to keep sharp.

- Carbon steel knives hold a razor edge, but are very brittle and can break if dropped or mishandled. They also discolor and can easily rust.

- High-carbon stainless knives combine the best of both carbon and stainless steel and, as a result, are more expensive.

Technique Is King

- The real trick after you pay big bucks for that Japanese hand-forged chef's knife is being able to use it without a trip to the emergency room.

- The knife is meant to move through food by sliding across it, not cutting straight down.

- When cutting with a chef's knife, the blade should touch your knuckles, and your fingertips should be tucked underneath so you can keep them.

- The knife should rock on its fulcrum, not guillotine straight up and down.

17

BOWLS, BOARDS & COOKWARE

The proper assortment of bowls, boards, and cookware is not as expensive as you think

Whether your kitchen is in a tiny apartment shared by two tired roommates, or an even tinier dorm room, you basically need a select group of items in order to be a successful cook.

There has been a lot of back and forth about the sanitation of cutting boards over the last few years. Some say that plastic boards are much safer than wooden boards in terms of harboring bacteria, and others say the opposite is true. The important things for you to consider when buying a cutting board (or boards) are 1) Is the board large enough to hold what you need? 2) Is it too large to store or so heavy that you need a helper to lift or clean it? 3) Will it comfortably fit in the sink you use for cleanup?

Chairman of the Board

- Wooden boards are easy on knife blades. Occasionally sand and coat them with mineral oil to increase their lifespan.

- Semisoft plastic boards are color coded, so you can separate those used for meats from those used for vegetables.

- Hard, clear plastic boards that are now popular are terrible to cut on and slippery for foodstuffs. Avoid them.

- Whatever board you use, secure it to the countertop with a moist towel between the board and counter to prevent slipping.

Tools the Pros Use

- You don't need all the tools a pro does, but there are some essentials: a large slotted spoon, large solid spoon, heat-proof rubber spatula, 2-ounce ladle, 6-ounce ladle, 8-inch pair of stainless tongs, standard wooden spoon, flat-topped wooden spoon, and 10-inch whisk.

- Place a stainless straight-sided container referred to as a "bain marie" on the counter and keep essentials like whisks, tongs, and spoons there.

- If you haven't used an item in a year, pitch it.

Discard any cutting boards that have large cracks, and always clean and sanitize between uses to kill all lingering bacteria.

Mixing bowls are a category unto themselves, as well. There are glass, ceramic, plastic, aluminum, and stainless steel varieties. There are also straight edged, pouring lipped, snap-tight lids, and a pile of other options out there. All you need are four or five stainless steel mixing bowls from 6 to 24 inches in diameter that will nest together.

The array of pots and pans can be a bit overwhelming. A good rule of thumb is not to buy a set of pots and pans, but to purchase piecemeal. Invariably, when a set is purchased there is always a pot or pan that is never used and collects dust or clinks around the cabinet. Someday it winds up in a yard sale. Save yourself the trouble and the money.

Spend Your Money Wisely

- If there was ever a place to splurge in the kitchen, it is on pots and pans. These "lifelines" will be with you forever if you buy quality and take care of them.

- The first test of a good pan is weight. Very light pans are poor conductors of heat and ineffective tools.

- "Clad" pans, which have a combination of metals including copper, stainless, and aluminum, are excellent choices.

- Enamel-coated cast-iron pans are excellent, although quite heavy and expensive.

Only What You Need

- Now is the time to outfit your kitchen.

- Look online for closeout or factory blemished cookware. eBay is also an excellent source.

- The following pots and pans make a good starter set: a 2-quart saucepan with lid, 5-quart saucepan with lid, 9-inch nonstick sauté pan, 12-inch straight-sided skillet with lid, and cookie sheet.

- Buy the best you can afford. Take your time to build a good collection.

OTHER SMALL MACHINES
Here are some other cool gizmos to make your kitchen life even smoother

A machine does not need to be a complicated device with moving parts or even require any power but your own hand. A machine can be defined simply as "anything used to accomplish a purpose." So you see, your knife is a simple machine. It is up to the operator to use the machine properly and eventually master its function.

It is sometimes difficult to ascertain what you actually need in your kitchen besides the basics. Cooking stores and Web sites continue to up their inventories, and inventors seem to have an endless supply of new-fangled choppers, roasters, and flippers, which seemingly simplify the cooking experience. Most of these claims are aimed at the complete novice

Bump and Grind

- Two simple machines that make a huge difference in efficiency and flavor are the peppermill and the coffee/spice grinder.

- A good peppermill is essential. Preground, store-bought pepper is no comparison for freshly ground. Always use the real deal.

- Freshly ground coffee can be an amazing and everyday treat. Practice getting the right grind for whatever method you brew with.

- An electric coffee grinder does double duty as a spice grinder. Make sure to clean well after uses.

From the Carpenter's Belt

- Sometimes inspiration comes from the strangest places. The "microplane" has been adapted from a woodworker's tool to a chef's tool.

- Shaving Parmesan cheese with a microplane showers the pasta with a fine snowy coat of the cheese.

- Nothing does a better job with citrus zest than the microplane. The key is that the blades do not grab the bitter pith.

- Finishing a dessert with a delicate topping of chocolate just got easier. Use the microplane; you'll be amazed at the results.

who does not understand basic techniques and is easily coerced. Don't fall prey to the hype.

Clutter is the hallmark of an inefficient kitchen. Too many machines and tools choke the workspace and hinder preparation. It is always advisable to be efficient at simple tasks like cutting and chopping with a knife and cutting board before purchasing the newest onion-flower maker or garlic-skin peeler. Learning those simple tasks makes you a true cook and limits your trips to the flea market or thrift store to donate your unused and unnecessary gadgets.

However, there are some machines you may want to invest in that are simple, perform their tasks well, and actually improve your time management in the kitchen. Take these suggestions, but never forget that learning basic techniques and tasks ultimately makes you the most successful cook. Being able to show up in a strange kitchen and bang out a great meal with a pot, cutting board, lousy knife, and hot plate makes you the hero of the day.

Fancy Pants

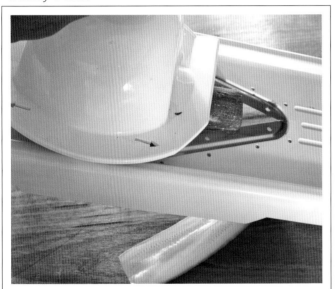

- A long-used secret in professional kitchens, the mandoline has gained favor with home cooks. While not a necessity, it makes slicing much easier.

- This tool is sharp and dangerous. Understand its functions thoroughly before attempting to use it.

- A mandoline makes julienning vegetables or making uniform slices easier than ever—and quick, too.

- This tool is great for making homemade french fries, potato chips, and even waffle fries. It can turn a pile of veggies into a finished product in no time.

A Worthwhile Investment

- The rice cooker is an amazing invention. It cooks all types of rice perfectly and takes all the guesswork out of it.

- It is worth it to get the programmable models. This way you can load the rice cooker before you go to class and come home to perfectly cooked rice.

- The rice can be held at optimum temperature for hours, making this device very versatile.

- Try adding flavoring, bullion, or even cooked veggies and meats to the rice before cooking.

ELECTRIC EXTRAS

Thank goodness for electricity; it has made the cook's life easier and more interesting

It is amazing how much we take electricity for granted. It is only when we experience a power outage that we realize how much we depend on it. Our lights, computers, televisions, and climate control are all dependant on electricity. Because people have been cooking in an organized way for thousands of years, most, if not all, our cooking essentials are powered by elbow grease and cooking fuel. But some really cool machines have been invented that cannot only increase productivity, but also allow us to create things that were once only possible in professional facilities.

Besides the aforementioned food processors, blenders, and others, the food industry is busy inventing and reinventing

Not Just for Tea

- Electric teakettles are great because of their speed and convenience. The water comes to a boil in an amazingly short time, and there is no need to discard excess water in the pot. Simply use it later.

- Many models have an adjustment that allows

- for boiling or sub-boiling water, depending on your needs.

- This is a versatile item—perfect for the tight dorm room—and is great for instant soups or whenever you need a quick shot of boiling water.

Some Things Never Change

- Perhaps one of the most versatile electric machines available to the home cook is the standing mixer.

- This machine is a perfectly paired down version of the big industrial mixers found in big bakeries and professional kitchens.

- Besides the obvious baking applications, this machine has myriad attachments available.

- Meat grinders, grain mills, and slicing and dicing blades are just a few of the possible options.

electric gadgets for the kitchen. Some machines have already been in existence in other industries and are now finding their way into the kitchens of the world's cooks. New technologies are revolutionizing cooking in ways that past generations could never have imagined. Just think of how long the microwave has been in use and how it has changed our lives.

When you buy that next electric gadget, think about how many times you will actually use it. If you are considering a piece of equipment that only performs one task, make sure it is a task you need performed quite often, like boiling water. Also, consider the size of your kitchen, the amount of storage space available, or if you have a supplemental area to store items. If need be, maybe Mom and Dad have a spot in the garage to store your budding collection of kitchen gadgets?

By George!

- The dual-sided grill or sandwich press has become one of the biggest selling cooking gadgets of all time, and for great reason.

- Modeled after the Italian-style sandwich presses, these grills do a lot more than make grilled cheese sandwiches.

- They are effective for grilling thinner pieces of meat and fish with little mess and in a short time.

- They are a great way to make inventive desserts like grilled bananas with whipped cream or grilled pears with honey.

Science Meets Art

- Induction burners use electromagnetic induction heat to heat certain metals.

- These burners can be used only with stainless steel cookware; they will not work with copper or aluminum.

- The heat is transferred only to the stainless cookware, making these safe if accidentally left on without a pan on the burner.

- Heat transfers quickly, making a quick sauté or pot of water for pasta easy. These are great if you need a portable and safe burner.

ABSOLUTE BASIC NECESSITIES

Every kitchen—be it in a dorm or apartment—needs a well-stocked pantry to avoid unnecessary trips to the market

A properly stocked pantry is essential not only for quick and efficient cooking, but for helping the creative process. When you have a pantry stocked full of essentials, creating new dishes becomes much easier and can get you out of the same old boring college food rut. As an example, if you have dry pasta, a jar of capers, and a can of tuna on hand, the addition of some fresh tomatoes can make a quick, healthful, and elegant dinner. Your only limitation is your own creativity. In fact sometimes the best dishes are created when there is seemingly "nothing to eat" in the house and a quick search of the pantry reveals a hidden treasure of ingredients.

Before refrigeration, the pantry was limited to the dry

Rice Is Nice

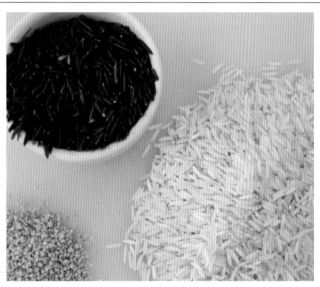

- Rice is an excellent pantry staple, as it will not spoil and can make a quick meal with a few simple additions.

- Mixing rice with beans makes an almost perfect protein and can sustain you with no meat.

- If you have no electricity to cook, you can "cook" rice by soaking it in water for 12 hours.

- Brown rice has more nutritional value than white rice, but takes longer to cook.

Worth a Hill of Beans

- Canned beans are an excellent pantry staple, perfectly cooked every time and loaded with protein and fiber. Many vegetarians get almost all their protein from beans.

- Canned beans can be transformed into soups in minutes with the addition of a little broth and seasoning.

- A quick puree of canned beans makes a satisfying spread for crackers or sandwiches.

- Drained and rinsed, several types of canned beans can make a quick and colorful salad.

goods, root cellar, home-canned items, and smokehouse, as these were the only way to preserve foods. It is important to realize that today's pantries are not just a cupboard full of dry ingredients, but have expanded to the refrigerator and freezer and maybe even the windowsill if you can keep certain essential herbs growing all year.

Since many items in the pantry are long lasting and do not require refrigeration, it is a good idea to mark them with the date you purchased them. This allows you to make sure the freshest items get used first and that foods do not sit too long or get buried in the back of the cabinet or shelf. Some cooks keep a running inventory list on the inside of the cupboard. When they use the last of something, they can mark it on the inventory list and then place it on their shopping list. This is a great budgeting trick to avoid buying duplicate items.

There are some items you should never be without. Some of these recommendations come from a sheer sense of survival. In case you are snowed in or worse and need to eat, these items will save the day.

Eggsellent

- As far as a refrigerated staple, eggs are on the top of the list. The number of uses for eggs is staggering.

- An omelet or scrambled eggs with some leftover meats, vegetables, or cheese tossed in makes a great lunch or dinner.

- Egg yolks are a great way to thicken sauces, like in the classic pasta carbonara.

- Many baked goods require eggs, and having them on hand opens up the baking world to you.

Thank Goodness for Freezers

- Frozen vegetables have many virtues that canned veggies do not. They are usually superior in color and texture.

- Unused portions can be returned to the freezer for later uses, unlike cans, which once opened, must be used.

- Frozen vegetables have higher nutritional values than canned.

- Frozen fruits make excellent pie fillings and are also great for smoothies. Don't thaw the fruit, and your smoothie will be thick and cold.

25

NO-NEED-TO-REFRIGERATE ITEMS

Items that require no refrigeration make up the largest part of the pantry

It is amazing to think about how people ate before refrigeration. Mechanical refrigerators are a very new invention, and while people figured out a long time ago that cold temperatures keep food cold, they were limited to ice boxes and winter weather. Even then, those who lived in warm climates and had no access to ice at any time of year had to find other

solutions to their food preservation challenges. In fact, the simple point that there was no refrigeration is what helped to spawn some of the world's greatest food products.

Many items were simply dried, as the removal of moisture from a food greatly diminishes the chance of bacterial growth and spoilage. Dried beans, grains, and pastas are

Ah, Pasta

- Pasta is one of the world's greatest no-need-to-refrigerate foods. Pasta made with or without eggs can be dried.

- Couscous is often mislabeled a grain but is actually a tiny pasta and cooks in only 5 minutes.

- Add pasta to broth soups to make the dish more hearty.

- The combination of pasta, butter, and Parmesan cheese is so stupidly simple and delicious. Use this as a "base" and add all manner of leftovers or vegetables and meats to make a quick and satisfying meal.

Canned Tuna

- Canned tuna is not just for sandwiches (although those are great, too); this versatile and handy protein has many uses.

- Drained canned tuna can be made into cakes using a crab cake recipe, but substituting in the tuna.

- Tuna packed in oil is wonderful tossed with hot pasta and a little garlic. Use the oil to coat the pasta!

- Tuna casserole has seen a huge resurgence in recent years and for good reason. It is wonderful and homey, perfect for the occasional homesick night.

what immediately come to mind. But myriad dried fruits, meats, fish, and shellfish have sustained countless people in many cultures. Beef jerky may be a great snack these days, but it was invented strictly out of necessity.

The beauty of nonrefrigerated items is that they almost never spoil, so your monies are usually safe in these food investments. They also have the added flexibility of being able to be stored anywhere, so the tight quarters of college living can accommodate your goodies in nooks and under beds and in closets if need be. Heck, sometimes your car trunk in the campus parking lot makes a great pantry!

If you find your stuff stored in a variety of places it is important to keep track of it all. If you forget that you have two boxes of granola under your bed and buy two more boxes, you are wasting hard-earned money. Keep a running list on paper or your cell phone.

Treasure Virginity

- Extra-virgin olive oil should be in everybody's pantry. This incredible food product acts as a conventional oil for sautéing and so much more.

- Sauté a little fresh garlic in the olive oil and toss with pasta; this is the simplest of Italian pasta sauces.

- Dip bread in olive oil instead of butter. The fat found in olive oil is one of the "healthy fats" that is good for your diet.

- Also, use olive oil in all your salad dressings for more flavor.

The Many Uses of Peanut Butter

- Peanut butter is an amazing food product. Loaded with protein and calories, it is a high-energy food with many other uses besides the traditional PB&J.

- Peanut butter makes an excellent sesame and sesame paste substitute for things like hummus and cold sesame noodles.

- Peanut butter is a key ingredient for a great satay sauce, and it is wonderful when brushed on grilling meats.

- You must try a crisp bacon and peanut butter sandwich.

LIFESAVING CONDIMENTS

Condiments have a way of making something out of nothing; have a key assortment on hand

Condiments play an essential role in cooking. They are the punch line to the joke and the exclamation point at the end of a sentence. Sometimes they are the main actor; other times they are the unseen understudy that saves the day. In any case, we need 'em.

One of the earliest references to a condiment is in an ancient Roman cookbook by Apicius. The condiment is garum, a fermented fish sauce made from the guts of oily fishes such as mackerel that was left to fester in pots in the sun. The smell of production was so offensive that is was relegated by law to the outskirts of the city. Luckily for us the evolution of condiments has been vast over the last two thousand years.

The Virtues of Mustard

- A Roman invention, which made its way to France, mustard has many uses besides as a great spread.

- Mustard is commonly used in vinaigrette dressings, both for flavor and to prevent the dressing from separating.

- Use some mustard in barbecue sauces and meat marinades for an extra punch. Or mix it with jam and use as a ham glaze.

- Add yellow mustard to crab cakes for an authentic Maryland flavor. Add some coarse mustard to a simple cream sauce for chicken.

MMMMmmmmayonnaise

- Mayonnaise is a French invention, which is almost nothing more than oil, emulsified in egg yolks. Almost no other condiment is as widely used.

- Try rubbing poultry with mayonnaise instead of butter before roasting. The color will be beautiful.

- Mayonnaise can be mixed with other condiments to create new condiments. Try sesame and soy, chipotle and lime, or mustard and dill.

- In Europe, french fries are dipped in mayo, not ketchup.

In Asia, condiments have evolved into high art. The array of soy-based sauces is staggering, from regulation soy sauce to hoisin sauces, oyster sauce, fermented soy curd, and the famous XO sauce of Hong Kong. There are also a head-spinning variety of chili sauces, pastes, and oils to satisfy those with a need for heat.

In the West, many other condiments were developed, and many were based on Asian techniques or even directly from Asian recipes. There are so many varieties of mustards and people who love them that there is even a store in Paris devoted entirely to this pungent condiment.

The ketchup we use today is strictly made from tomatoes, but early American cookbooks list ketchups made from everything from a watermelon peel to apples and mushrooms. And sauces, such as Worcestershire sauce and Tabasco, have made their way into recipes across the seas. And let us not forget mayonnaise. This sauce/condiment/universal solvent is the reason bread was invented and to which french fries are the ultimate vehicle.

Wooster Sheister Sheeser Sauce

- No matter how you spell it or pronounce it, Worcestershire sauce has a unique "meaty" flavor and soy sauce–like character that make it indispensable.

- Add it to almost any soup at the last minute instead of salt for a deeper flavor.

- Add it to marinades, barbecue sauces, and bloody Marys and other cocktails.

- It is excellent with beef and mixed in with hamburger meat for more savory-tasting burgers and meatloaf.

Dance the Salsa

- Salsa has eclipsed ketchup as the most popular condiment in the United States.

- Add salsa to your favorite chili recipe instead of canned diced tomatoes, as the chili is already loaded with Southwestern flavors.

- Add salsa and some cumin to your favorite meatloaf recipe for a Tex-Mex version of an American favorite.

- Dress hot dogs with salsa instead of ketchup and relish, or use it with Monterey Jack cheese in place of tomato sauce and mozzarella on pizzas.

BASES, BROTHS & SAUCES

Sauces are not easy or cheap to make; hence the array of already-made options

Making true sauces from broths and stocks takes many hours and huge bubbling pots filled with meats and veggies. Many times the meats and vegetables have to be roasted and the broths need to be tended to with skimming and simmering. In professional kitchens there is usually someone specifically assigned to this task, and it is a full-time job. Thankfully you do not have to do all this work.

The time it takes to make bases, broths, and sauces is the reason why so many innovations and inventions have been made in this department. This does not mean the intrepid cook should not attempt these classic preparations; it just means that you have options available at your fingertips and

Pecking Order

- Always have boxed or canned chicken broth in your pantry. Choose low-sodium versions to avoid salty finished products.

- Use chicken broth for soups, including vegetable soups, for a richer finished product as well as a protein boost.

- When making risotto, doctor the broth with spices, shrimp shells, saffron, or anything else to boost the flavor of the broth and hence the finished risotto.

- When making mashed potatoes use chicken broth instead of water for added flavor and complexity.

Instant Gravy Packs

- These can be a real lifesaver, especially when making stew. Most instant gravy packs call for one envelope per cup of water. Always add ¼ to ½ cup more water or broth if the stew will cook for a while.

- For stew, add several different flavored gravy packs for a more "rounded" flavor. Try onion, pork, mushroom, chicken, and herb.

- Add instant gravy packs to make a meatier chili.

- Mix gravy packs with curry powder for a curried stew.

in the supermarket aisles to assist in the endeavor.

Long and slow preparation of almost anything is bound to be superior to supermarket shortcuts, but we live in a fast-paced world, which sometimes demands the use of these shortcuts. By all means, learn how to make perfect stock when you have the time. The lesson learned will be an excellent baseline of flavor and texture that will allow you to use shortcut methods most effectively, as you will know the real McCoy.

MAKE IT EASY

Probably the most common and widely used "shortcut" is commercially made chicken broth. There are several excellent broth products on the market today, including low-sodium, organic, gluten-free, and "premium" varieties. Chicken broth is essential to making soups and sauces; and it's a great water substitute to more nutritious cooked rice and grains.

Round the Bases

- Bases are like bouillon but more moist and easy to stir into liquids. They are available in many grocery stores and online.

- Bases come in many flavors, such as crab, chicken, beef, and vegetable.

- Use a blend of bases when making soups. For instance, if you are making chicken soup, use some chicken, vegetable, and mushroom bases.

- Bases can be a bit salty, so be aware and taste your product before using or adding salt to your recipe.

Freezer Pantry Solutions

- Freeze leftover broth, sauce, or gravy in ice-cube trays and then store in ziplock bags in the freezer.

- After sautéing a piece of meat, add a splash of wine, a cube of sauce, and a teaspoon of butter. Boil for 30 seconds, and you have a quick pan sauce.

- The cubes are great when you need just a little bit and are great for saving a real killer sauce you made once.

- Sauces that are emulsified, such as hollandaise, do not freeze and will separate when defrosted. Tomato and gravy-type sauces freeze well.

CONVENIENCE ITEMS

Convenience foods are an important part of your college pantry

Since the life of a student is fast paced and action packed, it's important to shop smart and purchase items that both save time and offer good nutrition. Our markets are full of convenience items, and more are being developed daily.

The world of convenience foods probably opened up after the invention of the refrigerated boxcar train. For the first time ever, people could eat fruits and vegetables that were typically out of season in many locations but in season in places like California. Before then, when summer was over, people could no longer get their hands on tomatoes or watermelons, and when spring faded away, asparagus went away with it. Today, however, it's easy to forget that fruits and vegetables actually have distinct seasons.

Today's convenience foods have morphed into a blinding

Braising in Five Minutes

- Properly braising a piece of meat for a pot roast is a long and labor-intensive process. There are several great products on the market, such as Hormel fully cooked meats and roasts, that shorten this process. These items simply need to be heated.

- These are great for dinner when time is short. They also make great sandwiches.

- Look for these items near the meat section of the supermarket.

- Braised pork shoulders and short ribs of beef are also available.

Less Mess

- Prebreaded chicken cutlets, eggplant slices, and fish fillets are all over the market. Look for quality brands. With chicken, look for whole breast fillets, not ground patties.

- With these products, Italian dishes, such as chicken or eggplant Parmesan, are a snap to make.

- Many of these items can be oven fried instead of deep-fried, saving fat and calories.

- If baking prebreaded items, spray food with a foam of cooking spray to help create a crisp and brown crust.

array or frozen, dried, canned, cooked, semicooked, and otherwise prepared foods that keep us well fed despite the ever-increasing pace of our lives. In fact just about everything in the supermarket, with the exception of the fresh items found along the perimeter of the store, can be considered a convenience item. Although fruits like apples or bananas are of course pretty convenient. Never before have we had so many options.

For example, today there are some excellent cooked meats available that make certain dishes a breeze to prepare.

There are also breaded and frozen fish, meat, and vegetable items that eliminate the mess of breading your own. And in recent years, the availability of ethnic prepared foods has grown, which makes exploring different cuisines much more accessible.

For the Birds

- Besides the hot rotisserie chickens available at most supermarkets, there are great options for fully cooked, chilled, and packaged poultry that you simply need to heat.

- Fully cooked whole chickens in different flavors, including smoked, make quick meals

and simply need to be cut before heating.

- Fully cooked ducks are now readily available, saving a lot of time and headaches.

- Fully cooked grilled chicken breasts make for quick healthy salads and sandwiches.

Curry in a Hurry

- Fantastic Indian and other ethnic foods are now available fully cooked. Items such as curried lentils and legumes are popular.

- Look for them in the frozen, ethnic, and/or organic aisles of your market.

- Add some jarred chutney from the ethnic aisle and some cooked basmati rice, and you have a very authentic meal.

- Experiment with unfamiliar cuisines. It is like taking a culinary adventure. You can then learn to cook the dishes yourself.

DRIED SPICES & HERBS
Dried herbs and spices are a great way to experiment with flavor, so don't be afraid

Dried spices once had more value than gold. The spice trade was so important that wars were fought for prime spice routes and rights to the exotic spices of the Far East. The first routes were overland from India to Europe; the routes eventually shifted to the high seas, as the overland routes become fraught with danger.

Pepper was once so expensive that it was kept in small sachets around people's necks to avoid losing it to thieves. And saffron still remains one of the world's most expensive food products.

Although now readily available and relatively affordable, spices are a wonderful way to explore exotic cultures. Try

Seeds of Weeds

- Most dried spices are rendered from the dried seeds of plants. Many of these seeds are ground and sold this way. Grinding your own spices yields more potent flavors.

- Some plants yield spices and herbs. Coriander and dill are prime examples.

- Seed spices are excellent for adding to clear broths and pickling brines, as they deliver flavor without coloring the liquid.

- Toasting seeds in a dry skillet greatly increases their flavors.

Got Any Herb?

- Spices are made from dried seeds, bark, roots, flowers, or fruits. Herbs, on the other hand, are the leaves of plants.

- Dried herbs are much more potent than fresh herbs. If you are substituting dry for fresh, cut the volume in half, at least.

- A good starter selection of dried herbs includes thyme, rosemary, parsley, oregano, and dill.

- Dried herbs lose their potency after about one year, so only buy what you can use in that time.

spices you have never had; read about their uses. Food is an adventure and should be treated as such; spices can transport you.

While you're spending these years opening your mind to new ideas and knowledge, spend some time introducing your taste buds to new cultures. Adding spices to certain dishes is a budget-friendly way to experience entirely new cultures and countries. If you are out and taste something sensational, try to get the recipe or at least an ingredient list that you can experiment with.

ZOOM

Curry is actually not a spice, but a blend of many spices. There are hundreds of different curries in the world, and only some are native to India. There are Thai curries, which are more like pastes; Japanese curries; and many others. And, while there is a plant called curry, which yields the curry leaf used in Indian cooking, the plant has nothing to do with the yellow curries your may be familiar with.

The King of Spices

- Peppercorns have always been regarded as one of the world's most important spices. They are the dried fruit of a flowering vine.

- Black peppercorns are ripe fruits, white pepper is black pepper with the outer husk removed, and green peppercorns are the same fruit picked underripe. Pink pepper is an unrelated plant.

- Most recipes call for black pepper; even if unspecified, default to black.

- White pepper is a bit hotter and is widely used in Chinese cooking.

Grow Your Own

- Growing your own herbs to dry for the cooler months is a great way to keep freshly dried herbs on hand year-round.

- To get them at the peak of flavor, harvest your herbs before they flower.

- If flowers emerge, "dead head" them by lopping the flowers off to allow the plant to continue to produce leaves.

- Dry herbs very slowly to maintain the best flavors. Drying in a very low oven also works well.

PORTION CONTROL

The "freshman fifteen" are more like the freshman thirty these days; practice portion control

Perhaps the biggest health issue today is obesity and the diseases associated with it. Diabetes, heart attack, stroke, joint problems, certain cancers, and other ailments are all directly related to having a body mass larger than normal. When first arriving at college, it is quite easy to pack on the pounds. Changes in sleep, eating, and drinking habits are the catalysts for unhealthy weight gain. The added issue of late-night snacking on typically fatty foods such as pizza and burgers certainly do not help. We often forget portion control when we are in school. Remember: Don't load your plate to the top. Eat a bit and wait a few minutes before going back for seconds.

Look Before You Eat

- Understanding a few simple visual clues is an easy first step in understanding portion control.

- A portion of protein is about the size of a deck of cards or the area of the average human palm.

- A healthy portion of starches, such as pasta, potatoes, or rice, is about the size of your fist.

- It is a great idea to supplement all of your meals with plenty of vegetables. They will keep you full with few caloric consequences.

Serve Yourself

- Today's portion sizes are almost double those that were served in the 1950s.

- To monitor portion control, use smaller plates and bowls. Look for "thinware" dishes in your local department stores.

- If served a huge portion when eating out, ask for a take-out container right away and split your meal in half.

- Eat slower, chew, and enjoy your food. Mom was right about that one!

A gradual gaining of weight, starting in college, can pave the way for a lifetime of health issues. Be conscious, enjoy yourself, but also be aware. Some nutritionists recommend the 80/20 rule. This states that you should do all the right things 80 percent of the time and splurge a little 20 percent of the time. Try to keep at least a mental note of what you are eating in the cafeteria and try to get at least a half hour of good exercise in every day. These are good habits to develop and keep with you always.

Use your clothing as a guide rather than spending too much time on a scale. The human body can vary in weight, up to five pounds in a day. This is especially true for women whose bodies process water differently than men's. If your clothes get too tight, adjust your diet and exercise habits. One of the easiest ways to stay alert is to practice sensible portion control.

Calories Count

- Weight control boils down to this simple equation: the number of calories in and the number of calories out. The combination of too many in and not enough out equals weight gain.

- Higher calorie items require smaller portion sizes. You can have more of a skinless chicken breast than a fatty steak.

- If you must have dessert, split it with someone or opt for fruit. Small chocolates are also a good trick.

- A bowl of a healthful cereal makes a great midnight snack.

Knowledge Is Power

- Understand how much things weigh and what that means in terms of calories, fat, and nutrition.

- Read labels carefully and look at how much a serving is. Use a portion scale to measure a serving. You may be surprised.

- One tablespoon of olive oil, butter, vegetable oil, and any other fat all have the same amount of calories: 120.

- Use measuring spoons and cups until you can estimate servings on your own. Recheck every once in a while.

LIGHT & LOW FAT
There are many light and low-fat items that are excellent to use in a variety of dishes

Here is the conundrum: As humans evolved, they developed a taste for high-calorie and high-fat foods. This made plenty of sense, as life was very different until a few hundred years ago. First off, there was very little food available in general, and humans had to eat what they could find. High-energy foods such as honey, nuts, fats, and meat were premium items and our brains developed to crave and seek these foods out.

Second, our ancestors did not spend a lot of time sitting in front of computers, televisions, or video games. They were out, all day, running, working, building, farming, and generally expending many calories. They needed calorie-dense

Light or Low-Fat Mayonnaise

- Premium brands have managed to make lower-fat mayo almost as good as the real thing. Some folks even prefer it.

- Look for mayo made with olive oil for an even healthier option.

- Light or low-fat mayo can be used in any application as full-fat mayo, including in cooking, such as in crab cakes.

- One you switch over you won't miss the original. This is truly worth it.

Creamy Skim Milk

- For many, the words "skim milk" conjure up images of watery, tasteless milk that turns coffee gray and does nothing for a PB&J.

- Fortunately there is a new breed of skim milk on the market, which does not have the watery taste or texture.

- Look for brands such as "Skim Plus" and others that tout a creamy skim milk. You will be surprised at the great flavor.

- Beware, however, as skim milk in general is not good to cook with; it may separate.

foods in order to fuel their body's engine. These days we eat more than ever and expend fewer calories than ever. Thank goodness the food industries have begun to react and are now providing us with excellent low-fat, light, and lower-calorie options of the foods we crave.

It is a good idea to seek out these "lighter options" and see what appeals to you. Sometimes they are almost indiscernible from their full-calorie counterparts, while some have noticeable differences in flavor, texture, or aftertaste that make them unpalatable. There are no perfect solutions, but many lighter options will surprise you with how close they come to "the real thing." However, be careful not to overload on light foods simply because they're half the calories; that would be counterproductive.

It is also recommended that you go for "low-fat" rather than "fat-free" items. Some studies show that an absence of fat may actually trigger cravings for more fat. So if you have a "low-fat" item, you may get just enough fat to be satisfied and not leave the table feeling deprived.

Low-Fat Cheeses

- Many cheeses are already low in fat by design. A general rule of thumb is that the harder the cheese, the lower the fat content.

- Spreadable Swiss cheeses, such as the Laughing Cow brand, make excellent sandwich spreads in place of butter or mayo.

- Part-skim ricotta makes excellent lasagnas, raviolis, and other stuffed pastas.

- Parmesan cheese packs a ton of flavor with few calories. Try it as a snack on its own in small chunks.

Light Oil

- A common misconception is that "light" olive oil has fewer calories or less fat or is in some way healthier.

- The truth is that extra-light, light, and extra-virgin olive oils all have the exact same amount of calories and fat. The main difference is flavor. Extra-light has almost no flavor, while extra-virgin has the most flavor.

- Light and extra-light olive oils are more processed than extra-virgin olive oil.

- Use light or extra light if you do not want the strong flavor of extra virgin, such as when frying.

LOW-FAT SALAD DRESSINGS

Besides using low-fat dressing in moderation, you can also make your own quite easily

Salad is healthy, right? Loaded with vitamins and essential nutrients, fresh veggies should be a large part of your diet. They not only provide you with all those great vitamins and minerals, but the roughage and fiber that raw veggies bring to your diet are essential for a healthy digestive tract.

There is, however, one small problem. Salad dressings are notoriously high in fat, and most people absolutely drown their salads in so much dressing that the flavor of the vegetables is lost in the flood. However, hope is not lost. There are many solutions to this seemingly unfair problem.

First and foremost: Put less dressing on your salads for cryin'

Fat Free Can Work

- A great and simple fat-free dressing is 1 teaspoon honey, 1 teaspoon mustard, and 1 tablespoon balsamic vinegar with a dash of salt and pepper.

- You can add 1 teaspoon oil to this dressing if you really crave the fat.

- Mustard is a natural emulsifier and helps give dressings body without adding fat or calories. Try experimenting with different mustards in your dressings.

- This dressing also makes an excellent marinade for meat, chicken, or vegetables.

The Starch Trick

- Since salad dressings use an emulsion of oil to make them creamy, achieving this result is difficult without fat.

- Here's how to do it: In a small saucepan, mix 2 tablespoons cornstarch into 1 cup cold water and stir well. Bring to a boil and cool down. The mixture will have thickened.

- Into this mixture you can blend all manner of spices, some vinegar, and a smidgeon of extra-virgin olive oil. Taste as you go.

- The dressing will be a bit thick and not watery.

out loud! In Europe a perfectly dressed salad is one where the dressing barely coats the leaves and veggies, and the flavor of the actual salad comes through; the dressing acts as an enhancement, not a dominating flavor. After all, it is a salad, so you should taste the greens. Try tossing your salad with a very small amount of dressing and see how you like it. Also, toss a little salt and freshly ground pepper in with your dressing. The salt enhances the flavor and allows you to put less dressing on your salad while still enjoying the flavor of the salad.

There are also some great tips for making your own dressing that have very little fat and yet are still wonderful and satisfying. The trick is to find a substitute for most or all of the oil in the dressing, as oil is the main calorie culprit. It is okay to keep some of the oil, as you crave the silky feeling the oil gives your taste buds. Just don't keep all of it.

Flavor Bombs Away

- Items that pack tons of flavor in small amounts are an excellent way to maximize flavor without adding too much oil.

- Try cutting the amount of oil in your salad dressing in half and adding 1 tablespoon grated cheese or 2 teaspoons blue cheese. You will reduce calories.

- Fresh herb leaves tossed in with your greens provide a huge burst of flavor with zero calories.

- Anchovies add a "deep saltiness" to salad dressings. Try adding them in place of salt.

Creamy and Delicious

- You can still have creamy salad dressings and reduce calories and fat. The key is to dress your salads sparingly.

- Substitute low-fat mayo for the oil in your dressings and blend well. If needed, thin out with a little water.

- Adding low-fat sour cream in place of three quarters of the oil works well, especially with ranch-style dressings.

- Low-fat yogurt, yogurt cheese, and skim buttermilk are all excellent ingredients in creamy dressings. Experiment!

SMART PROTEIN CHOICES
Learn to make smart choices whether you're eating at home or out

Take a look at the diet in Asia: The bulk of food consumed is vegetables, a bit of rice or noodles, and a small amount of animal or soy proteins. Asian cultures tend to be thinner, healthier, and live longer and the key is to eat with more of a balance, with emphasis on portion control. Remember, the palm of your hand or a deck of cards is about the right size for a portion of protein.

Understanding how protein works and what it does to your body is important. Protein is an excellent fuel source for your body. The protein you eat builds and maintains important tissues and systems in your body including your muscles and immune system. Protein is also a very efficient burning fuel because it slowly releases its energy, which is a great way to keep you from getting hungry.

The Incredible Edible Egg

- Eggs are one of the best and cheapest sources of protein available to us. The white part contains the protein, and the yolk contains the fat.

- A medium egg contains about 6 grams of protein and about 70 calories.

- Eggs are also loaded with omega-3 fatty acids, which are very good for brain function. Some eggs are actually fortified with extra omega-3s.

- Try using just egg whites, which are available in cartons, if you do not want the fat from the yolks.

Perfect Poultry

- Poultry is an excellent source of lean protein. The skin is where most of the fat is, so pull off the skin either before or after cooking.

- White meat has less fat than dark meat, but dark meat will remain moister after cooking.

- Duck has a high external fat content, but it is low in saturated fat. Rendered duck fat is an excellent frying fat, especially for potatoes.

- Five ounces of poultry is about the size of your palm.

Here is how it works: If you eat a couple of slices of toast, which is almost entirely made of carbohydrates, your body very quickly burns the carbohydrates (sugars) in the bread. The fuel burns, gives your body a quick energy boost, raises your blood sugar, and then quickly fizzles out. Your blood sugar drops and you become hungry again quickly. On the other hand, if you eat a couple of scrambled eggs, you body burns this fuel more slowly, allowing for a much less drastic change in blood sugar and, hence, you do not feel as hungry as soon as you do with the toast. This clearly illustrates how important protein is as part of a balanced diet. This chapter should help you make good choices when shopping or eating.

Good for the Heart

- Beans are one of the most incredible protein sources available to us today. A half cup of cooked beans has as much protein as 3 ounces of steak.

- Beans also have the extra benefit of being packed with fiber, which helps you feel full longer and is good for digestion.

- Try adding some canned beans to salads for a quick and healthy shot of protein.

- Soybeans and tofu, which is made from soybeans, are excellent sources of protein.

Moo

- Dairy foods are great sources of protein. Be aware of fat content when choosing dairy foods.

- Some studies have shown a link between consuming dairy products and weight loss. Adults who ate two to three servings of low-fat dairy a day had an easier time losing weight.

- Cultured dairy products, such as yogurt, have positive effects on your digestive tract and help with regularity.

- Dairy also has the added bonus of being a great source of calcium.

FIBER IS YOUR FRIEND

Become a label reader and be conscious of the recommended daily amount of fiber

Fiber really is your friend. When our ancestors roamed the planet, eating a high-fiber diet was easy. Meat was scarce, and whole grains and vegetables made up the bulk of the diet. Nowadays, there is so much meat and starch in our diets, that fiber has slipped by the wayside, and with real health consequences.

Fiber is important for regularity in the body. It helps the body eliminate solids. This is very important, as studies show that people who maintain a high-fiber diet have a much lower incidence of many diseases, including colon cancer, diverticulitis, diabetes, constipation, and hemorrhoids.

Start with the Bread

- For years, high-fiber bread was strictly grainy, dry, crumbly European bread that was not palatable to most. This has changed.

- "Whole wheat" or "made with whole grains" is not enough. High-fiber bread should have between 3 and 6 grams of fiber per slice.

- Pairing high-fiber bread with lettuce, tomato, and other veggies suddenly makes that ham sandwich a lot healthier.

- Look for "double fiber" breads in the bread aisle. They are soft and not at all grainy.

Rice Is Nice

- White rice is simply brown rice with the bran and germ (the healthful parts) removed. This was done to increase shelf life but doesn't contribute to your nutritional needs.

- Brown rice has a wonderful nutty flavor that is easy to love. It has much more fiber than white rice.

- Brown rice takes longer to cook than white rice and requires more liquid.

- If the rice seems too crunchy, add more water and cook longer for softer rice.

The recommended daily intake of fiber is about 25 to 30 grams. Most Americans get between 5 and 10 grams of fiber daily, and the incidence of gastrointestinal cancers and other gastro diseases reflect it.

These days many products have fiber added to them, as people are catching on to the importance of a high-fiber diet. Some items are marketed specifically for their high-fiber content, and many are excellent. So remember to read labels, eat your whole grains, and for goodness sakes, stop eating that terrible, tasteless white bread.

GREEN ● LIGHT

In general, "white foods" such as white bread, white rice, and potatoes are much less healthy than their "brown" counterparts. Whole wheat and grain breads, brown rice, and whole grains are the better option. Many people prefer the heartier and nuttier flavors that these whole wheat and whole grain foods provide. There are also whole wheat mixes such as muffin or pancake mixes.

Eat Your Veggies

- Fruits and veggies have a high amount of insoluble fiber, which helps prevent colon cancer. Soluble fiber, which is found in breads, binds with fatty acids and helps control blood sugar.

- Veggies such as carrots, celery, cabbage, eggplant, and artichokes are great fiber sources.

- Potatoes, especially sweet potatoes, are great fiber sources.

- Try to eat fruits with the skin on, as much of the fiber is contained there. The skin of fruits also contains many important nutrients.

Nuts about Nuts

- Nuts and seeds are excellent sources of fiber.

- Many seeds are high in fiber, and many have the added benefit of being high in omega-3 fatty acids. Flaxseed is an excellent source of both.

- Be aware that nuts are high in calories and fall under the "a little goes a long way" rule.

- Toasting nuts briefly in a dry pan at 350°F for 5 minutes intensifies their flavor.

HEALTHY TIPS

TOFU ROCKS

Many have limited exposure to tofu, but there's much to learn about this great food

Tofu is one of the world's great food products. It is made in much the same way cheese is produced. In fact, tofu is soybean curd, just as cheese is milk curd. An easy way to think of tofu is as soy milk cheese, which is really what tofu is. And, as in the world of cheeses, there are hundreds of different types of tofu. Besides what we typically see in the grocery store, there is smoked, fermented, dried, sheet, marinated, and countless other types of tofu. Look for them all in Asian supermarkets, and play around.

You cannot talk about tofu without talking about the miracle of the soybean. Soybeans contain about 35 percent protein, which is higher than any other crop. In fact, it is higher

Chinese-Style Tofu

- Packages of firm water-packed tofu are widely available in today's supermarkets. These are great for grilling and stir-frying.

- Try marinating tofu in anything from an Asian-style soy sauce to barbecue sauce, and grill away.

- You can press the tofu between heavy plates and some towels in the fridge overnight to make it even firmer.

- Try crumbling it into chili, replacing some of the meat. The tofu will soak up the flavor of the chili.

Boxed Silken Tofu

- Silken soft tofu is excellent for dips, dressings, and drinks. Try adding it to your favorite onion dip or creamy salad dressing.

- Blended with fruit, a little ice, and some soy milk, tofu adds a super jolt of protein to smoothies.

- Scramble 2 ounces of silken soft tofu with an egg to reduce calories and cholesterol without sacrificing flavor or texture.

- Cut it into small cubes and add to miso soup for an authentic Japanese experience.

in protein than almost any animal protein, as well. A ½ cup of regular canned beans has as much protein as 3 ounces of steak, while a ½ cup of soybeans has as much protein as 5 ounces of steak! Tofu truly is a superfood, and more people should embrace the soybean and tofu.

Tofu can basically replace meat entirely in a diet. Many vegetarians rely on tofu as their main source of protein. Vegetarian Chinese Buddhist monks have come up with incredible tofu recipes, such as "mock chicken" and "mock duck," which are incredibly complex and could easily pass as meat.

You can find small boxes of Japanese-style "silken" tofu in different degrees of firmness in most supermarkets, as well as water-packed Chinese-style tofu in different degrees of firmness. Both have myriad uses. Firmer tofu tends to be better for grilling and stir-frying, and softer tofu is better for eating as is or using in dips, dressings, and smoothies.

Fakin' Bacon

- Tofu has been transformed into many pseudomeat products for hard-core vegetarians.

- Tofu sausage, bacon, and hot dogs are widely available in organic and natural markets.

- Some of these items are just as high in calories as the foods they're trying to replace, so read labels carefully.

- Try going to a great Chinese restaurant that specializes in tofu to see what the hype is all about.

Relatives Make Good Company

- Since tofu is made from soybeans, you should get familiar with its cousins.

- Soy milk is an excellent dairy substitute. It is great in cereal and in baking. Chocolate soy milk is yummy.

- Soy milk can be cultured into yogurt. It has a slightly looser texture and makes a great smoothie. All soy products contain no lactose.

- Miso is a fermented soybean paste that is more of a seasoning. It makes a great soup but is also great in marinades.

NOT YOUR MOM'S OATMEAL

This is an amazing and delicious energy-boosting breakfast, especially nice on a cold morning

Eating a bowl of hot cereal has been a breakfast staple for much of the world for centuries. In Asia, for example, rice porridge is commonly served for breakfast and is usually a savory affair with meats, vegetables, and even hot sauce mixed in.

Hot cereals are a great way to start your day. Many of us remember being force-fed oatmeal, Cream of Wheat, and Wheatena while wishing for the bacon and eggs that Dad was eating at the breakfast table. This incredibly hearty, nutty, and satisfying breakfast bowl will not leave you feeling deprived, however. Grape-Nuts, used in this recipe, have long been a favorite cold cereal, but serving them hot morphs these nuggets into a wonderful breakfast. *Yield: 1 portion*

Ingredients

1 cup Grape-Nuts cereal

¼ cup low-fat granola

1 tablespoon raisins

3 dried apricots, roughly chopped

8 pecans, chopped

1 cup low-fat milk, plus a few tablespoons for topping

Pinch of salt

1 medium banana, sliced

1 tablespoon honey

Dash cinnamon

Not Your Mom's Oatmeal

- Place all ingredients except banana, honey, and cinnamon in a microwavable bowl and microwave for about 30 seconds. If you like your cereal very soft, microwave for 60 seconds, otherwise the cereal will have a pleasing crunchiness to it.

- Stir well and allow to rest for 20 seconds.

- Place cooked cereal in a serving bowl, and top with banana slices.

- Drizzle with honey and a little milk and dust with the cinnamon. Serve immediately.

Oatmeal with Cooked Fruit: Try adding cooked fruits to the bowl by making a compote with fruits on hand. In a saucepan, combine ¹/₂ cup orange juice and 2 tablespoons sugar. Add ¹/₂ a chopped apple, 6 prunes, and ¹/₂ a banana; boil for 5 minutes. This compote will last for a week in the fridge. It's a great way to clean out the crisper.

Grape-Nuts Cobbler: Once you have made the compote, you can transform the same ingredients into a healthy dessert. Bring the compote to a boil. Thicken by gently stirring a mixture of 2 teaspoons cornstarch and 2 teaspoons cold water into the boiling compote. Pour over hot Grape-Nuts and bake at 375°F for 15 minutes to make a cobbler.

Dried Apricots Are Versatile

- Dried apricots are an excellent item to keep on hand, as they almost never go bad. If they become too hard, simple microwave with a little water to reconstitute.

- When cutting apricots or other dried fruits, be careful, as the fruit can slip on the board and may have a tough skin.

- Dried apricots also make an elegant and simple treat to eat with cheeses before or after a meal.

- Dried peaches are an excellent apricot substitute.

The Magic Banana

- Bananas are incredibly nutritious and full of helpful vitamins and minerals, especially potassium.

- Look for green-tipped bananas with an even colored skin. These should ripen properly.

- If bananas get too cold in transport they will ripen unevenly and may get too soft before becoming sweet.

- A perfectly ripened banana has an even mottling of tiny brown spots all over the skin.

DOCTORED-UP GRANOLA

This is just what the doctor ordered—who thought healthy could taste so good?

Granola has a long history. From as early as 1863, a New York doctor invented what he called "granula," which was a healthy graham flour cereal of sorts. Forty years later, the famous Mr. Kellogg also created a cereal and took the same name, granula. He was sued and as a result changed the name to "granola."

In Europe, the cereal "muesli" was also invented in the 1800s and is a close relative of American granola. In the 1960s in California, granola boomed with the huge numbers of vegetarians and their culinary movement. Many different recipes, including all sorts of nuts, grains, and oats, were being sold in health food stores. *Yield: 1 serving*

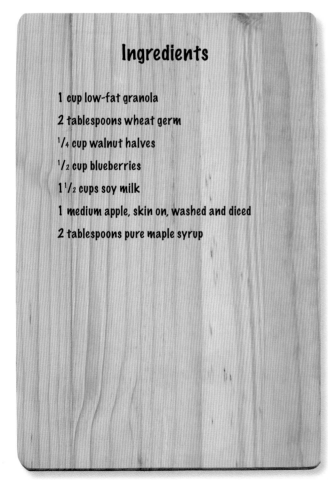

Ingredients

1 cup low-fat granola

2 tablespoons wheat germ

1/4 cup walnut halves

1/2 cup blueberries

1 1/2 cups soy milk

1 medium apple, skin on, washed and diced

2 tablespoons pure maple syrup

Doctored-Up Granola

- Pour the granola into the bowl you will be serving it in. Toss in the wheat germ and walnuts.

- Carefully wash the blueberries and pick out any blemished fruit. Add to the granola.

- Pour soy milk over the granola.

- Top with the apple dices and drizzle with maple syrup.

Sometimes it's just easier to pour some granola out of the box and not take the time to cut apples, wash blueberries, and open the cupboard for additional ingredients. But what do you do if want something a bit more special? A nice time-saver is to "doctor" your granola with dried apple pieces, dried blueberries, dried strawberries, and some toasted nuts. You can do this ahead of time and store.

Hot Granola: Since muesli and granola are such close relatives, try buying both and mixing them together. The interesting thing about muesli is that it can be served hot or cold. Try heating some milk or soy milk and cook the granola and muesli together. The granola will get quite soft, but the muesli will retain some texture. You can then top with all manner of fruits and nuts.

Superfood

An Apple a Day

- Blueberries are a so-called "superfood," as they are loaded with antioxidants and phytoflaviniods, which are the darlings of doctors and nutritionists.

- It is important to wash blueberries thoroughly, as pesticides are usually used to grow them.

- You can freeze fresh blueberries. Place them well spaced on a cookie sheet, freeze, then place in a ziplock bag. You can also find frozen blueberries in the supermarket.

- Dried blueberries have the same nutrients as fresh, but do not spoil.

- Wash apples and do not remove the skin. The skin contains many valuable nutrients as well as fiber.

- If you are saving cut apples for later, sprinkle them with a little lemon juice, and they will not turn brown or oxidize.

- Practice your cutting technique by seeing how uniform you can make your apple dices.

- There are many new "heirloom" apples on the market these days. Try Honeycrisps and Fuji apples for a nice change.

51

YOGURT "CHEESE," SWEET/SAVORY

A true Mediterranean treat, this simplest of cheeses makes for a wonderful breakfast

This straining technique for making a rudimentary cheese is an ancient one. In the Middle East, yogurt has been eaten for at least four thousand years. The first yogurt was probably made by accident with a strain of wild bacteria "culturing" the milk into yogurt. Yogurt has been credited with having unique health benefits that could aid longevity. It is very rich in calcium, protein, and B vitamins. In fact, there has been speculation that the long life spans of one group of people from Bulgaria is due to the group's high consumption of yogurt.

Making this cheese from store-bought yogurt is excellent, but if you can, seek out artisan yogurts or Greek yogurts. *Yield: About 1 cup*

Ingredients

1 1/2 cups plain yogurt, strained

Savory Option
1/2 cup diced cucumber
6 cherry tomatoes, sliced in half
2 green onions, finely sliced
1 tablespoon extra-virgin olive oil
Few grinds black pepper
1 whole wheat pita, cut in quarters

Sweet Option
3 tablespoons honey
1/2 cup sliced strawberries
2 tablespoons sliced almonds
1 whole wheat pita, cut in quarters

Yogurt "Cheese," Sweet or Savory

- Place the yogurt in your coffee filter cradle and place directly over the coffeepot. Cover; put in the fridge and allow to drain overnight.

- In the morning the coffeepot will have a puddle of whey, or liquid, strained off the yogurt, and the filter will contain the firm curd. Place the curd in a bowl for storage. The yogurt cheese is now ready to eat.

- Top with either the sweet or savory ingredients.

- Serve immediately with warm pita.

In the Middle East a very traditional way to serve yogurt cheese is with an amazing spice blend called za'atar. The blend consists of dried oregano, basil, thyme, dried sumac, sesame seeds, salt, and lemon zest. Experiment with your own mix, but always keep the oregano and sesame seeds. Spread a warm pita with yogurt cheese and generously sprinkle with za'atar.

MAKE IT EASY

You can make this cheese in bulk, and it will keep for a long time in the fridge. In order to extend the shelf life, make sure to sanitize all the utensils and vessels you use in food prep. Add $\frac{1}{2}$ teaspoon salt to each cup of yogurt before straining and pack tightly into small jars. You can cover the top of the cheese with a $\frac{1}{4}$ inch of olive oil for an even longer life.

Curds and Whey

- Whey is the liquid left over when the straining is complete. It has many nutritional benefits.

- Little Miss Muffet ate both the curds and the whey.

- Many people save this liquid and use it as a water substitute when baking breads and muffins. Some folks use it to water their plants or give it to their pets.

- Some folks simply drink this liquid, as they claim it helps everything from energy to digestion.

Mix It Up

- The savory aspect of this cheese is new to most people, who tend to think of yogurt as strictly sweet.

- Try different toppings besides fresh veggies, such as cooked vegetable stews or curries.

- This cheese makes a great sauce for Middle Eastern spiced meatballs, skewers, and gyros. Season with some herbs and garlic.

- Use as a dressing for a grilled vegetable salad with some fresh cilantro and cumin, or try a simple sauce of chopped onion, salt and pepper, and yogurt cheese.

MICROWAVE EGG TRICKS
Eggs are great any time of day and cook well in the microwave

Eggs have many virtues. One thing you will notice when shopping is that eggs are cheap! They are such a bang for the buck and can provide you with valuable and healthy protein for just a few cents. The other great thing about eggs is that they are a snap to prepare and can be made ahead of time for a quick meal or snack. Remember: A hard-boiled egg is one of the world's most convenient foods. It even comes with its own wrapper! And, of course, egg salad is always a wonderful treat. Don't overlook these little treasures—enjoy the egg. *Yield: 2 eggs*

Ingredients

Cooking spray

2 eggs

Salt

Pepper

Microwave Egg Tricks

- Fried eggs: Spray a microwavable, small shallow bowl with cooking spray and break 2 eggs into it. "Pop" the membrane and season with salt and pepper.

- Cover with plastic wrap or a loose lid and microwave 2 minutes, or until desired level of doneness. Let rest 1 minute; serve.

- Scrambled eggs: Beat two eggs with 2 teaspoons water; season with salt and pepper. Place in a shallow bowl and cover as for fried.

- Cook 1 minute, stir, and cook 1 more minute. Let rest 1 minute; serve.

······· RED ● LIGHT ·············

Salmonella is a real risk when eating undercooked or raw eggs. Most egg producers take many precautions to avoid the risk, but nevertheless it remains real. Practice common sense when preparing eggs. Be sure you always keep eggs refrigerated and heed the expiration date on the carton. When cracking eggs, make sure that any stray egg is cleaned and the area sanitized before cooking other foods.

· · · · · RECIPE VARIATION · · · ·

Scrambled Egg Cakes: Scrambled eggs are a blank canvas that can be mixed with all manner of ingredients. In Europe, there is the omelet; in Italy, the frittata; and in Spain, the tortilla. These are simple scrambled egg "cakes" with goodies added to them. Try mixing 3 scrambled eggs with a $1/2$ cup cooked mushrooms, leftover cooked vegetables, or meats.

Anatomy of an Egg

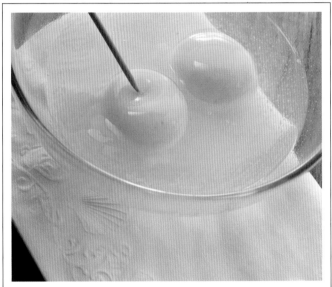

- The egg is truly a masterpiece of nutrition, but it is also a masterpiece of design.

- The yolk contains all the fat and omega-3 fatty acids

- The white is pure protein and has no fat. Look for cartons of egg whites at your supermarket.

- To avoid shell bits in your dish, break eggs on a flat surface instead of the edge of a pan.

The Wave

- Microwaves are funny things, and many of them cook in an almost uneven manner.

- Be sure to stir your eggs at least once through the scrambling process to avoid tough pieces.

- Halfway through the cooking process, add any cheeses or other mix-ins.

- If you do add mix-ins, your cooking time may vary. To make cooking even, heat the mix-ins before adding them to the eggs.

BACON IN THE MICROWAVE
This is one of the best ways to cook bacon, even if you don't live in a dorm room

Bacon is truly one of the world's most amazing foods. It's basically the cured and smoked belly of the pig. Most bacon we buy is presliced, but bacon can be bought in one piece; this is called "slab" bacon. The curing process can include all manner of spices and sweet components including honey, maple syrup, and molasses, but most bacon we buy has been cured in simple salt and sugar. In Italy the most popular bacon is not smoked and is called pancetta; it is also rolled and not left flat. This recipe utilizes turkey bacon for the health conscious.
Yield: 1–2 servings

Ingredients

6 slices turkey bacon

Bacon in the Microwave

- Line a microwave-safe plate with a layer of paper towel.

- Arrange the bacon in rows on the towels, leaving about ⅛ inch between slices. Top with a paper towel and repeat the process. If making more for a crowd, you can build up to four or five layers of bacon.

- Microwave in 2-minute increments, checking the bacon between microwavings to check doneness.

- Cook until bacon is dark and crisp; allow to rest for a minute or so before handling. Carefully peel off paper towels and enjoy.

RED ● LIGHT

Although bacon and turkey bacon have been cured and smoked, the possibility of bacteria and food-borne illness is real. Always make sure you thoroughly cook your bacon and clean and sanitize any cutting boards or knives that have come in contact with raw bacon. Some recipes call for wrapping raw bacon around an item before broiling or grilling. A trick is to blanch the bacon for 30 seconds; this makes a crisper slice.

• • • • RECIPE VARIATION • • • •

Custom-Flavored Bacon: Making custom-flavored bacon is fun and can yield some amazing results. Bacon pairs very well with sweet flavors, which is why we love to dip bacon in our maple syrup on our breakfast plates. Try marinating bacon overnight in a little brown sugar and brandy for a sophisticated treat. Or sprinkle it with cinnamon and a little maple syrup.

Space, the Final Frontier

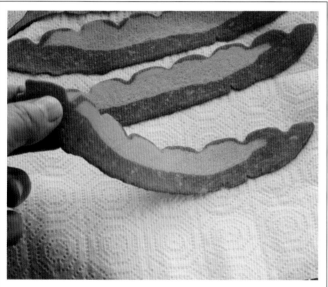

- It is important not to overload your microwave or plate of bacon before cooking.

- Lay the bacon out with small spaces between each slice to allow for better cooking. This will prevent steam from building up and making the bacon soggy.

- Depending on the power of your microwave, you may need to limit the number of layers of bacon when cooking.

- For added doneness, carefully flip the whole plate of bacon over during cooking.

How You Like It

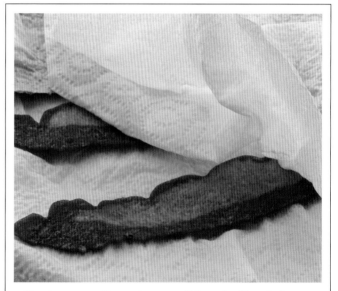

- The doneness of bacon is a personal choice. Some like it crispy, while others like it limp. Adjust your cooking time to your preference.

- If you like your bacon limp, make sure it heats to at least 165°F, which is considered safe to eat.

- When checking during cooking, be very careful, as the fat and steam generated can burn you.

- If you marinated the bacon in something sweet, it may be a bit difficult to peel off the towels; be gentle.

BREAK YOUR FAST

SALSA VERDE BREAKFAST BURRITO

Combine your new skills for a portable breakfast that's perfect for students on the go

The burrito is an excellent way to eat on the go. The name, which translates to "little burro," is a small donkey. Some say the wrapped tortilla resembles the donkey's ears or maybe the packs the donkeys carried. In any case, the burrito made its way from Mexico to California, and gained a large following in the San Francisco Mission District, where burritos quickly found their way onto menus.

The beauty of these portable packages is that they can be stuffed with just about anything. Traditionally beans, a little meat, and rice were stuffed into the tortillas, but these days there are all sorts of burritos. *Yield: 1 burrito*

Ingredients

2 eggs

2 strips microwave bacon

1 12-inch flour tortilla

¼ cup shredded Monterey Jack cheese

1 tablespoon sour cream

2 tablespoons jarred salsa verde

Salsa Verde Breakfast Burrito

- Scramble two eggs in the microwave according to recipe on page 54. Microwave the bacon, too. Keep warm.

- Gently warm the tortilla in the microwave for 10 seconds to allow for easier rolling.

- Place the eggs, bacon, and cheese in the center of the tortilla; top with sour cream and salsa verde. Roll by tucking two ends in to make an enclosed pocket, then roll up tightly.

•••• RECIPE VARIATION ••••

Chorizo Sausage Burrito: For a truly traditional Mexican breakfast burrito, try raw, finely ground chorizo sausage. This sausage is very fine, almost paste-like, and very flavorful. Cook a few tablespoons and then add your eggs and continue to cook until done. Splash with a little real Mexican hot sauce and wrap in a warm flour tortilla. This is as authentic and real as it gets.

YELLOW LIGHT

Many folks have trouble deciding when to use flour tortillas in a recipe and when to use corn tortillas. Flour tortillas are made from much softer dough than corn tortillas and tend to be more elastic and less prone to breakage, especially when warmed. Avoid using corn tortillas for burritos and, if using for tacos, do as they do in Mexico—double up on them, as one will surely break.

More Cheese Please

- If you cannot find Jack cheese, sharp white cheddar makes a great substitute.

- Grating your own cheese saves you money, as pre-grated cheese tends to be much more expensive than block cheese.

- Store your grated cheese in a ziplock bag wrapped tightly in the fridge; discard if any mold forms.

- If you cook your cheese with the eggs, it can get tough or even separate slightly and get greasy. Sprinkling the cheese right before rolling is best.

Rock and Roll

- There are two methods for burrito rolling: One has an open top, the other is closed on both ends.

- Be sure the tortilla is warm, as it will roll much easier. A warm tortilla also tastes better.

- Place the filling in the bottom third of the open tortilla and then fold the tortilla over the filling.

- Tuck either one or both sides in and roll as tightly as you can without tearing the tortilla.

BRUTUS SALAD WITH CHICKEN

Thank goodness for pregrilled chicken strips, which make this unique salad a snap

"Et tu, Brute?" Caesar uttered these words when his former friend, along with a slew of others, murdered him on the senate steps. At least Shakespeare wants us to believe this. This salad, with the addition of chicken and avocado, simply kills all the regular Caesar salads out there. While traditional Caesar salad uses raw eggs in the dressing, along with anchovies,

lemon juice, garlic, and Parmesan cheese, store-bought dressing contains no raw eggs. Romaine lettuce is traditionally used, but any sturdy lettuce works just fine. While you may be skeptical about having anchovies in your salad, don't be afraid to give them a shot. They rock! *Yield: 1 big salad*

Ingredients

¹/₂ avocado, cut into ¹/₂-inch dices

¹/₄ cup Caesar dressing

1 teaspoon chipotle hot sauce

3 cups chopped romaine lettuce

¹/₂ cup prepared croutons

6 grilled chicken strips

2 tablespoons shredded Parmesan cheese

Brutus Salad with Chicken

- Prepare avocado by cutting it in half lengthwise and twisting halves apart. Insert the blade of the knife into pit, twist and pull out the knife, pulling the pit with it. Peel off skin; dice.

- In a small bowl, mix together the dressing and hot sauce.

- Toss in the avocado and remaining ingredients, except the chicken and cheese. Transfer mixture to a serving bowl

- Top salad with the grilled chicken strips and cheese, and serve.

• • • • RECIPE VARIATION • • • •

Tex-Mex and Chinese Caesar Salad Versions: The cool thing about Caesar dressing is that you can tweak it with a slew of other flavors. One option is to add a pinch of pureed chipotle peppers and a dash of cumin; the salad instantly becomes a Tex-Mex version. For a Chinese version, add a dash of soy sauce and sesame oil and garnish with some bean sprouts.

ZOOM

Interestingly enough, the Caesar salad, which most people assume is an ancient Italian invention, probably finds its roots in the Mexican town of Tijuana. An Italian who was living in Mexico supposedly invented the salad during a very busy night in the restaurant and had to make do with the ingredients available to him. Whatever the case may be, it is a worldwide success.

The Mighty Avocado

Hail Caesar

- Avocados are an incredible food loaded with healthy fats. Some studies that show diets rich in avocados can actually lower serum cholesterol.

- Choose avocados that are yielding but not mushy. The little nub of a stem, if intact, should dislodge easily.

- Avocados have sweet applications that make them good ingredients for milkshakes and cheesecakes.

- Cut avocados by "scoring" the flesh inside the "shell" and scooping out with a spoon.

- You can make your own Caesar dressing easily with a bowl and whisk or a blender or food processor.

- If you use raw egg yolks, understand that there are risks of salmonella contamination.

- You can use a soft-boiled egg yolk, as it is partially cooked, to avoid issues.

- Another trick is to substitute mayonnaise for the egg yolks and simply add a bit of water to thin out the recipe. This works well.

SUPERMARKET NIÇOISE
This salad is sophisticated and rustic all at the same time—and a real treat

There are many stories about when the salad became famous or which recipe is authentic. Most agree that the salad was inspired by and made in the city of Nice, France, hence the name Niçoise. This salad always contains tuna, anchovies, hard-boiled eggs, and tomatoes as well as small black olives, but there are countless variations. Of course, if you hate anchovies, omit 'em.

This is a beautiful salad, often arranged very artfully on a large plate. A big platter of "salade Niçoise" on a brunch buffet always draws oohs and ahhs. You can construct the salad and leave the dressing on the side so your friends can add dressing as they serve themselves. *Yield: 1–2 servings*

Ingredients

1 5 to 6-ounce can of tuna packed in olive oil, drained, oil reserved

Extra-virgin olive oil

1/2 lemon

Salt and pepper to taste

2 cups mixed washed greens

3 small new potatoes, microwaved 3 minutes, cooled, and sliced thinly

12 kalamata or nicoise olives, pitted

8 grape tomatoes, halved

4 anchovy fillets

1/4 cup red onion, thinly sliced

1 hard-boiled egg, cut in quarters

12–15 frozen French green beans, thawed and patted dry

Supermarket Niçoise

- Drain oil from tuna into a small bowl; set aside tuna. Add enough olive oil to the tuna oil to make a total of 4 tablespoons oil.

- Squeeze half the lemon into the oil; season with salt and pepper. This is the dressing.

- In another bowl, toss greens with dressing and then arrange on a large plate.

- Artfully arrange the remaining ingredients, except the tuna, on the salad in any way you like.

- Place the tuna in the center of the salad, and eat!

•••• RECIPE VARIATION ••••

Tuna Niçoise: Many restaurants today serve this salad with a piece of rare seared tuna instead of the traditional tuna packed in oil. In fact many chefs think this is the original recipe. To try this, simply get the best piece of tuna you can find. Season it with salt and pepper and cook for 30 seconds on each side on a hot surface. In a dorm, it just might have to be your iron!

YELLOW ● LIGHT

There is much controversy about the safety of tuna. This incredibly large and powerful fish is full of healthy fats and nutrients, but also may be a source of the poison mercury. Pregnant women are usually told to avoid tuna. The other issue with tuna is that the world's love affair with sushi and sashimi has caused a huge decrease in the tuna population. Some researchers speculate that the world will have no tuna left in less that thirty years. Bogus!

Basic Vinaigrette

- Adding lemon juice to oil is one of the simplest vinaigrettes.

- Vinaigrettes always contain oil and some acid, such as vinegar or lemon juice.

- The classic ratio for oil to vinegar (or lemon juice) is three times as much oil as vinegar.

- Always season your vinaigrette.

Eat with Your Eyes

- Food can be considered an art or even a craft. Making a salad like this is definitely considered an art form.

- Try arranging the ingredients in a geometric pattern on the plate, especially if you are serving a special someone.

- Try not to let items of the same or similar color sit next to each other; separate them with strips of red pepper or black olives.

- Be creative and have fun with this salad. No two need ever be the same.

GOAT CHEESE & BEET SALAD
This is an upscale salad with an amazing combination of flavors

Goat cheese?! Sure, it may not be one of your daily food choices or on the menu at the cafeteria, but it has a uniquely pungent flavor and semicreamy texture that is guaranteed to liven up your average college meal.

The different varieties and textures of goat cheeses are incredible, and there are many domestic cheese makers who make excellent goat cheeses. The cheese in this recipe is a fresh goat cheese, or chèvre, but there are all varieties of aged goat cheeses, goat cheeses rubbed in ash or coated in grape leaves, and even blue goat cheeses. They are worth seeking out and trying. Cheese is one of life's pleasures that you should come to know. *Yield: 1–2 servings*

Ingredients

1 14-ounce can whole baby beets, drained and sliced into four wedges each

1 small red onion, sliced as thinly as possible

3 tablespoons walnut oil or sesame oil

1 tablespoon sherry vinegar

Salt and pepper to taste

2 cups washed baby spinach leaves

4 ounces chèvre goat cheese, in large crumbles

12 walnut halves, lightly crushed with the back of a knife

Dash pepper

Goat Cheese and Beet Salad

- Toss the beets and onion with the oil and vinegar. Season with salt and pepper.

- Place the spinach on the bottom of a serving bowl and nest the beet/onion mixture on top in a nice pile.

- Sprinkle the goat cheese crumbles over the salad and top with the walnuts. To finish, grind a little pepper over the top.

- Be sure to get a little of everything in each bite to truly appreciate the combination.

• • • • RECIPE VARIATION • • • •

Goat Cheese and Butternut Squash Salad: Some people have such an aversion to beets that they simply cannot bring themselves to even try them. For those folks (maybe you included), try substituting pieces of cooked butternut squash for the beets. Another good substitute is sweet potato slices cooked in the microwave. The sweetness is a key component.

ZOOM

Beets have been grown as a food crop for over two thousand years. There are several varieties, including a bright yellow beet now known as the golden beet. Golden beets taste the same as red beets but do not have the red pigment. Beet juice is a common ingredient in red food colorings and shows up in many food labels in surprising places.

Toss It Up

- Beets and onions can be marinated and stored for at least a week in the refrigerator. Be sure there is some vinegar in the marinade to preserve it.

- Try different vinegars, such as balsamic, apple cider, tomato vinegar, or red wine.

- The red pigment in beets is water soluble, and if you get a stain on your clothing, cold water and soap will get it right out.

- Try adding potatoes to the beet salad for a funky and delicious purple potato salad.

Brain Food

- For years walnuts were thought to be good for the brain because a half a walnut looks eerily like a brain.

- It turns out that walnuts are excellent "brain food" because of the high concentration of good fats and omega-3s.

- If you have an oven or toaster oven, toasting the walnuts for 5 minutes at 350°F greatly increases their flavor.

- Try pecans as a substitute for walnuts.

DILLED CUCUMBER SALAD
This salad also works well as a side dish for a cookout or picnic

Cucumbers have been an important food crop for centuries. Summer is the traditional season for them, but hothouse cucumbers are available all year-round. This dish is particularly well suited for a summer meal side dish, as the pleasant cooling crunch of cucumbers makes a great foil to grilled meats during a barbecue.

Since cucumbers have so much water in them, many cooks "purge" the cucumbers by lightly salting them and allowing some of the water to leave the vegetable. If this is not done, the cucumbers will purge themselves after being tossed with the sauce or marinade, making the dressing very watery. This recipe gets its inspiration from Eastern Europe. *Yield: 2 servings*

Ingredients

1 large "English" or seedless cucumber

$1/2$ cup thinly sliced Vidalia onion

Salt (to purge)

$1/2$ cup low-fat sour cream

$1/2$ teaspoon sugar

1 teaspoon white wine vinegar

Pepper to taste

1 tablespoon fresh or 1 teaspoon dried dill

Dilled Cucumber Salad

- Slice the cucumber into ¼-inch slices. Toss in a mixing bowl with the onion and add 1 teaspoon salt. Place in a strainer over a bowl and allow to purge its water for 10 minutes.

- In a small bowl, mix together the sour cream, sugar, and vinegar into a nice thick dressing.

- Toss the cucumber mixture with the dressing and season with pepper. Add salt if you feel it needs some. It may not as you already added salt in the beginning.

- Place in a serving bowl and top with dill.

• • • • RECIPE VARIATION • • • •

Varied Herb Cucumber Salads: Dill has a very particular taste, and many people without some Eastern European relatives or friends find the flavor alien. If you don't like dill, still experiment with this salad but use some other herbs. Some good choices are parsley, basil, tarragon, chervil, or cilantro. These lighter, less "wintery" herbs work well. Avoid herbs like rosemary.

• • • • • • • • • GREEN ● LIGHT • • • • • • • •

Cucumbers are really good for you. With the skin, they are loaded with vitamin C, potassium, and magnesium. They are also great sources of fiber and full of water, which helps you feel full longer. Add 'cukes to your salads all year long to capitalize on all of the health benefits.

Purging Is Good

- Purging cucumbers with a little salt over a strainer helps get rid of excess water that may make your dressing weak and watery.

- Taste the liquid; if it is not too salty, mix it in with some tomato juice or V8 for a tasty drink.

- If you are over age twenty-one, the liquid makes an excellent addition to a bloody Mary or even a Martini with a slice of cucumber in the drink.

- Purged cucumbers also keep their crunch longer.

Let's Play Dress Up

- Cucumbers do well in creamy-style dressing. Sour cream is traditional in Eastern European recipes.

- Good substitutes for the sour cream include yogurt, yogurt cheese, and low-fat mayonnaise. You can even use a combination of all of them.

- If you do not like creamy dressings, make the same salad with oil instead of sour cream.

- If the dressing is too thick, add back a little of the purged liquid.

THE BIG SALAD

For all you *Seinfeld* fans, this could be the prototype salad for the episode

What better way to enjoy a dish than to pay homage to one of the best television shows in history? To honor "The Big Salad" episode from *Seinfeld,* try this dish.

The key to the success of this salad is to use many different vegetables of differing colors and textures. This salad has a simple vinaigrette and relies on the tastes and textures of the vegetables to be the main flavor players as opposed to an oppressive dressing. This is the type of salad that can turn the most ardent salad hater around. Keeping the vegetables in large chunks adds to the "meal-like" character of this salad. This is a crunch lover's dream. *Yield: 1–2 servings*

Ingredients

For Salad:

$1/2$ small head iceberg lettuce, cut into 1- to 2-inch chunks

1 sweet yellow bell pepper, cut into 1-inch chunks

$1/2$ cup diced jicama

$1/4$ cup diced cucumber

2 scallions, minced

8 grape tomatoes, halved

8 baby carrots, halved lengthwise

For Dressing:

1 small garlic clove, ground into a paste with $1/2$ teaspoon salt

2 tablespoons red wine vinegar

1 teaspoon Dijon mustard

6 tablespoons extra-virgin olive oil

Salt and pepper to taste

The Big Salad

- Be sure all your veggies are cut into nice 1-inch dices.

- Prepare the vinaigrette by grinding the garlic into a paste with the back of a knife on a cutting board. Sprinkle with salt. Place the garlic in a small jar with a lid.

- Add the vinegar, mustard, oil, and some pepper to the jar. Place the lid on top and shake well.

- Toss the salad ingredients together with the vinaigrette and a little more salt and pepper.

GREEN ● LIGHT

A big salad may be one of the healthiest things you can eat. The different veggies and greens provide you with so many essential nutrients as well as valuable fiber. When making vegetable salads, try to incorporate as many different colors of veggies as possible. Each color represents different vitamins and minerals that each vegetable contains. This is a great trick to maximize your nutritional bang for the buck.

• • • • RECIPE VARIATION • • • •

Packed-with-Protein Salad: Boosting your salads with a dose of protein can turn your salad into a meal, as protein keeps you full longer than just veggies. Try adding ½ cup beans or chickpeas to this salad, or 4 ounces chicken breast. A couple of hard-boiled eggs will also do the trick, as well as 1 cup cooked mushrooms or 4 ounces of any leftover meat or fish.

Grind into a Paste

- Fresh garlic is an integral part of a great salad dressing. The key is to not have big chunks of garlic in the dressing.

- Smash a clove of garlic with the back of a knife and then sprinkle with kosher salt.

- Grind the knife into the cutting board, slowly rubbing the garlic with the salt into a fine paste.

- This garlic paste is also great to use in marinades as well as rubbed right into meats before grilling.

Jicama?

- Jicama is a very interesting vegetable used mainly in Mexican cooking.

- It is almost always eaten raw and is traditionally shredded and then tossed with a simple lime dressing. It is also eaten with radishes as an accompaniment to tacos.

- Some say it has the flavor of a potato crossed with an apple. It has a great crunch.

- Look for a jicama with smooth skin and no blemishes. Peel before cutting, as the skin is very tough.

FIVE-BEAN PROTEIN BLAST

Beans are an amazing source of low-fat protein and fiber; plus they are quite tasty

Canning has been widely used for foods since the late 1800s. The fact that canned foods may last for years on a shelf is the reason canning is so popular. Canned fruits, vegetables, and legumes are all fully cooked, and can be eaten directly from the can with no further cooking. Canned beans are especially helpful to college students because beans typically require

sorting, hours of soaking, and then a slow and gentle cooking process to ensure a good finished product. But even if all these steps are followed, many experienced cooks still have poorly cooked beans with tough skins, undercooked centers, or overcooked mush. The beauty of the canned bean is that it is perfect every time. *Yield: About 2 cups*

Ingredients

$1/4$ cup canned black turtle beans, rinsed and drained

$1/4$ cup canned butter beans, rinsed and drained

$1/4$ cup canned black-eyed peas, rinsed and drained

$1/4$ cup canned red kidney beans, rinsed and drained

$1/2$ cup frozen French green beans, thawed under cold water and dried

1 small garlic clove, ground into a paste with 1 teaspoon salt

$1/4$ cup finely diced red onion

1 tablespoon sugar

4 tablespoons extra-virgin olive oil

2 tablespoons red wine vinegar

Salt and pepper to taste

1 cup shredded iceberg lettuce

2 tablespoons fresh Italian parsley leaves, chopped fine

Five-Bean Protein Blast

- Drain all beans and rinse under cold water in a strainer. Allow to dry well, or the vinaigrette will not cling well to them.

- In a large bowl, mix the beans together with the garlic, onion, sugar, oil, vinegar, and salt and pepper and mix well.

- Place lettuce in the bottom of a serving bowl and pour bean salad over the top.

- Top with parsley.

········ RED ● LIGHT ··············

Botulism bacteria may be used for Botox injections around the eyes, but it is no friend to food. Cans are the main culprit for botulism poisoning, because the bacteria typically like to live in an environment that is lacking oxygen. Cases of botulism are rare, but they do pop up every once in a while, and it is important to understand when you should not trust a can of food. The rule is this: Never use a dented, rusty, or bloated can.

···· RECIPE VARIATION ····

Southwestern Bean Salad: This bean salad has a very neutral flavor base with a nice balance of sweet, sour, and oniony notes. Make a great Southwestern version by simply adding a few ingredients. Add 1 drained can of diced tomatoes, 1 teaspoon each cumin and coriander, and $1/2$ teaspoon chili powder. Substitute lime juice for the vinegar and cilantro for the parsley leaves.

Color Is Key

- One of the great things about this salad is that is it visually appealing.

- Try substituting other beans you find in the supermarket. Look in the Latin foods section for some varieties you may not be familiar with.

- Always drain and rinse the beans well before using to get rid of the starchy liquid that is in the cans.

- If you save this liquid, it is excellent added to vegetable soups and even pasta sauce. The starch adds nice body to these liquids.

Options Are Good

- Shredded lettuce is just one way to serve this salad. Be creative.

- Try placing a few tablespoons of the bean salad in little cups of butter lettuce or radicchio leaves and eat with your hand like lettuce tacos.

- Slightly warmed, this salad makes a nice side dish for roasted meats or poultry.

- The Southwestern version can be added to chili and the traditional version added to vegetable soups.

NUKED PHILLY CHEESESTEAK, "WIT"

"Wit" or "wit out": That's how you order a cheesesteak in Philly

Pat's or Gino's? That's what most folks ask when you tell them you are going to Philly to get some cheesesteaks. Truth be told, these are simply two of the most prominent places in the city; there are tons of little joints all over and around Philly that many say have as good or even better steaks.

The meat used in most traditional steaks is very thinly sliced rib eye, which has a good deal of fat within the meat that helps make the sandwich just greasy enough to have to eat it standing over a paper plate. The cheese of choice is warm Cheez Whiz sauce, and that's about it. This sandwich is leaner and of course uses precooked meat you can find at the store.
Yield: 1 sandwich

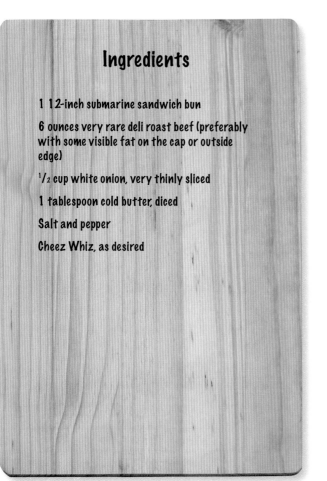

Ingredients

1 12-inch submarine sandwich bun

6 ounces very rare deli roast beef (preferably with some visible fat on the cap or outside edge)

$1/2$ cup white onion, very thinly sliced

1 tablespoon cold butter, diced

Salt and pepper

Cheez Whiz, as desired

Nuked Philly Cheesesteak, "Wit"

- Split the bun, but not all the way through. Open like a book.

- Tear each slice of beef into 3 or 4 shreds and toss with onion, butter, and salt and pepper. Place on a microwavable plate; cover with plastic wrap. Microwave 1 minute, stir, then micro-wave 1 minute.

- Place as much Cheez Whiz as you want in a cup and microwave 30 seconds.

- Place the meat on the bread and pour cheese over. Squash together and eat standing up, preferably late at night.

Light Philly Cheesesteak: For a lighter approach to this sandwich, substitute turkey or grilled chicken for the beef. The best approach is to make sure the meat is sliced very thin. You can also substitute sliced Swiss or cheddar cheese by layering the cheese between layers of meat, as you will not have the soft cheese sauce. It won't be the real thing, but it will still be yummy.

Vegetarian Cheese "Steak": A vegetarian cheese "steak" can be delicious. Some of the best recipes utilize the meaty portobello mushroom. Peel the skin off the top of the mushroom cap and scrape off the bottom black gills. Slice the mushroom thinly and toss with a little Worcestershire sauce. Cover and microwave for 3 minutes. Build your cheese "steak" as described in the recipe.

A Little Butter Helps

- Using butter in this sandwich makes up for the missing fat inherent in the traditional rib eye used for cheese steaks.

- Do not use light butter, as it will not hold up to microwaving.

- Be sure the butter is evenly distributed between the meat pieces for better results.

- You can drizzle the meat with a little oil in place of the butter, but it won't taste as good.

Gooey Is Yummy

- Cheez Whiz is ultra creamy and smooth when melted.

- This processed cheese food has to be at least 51 percent cheese by law. The other components are emulsifiers, oil, and whey.

- American cheese and Velveeta are also processed cheese foods that melt exceedingly well. Laughing Cow is the French version, showing how processed cheese has gone international.

- There is nothing wrong with enjoying these foods occasionally, just not as your main protein source.

SEMI-LEGAL GRILLED CHEESE

If you have an iron in your room, try this ingenious grilled cheese

Sometimes you just need a grilled cheese sandwich, but the cafeteria is closed. You are too tired to make the trek to the all-night diner, but you don't have a grill in your room. The frustration builds and the thought of another white bread and American cheese sandwich is not half as appetizing as a nice and crispy/gooey grilled cheese. This recipe was developed by an ingenious college student who found himself in

this same predicament. The brilliant solution was to find a nice flat, even heat source. After all, an iron is just like a flat griddle, just smaller (and designed for something totally different, but hey, college students are supposed to improvise). The results were spectacular. *Yield: 1 sandwich*

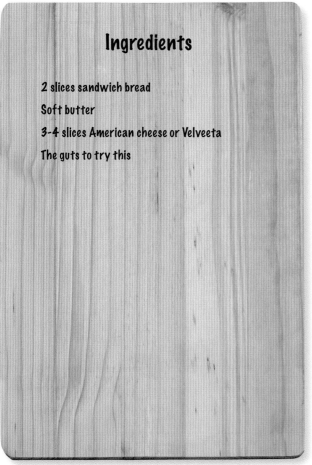

Ingredients

2 slices sandwich bread

Soft butter

3-4 slices American cheese or Velveeta

The guts to try this

Semi-Legal Grilled Cheese

- Turn iron onto highest setting and heat for 5 minutes. Lay out a sheet of heavy aluminum foil.

- Butter each slice of bread on one side; lay one slice, buttered side down, on the foil. Top with cheese and the other slice of bread, buttered side up.

- Wrap the foil around the sandwich. Press the iron to each side of the wrapped sandwich for about 45 seconds, or until the sandwich is toasted on both sides.

- Rest for 1 minute to melt the cheese.

RED●LIGHT

The iron was not actually designed to be a cooking tool, if you can believe it. It is important to understand how your iron works, and if you are even allowed to have one in your dorm. Check your school's rules. That being said, be sure your hot iron is always in a safe, stable place and is not in danger of tipping over. Also, always turn your iron off immediately after use.

• • • • RECIPE VARIATION • • • •

Semi-Legal Varieties: Your semi-legal panini maker can be used to make a variety of grilled sandwiches. Try adding a few slices of ham between the cheese. Or add turkey and bacon for a club sandwich–style grilled "sammie." You can also use roast beef and onions to make a cheese steak–style grilled sandwich. The key is to always use the butter on the outside of the bread.

Construction Is Key

- Building this sandwich is the first and most important step to success.

- The bread must be buttered on the outside in order for the bread to grill and toast. Don't make it inside out, or you will have a soggy sandwich.

- Wrapping the foil in a tight package is key, as you do not want melted butter burning on the iron.

- Be sure to monitor your sandwich during the entire cooking process to prevent burning!

Keep Your Eyes Open

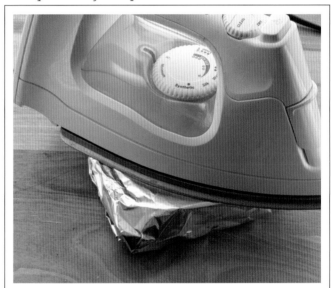

- Cooking the sandwich in foil is a tough technique because you are essentially blind while cooking this sandwich.

- Be sure you carefully unwrap a portion of the foil after 30 seconds or so to see how your particular iron is doing.

- You can double up on the foil if your sandwich burns before cooking. Two layers of foil will help.

- The amount of butter can also be varied to achieve different results.

WON'T-MISS-THE-MEAT VEGGIE SUB
This sandwich is for those who never thought you could make a good meatless sammie

There are many meatless sandwiches in the world, some better known than others. The classic Italian-American eggplant Parmesan is an irresistible mixture of fried breaded eggplant, tomato sauce, and gooey mozzarella cheese. The Israeli falafel is an amazing mixture of fried chickpea "meatballs" nestled in pita bread with an assortment of fresh vegetables and smooth sesame tahini sauce.

This recipe uses quick supermarket ingredients for easy preparation. When buying canned or jarred vegetables, remember that many of them are packed in copious amounts of water, oil, or marinades. It is always a good idea to drain these items and rinse well. *Yield: 1 sandwich*

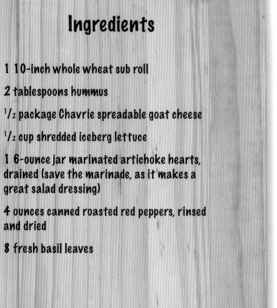

Ingredients

1 10-inch whole wheat sub roll

2 tablespoons hummus

¹/₂ package Chavrie spreadable goat cheese

¹/₂ cup shredded iceberg lettuce

1 6-ounce jar marinated artichoke hearts, drained (save the marinade, as it makes a great salad dressing)

4 ounces canned roasted red peppers, rinsed and dried

8 fresh basil leaves

Won't-Miss-the-Meat Veggie Sub

- Split the roll totally in half. Spread the hummus on the bottom of the bread and the goat cheese on the top half.

- Lay the lettuce on the hummus and top with the artichoke hearts and peppers. Top with basil leaves.

- Lay the top slice of bread that has been spread with the goat cheese on top.

• • • • **RECIPE VARIATION** • • • •

Switching up the Veggies: If you have a supermarket near you with a great salad bar or a large prepared foods/deli section, you can hunt for many vegetarian options to fill your sandwich. Many shops sell grilled and chilled vegetables. Many times they are eggplant and summer squash, such as zucchini or yellow squash. These make an excellent sandwich filling.

ZOOM

Roasted peppers are readily available in jars and cans, but they are easy to make. If you have a kitchen or access to a barbecue grill, you can make these easily. Simply place the peppers over an open flame, turning occasionally, until they are completely black and charred all over. Place in a bowl, cover with plastic wrap, and allow to steam for 5 minutes. The skin will then peel right off.

The Mighty Choke

- Artichokes are an interesting food item. They are the largest member of the thistle family.

- The edible parts of the plant are the stem, bottom, and heart. The "choke" and the leaves are the inedible portions.

- Raw artichokes rapidly discolor or oxidize and need to be doused with lemon juice when you work with them.

- Most artichokes are grown in California, although some marinated and jarred varieties come from Italy or the Mediterranean.

Goat's Milk

- Goats have been raised for thousands of years for their milk and meat.

- Goat's milk makes excellent cheese that has a slightly tangy flavor. Most goat cheese is "fresh" goat cheese. Goat's milk yogurt is also available in many markets.

- Aged goat cheese develops a firmer texture and more complex flavor. It becomes drier and crumbly.

- Goat's milk is found in many health food stores and in some supermarkets. It is worth trying.

LOX & AVOCADO SANDWICH

Try this wonderful combination that borrows from New York, Japan, and Eastern Europe

Smoked salmon, or lox, is one of the world's great foods. Silky and smoky, the salmon takes on an incredible character after being cured with salt and sugar and smoked over hardwood. There are many different styles of smoked salmon. The most popular is Nova style, or Nova Scotia. It has a mild smokiness and is quite moist. Scottish style is much more deeply smoked and cured for slightly longer. It has a much stronger and dryer flavor and is popular in Europe. There are also unsmoked lox varieties, including Graved Lachs, which is a Scandinavian version marinated with dill, and Bell lox, which is simply salted salmon. All have their fans and applications, and all are great on a bagel. *Yield: 1 sandwich*

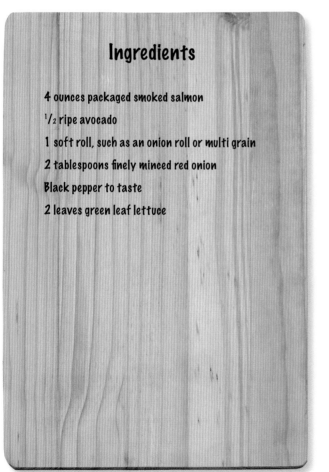

Ingredients

4 ounces packaged smoked salmon

1/2 ripe avocado

1 soft roll, such as an onion roll or multi grain

2 tablespoons finely minced red onion

Black pepper to taste

2 leaves green leaf lettuce

Lox and Avocado Sandwich

- Take the salmon out of the package and cut out any small spots of dark flesh on the underside. This flesh is stronger in flavor and is typically removed.

- Score and mash the avocado in its skin. Split the roll and spread the avocado on one half of it. Top with the onion and black pepper

- Lay the salmon on top of the avocado; top with lettuce and the top of the roll.

78

•••• RECIPE VARIATION ••••

Swap out the Lox: Smoked salmon, or lox, is simply smoked and cured meat. Its flavor profile pairs well with the rich and creamy avocado, which acts as a foil for the salty and smoky fish. Some great substitutions for salmon are prosciutto, smoked ham, smoked turkey, Serrano ham, or salami. Be creative and pair smoked meats with avocado for a real treat.

YELLOW LIGHT

Most smoked salmon available on the market is prepared from farm-raised Atlantic salmon. There are many debates about farmed salmon and the salmon farming industry as a whole. Salmon farms are responsible for a great deal of ocean pollutants. Farmed salmon sometimes escape their pens and interbreed with wild salmon, diluting the wild DNA. However, farmed and wild salmon both have healthy fats and omega-3 fatty acids.

The Dark Side

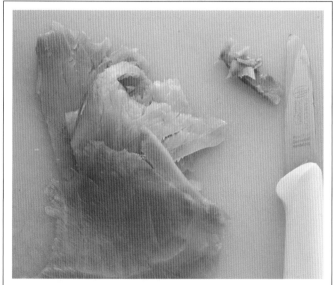

- The dark meat usually found on the skin side of fish fillets is known as the bloodline.

- This part of the fish's flesh has a stronger flavor than the lighter side of the flesh.

- The bloodline is also the area of the flesh where toxins and heavy metals can build up in fish flesh.

- In smoked sliced salmon this dark flesh is easily removed by using the tip of a knife to cut a small V into the meat.

Green Butter

- The rich flesh of the avocado can be referred to as "green butter." It makes for an excellent spread on toast with a little salt and pepper.

- The mashed flesh of avocado is also the main ingredient in the dip/sauce guacamole.

- Avocado turns brown, or oxidizes, quickly when cut; a little lemon or lime juice slows that process.

- Haas avocados are small and nubby, while Bacon avocados are large, smooth, and have a more watery flesh.

CURRIED TUNA SALAD WRAP

This sandwich is full of complex flavors and textures; the water chestnuts make it crunchy

Tuna salad has been a staple of the American lunch for decades. The classic recipe calls for tuna, mayonnaise, celery, and salt and pepper and is a classic for good reason. When buying prepared tuna salad, read the ingredients on the label carefully. Some manufacturers add large amounts of bread crumbs to the tuna salad to both soak up excess water and

bulk up the tuna, as bread crumbs are cheaper than fish. Tuna salads with bread are not suitable to people with gluten intolerance or celiac disease. Look for albacore tuna, which is of higher quality than commonly used tongol tuna.

Yield: 1 sandwich

Ingredients

1 5 to 6-ounce can tuna packed in water

1 small can water chestnuts

3 tablespoons mayonnaise

1 tablespoon Madras curry powder

2 teaspoons sweet pickle relish

Salt and pepper to taste

1 10-inch whole wheat tortilla

1 cup mixed baby greens

Curried Tuna Salad Wrap

- Drain the tuna well and flake into a bowl

- Drain the water chestnuts and chop roughly. Add to the tuna.

- In a separate bowl, mix the mayo, curry powder, and relish into a thick sauce.

- Pour onto the tuna and mix until combined. Season with salt and pepper.

- Warm the tortilla for 5 seconds in the microwave. Top with baby greens, then the tuna mixture. Roll up and tuck in the ends.

•••• RECIPE VARIATION ••••

Added Crunch: The crunch component is a key player in any tuna salad. The classic uses celery, and this salad uses water chestnuts. There are many vegetables that can be used to add crunch to your salads. It is fun to play around with these. Open your fridge; you probably have something crunchy such as pickles, onions, radishes, or peppers.

YELLOW ● LIGHT

There is much in the news these days about mercury in tuna. Mercury is a heavy metal found naturally in the environment. Mercury manages to go to the top of the ocean food chain and, since tuna are an apex predator, there have been instances of higher than acceptable levels of mercury in the fish, especially larger tuna. It is a good idea to keep abreast of this issue by checking Web sites devoted to this issue. One good one is www.healthytuna.com.

What's a Water Chestnut?

- The water chestnut is a member of the sedge family that grows in flooded fields, mostly in Asia.

- It has an unusual cell structure, which allows it to stay crispy even after it's cooked.

- Water chestnuts can also be dried and ground into a type of flour, which is used in some Chinese dishes.

- Rumaki is one of the most famous appetizers and is made from water chestnuts, chicken livers, and bacon.

Flavored Mayonnaise

- Adding flavors to mayonnaise is a quick and easy way to make some great sauces.

- Besides curry powder, try adding hot sauce, pesto, garlic, mustard, Parmesan cheese, horseradish, soy sauce, and so on.

- One of the most famous flavored mayonnaises is aioli, which is a garlicky mayonnaise from France.

- In Japan, flavored mayonnaises are very popular and are used in the classic spicy tuna roll, which is mayo, sriracha hot sauce, and sesame oil.

CHEATERS' CHICKEN PARM

Frozen breaded and cooked chicken cutlets are the key to this sandwich

Parmigiana or Parmesan is not only a cheese, but also a style of cooking food products in the style of Parma, a region in Italy. This technique has been made popular, especially on the East Coast, and has spread across the country.

Typically, veal, chicken, or vegetables are breaded in flour, eggs, and bread crumbs (sometimes with Parmesan cheese mixed in) and then fried in olive oil. These cutlets are then layered into casserole dishes with tomato sauce and mozzarella cheese and baked in the oven until the top is browned and bubbling. These items are sometimes piled into rolls and toasted in the oven for a hearty and satisfying meal on a roll.

Yield: 1 sandwich

Ingredients

About 8 ounces frozen breaded, fully cooked chicken cutlets

$1/2$ cup jarred marinara sauce

$1/4$ cup shredded Parmesan cheese

1 4-ounce ball fresh mozzarella, cut into 3 or 4 slices

1 10-inch white sub roll, split through

Salt and pepper to taste

6–8 fresh basil leaves

Cheaters' Chicken Parm

- Cut the chicken into 2-inch strips. Toss with sauce and Parmesan.

- Lay chicken onto a microwavable plate in the same shape as the roll. Cover and microwave for 1 minute.

- Lay the mozzarella slices on a paper towel and cover with another towel; press to drain off excess moisture. Lay the cheese over the chicken. Season with salt and pepper.

- Microwave, covered, for about 2 minutes. Slide onto the bottom of the roll and top with the basil leaves and top of the roll.

· · · · RECIPE VARIATIONS · · · ·

Eggplant Parm: It is becoming easier to find pre-breaded and cooked eggplant cutlets in the freezer section. Try a sandwich with these cutlets for a vegetarian option. Be aware that even though you will not be frying these cutlets, they often have been prefried and contain a fair amount of oil and calories from fat despite being a vegetable. You can also use grilled chicken breasts for a healthier option.

Leftover Delight: If you have made it to an apartment where you have a better-equipped kitchen, you can transform any of these Parm sandwiches into a host of other dishes. Try preparing the dishes in a casserole and then using the leftovers. Spread leftovers on a pizza crust and bake at 450°F until hot.

Fresh Mozz

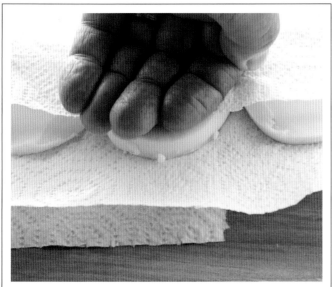

- Fresh and creamy white, mozzarella is unknown to many people, which is unfortunate because it has a delicious taste.

- It is one of the simplest cheeses to make, using only fresh curd, water, and salt.

- It takes a practiced hand to knead the cheese just long enough so that is comes together but still remains tender.

- Fresh mozzarella contains a great deal of water that can leak out when cooked, which is why it is pressed in this recipe.

Bread Makes the Difference

- Bread with a crunchy crust is especially important when making this type of sandwich, as the sandwich is heavy and wet and the crust will help hold things together.

- If your bread is not crusty enough, toast it to make it sturdier.

- Not storing bread in plastic bags and allowing it to "breathe" will help preserve the crust. Paper bags work great.

COFFEEPOT MISO SOUP
Your coffeepot works to make boiling water, so use if your microwave is on the fritz

Miso is another food product made from the incredible soybean. Miso's roots probably trace back to China, but it was in Japan that it became the refined seasoning that it is today.

Miso is made by grinding and fermenting soybeans. Any type of bean or grain can be used to make miso, but soybeans are the most popular and widely used. There are several varieties of miso, including white, red, and brown. Each has a different intensity of flavor.

Miso soup is probably the way most of us first encounter this flavoring. It is commonly given as a first course in Japanese restaurants and usually contains small cubes of silken tofu and seaweed. *Yield: 1 large or 2 small bowls*

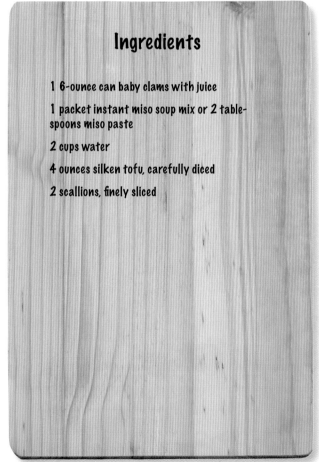

Ingredients

1 6-ounce can baby clams with juice

1 packet instant miso soup mix or 2 tablespoons miso paste

2 cups water

4 ounces silken tofu, carefully diced

2 scallions, finely sliced

Coffeepot Miso Soup

- Be sure your coffeepot is clean. Place the clams and juice in the bottom of the pot and whisk in the miso paste or stir in the instant miso.

- Pour the water into the top of the coffee machine and brew into the pot. When finished, mix well.

- Dice the tofu, very gently without moving it from the board. Just pass the knife through it. Add to the soup

- Pour soup into a bowl and top with scallions.

ZOOM

Miso is used in Japan for much more than soup. It is an important ingredient in many broths, such as ramen, and stews. But, most interestingly, miso is used as a pungent addition to sauces and glazes. One of the most popular dishes is eggplant broiled with miso. The flesh of small Japanese eggplants is scored and then rubbed with miso and passed under the broiler until very brown.

Miso Mix-Ups: If you are not a clam or seafood person, miso soup can be made with many other ingredients and be just as wonderful. Try adding 1 cup of raw baby spinach to the bowl with a few sesame seeds, or add $1/2$ cup of any cooked vegetable (mushrooms top the list). Or add 3 ounces of leftover chicken or even slices of 1 hard-boiled egg.

Learning to Boil Water

- Boiling water is an essential cooking medium for countless dishes, including pasta, rice, soups, and coffee. It is nice to know a few ways to get it done.

- Your coffeepot actually brews to just under boiling, which is good for coffee and miso soup.

- A 12-ounce cup of water will come to a boil in about 2 minutes in a typical microwave oven.

- The new electric kettles on the market are excellent tools for bringing water to a boil very rapidly.

Slicing and Dicing

- Learning to dice in uniform cuts while keeping your fingers intact is important.

- Tofu is a nice medium to learn on, as it has very little resistance and is a uniform shape.

- Be sure to keep the blade of the knife perpendicular to the cutting board to avoid making uneven cuts. A thin-bladed knife is easier to practice with at first.

- Keep your fingertips curled under your hand and out of the way of that blade!

SOOTHING SOUPS

BLT SOUP

The BLT is a perfect combination of flavors that works amazingly well as a soup

Soup is the ultimate comfort food. And an excellent comfort meal, perhaps during stress-filled final exam time, is this great BLT soup. Soups have been soothing souls for as long as people have been cooking. A pot of water was set over the fire and then whatever was around was added to stretch out the ingredients to feed a group of people. Soups can be made from almost any ingredients: meat, fish, fowl, or vegetables. There are broth soups, puree soups, creamed soups, and even dessert soups made with fruits and served chilled. Soups are probably the most calming of all the foods, and many are reported to have medicinal powers. *Yield: 4 medium bowls of soup*

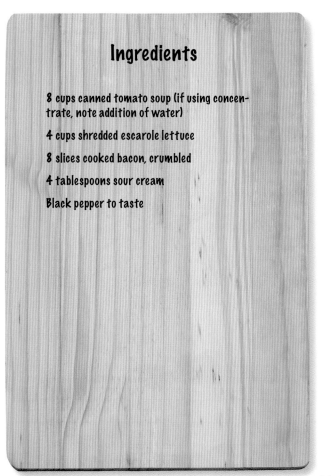

Ingredients

8 cups canned tomato soup (if using concentrate, note addition of water)

4 cups shredded escarole lettuce

8 slices cooked bacon, crumbled

4 tablespoons sour cream

Black pepper to taste

BLT Soup

- Heat soup in the microwave in a bowl you will not use to serve the soup in.

- Divide the escarole among four serving bowls.

- Pour the hot soup over the escarole and allow some of the lettuce to protrude from the soup for visual effect.

- Crumble the bacon evenly over the bowls and place 3 teaspoon-size dollops of sour cream equally around the soup. Sprinkle with black pepper and serve immediately.

Manhattan Chowder or Southwestern Chili Soup:
Tomato soup can be treated like a blank canvas. Besides adding bacon and lettuce to tomato soup, you can use this base for a variety of incarnations. Try adding 1 can of clams and a diced cooked potato for a quick Manhattan chowder. Or add 1 can of beans, some chili powder and cumin and ¼ cup of Jack cheese for a Southwestern chili soup. The possibilities are endless.

Tomato soup also has myriad other culinary applications besides actual soup. Some folks add it to slow cookers with a big hunk of meat and a little broth for a delicious tomato gravy. It also makes a great sauce for stuffed cabbage.

Bacon, the Universal Yum

- Smoky, salty, meaty, and porky, bacon is truly a can't-do-without food that has so many uses.

- Try cutting raw bacon and cooking with a few diced onions for the base of a soup. Just add other ingredients in afterward and cook as directed.

- Bacon makes an excellent wrapper for roasted meats, burgers, or appetizers. You can briefly blanch the bacon by dropping it in boiling water for 1 minute for quicker cooking time.

- Some folks are wrapping hot dogs in bacon.

Soup Garnishes

- It is very elegant to finish off a bowl of soup with a nice floating garnish. It elevates a humble dish to something special.

- Try making your own croutons by baking bread cubes in a 350°F oven with a little butter and garlic; use as a soup garnish.

- Pesto makes a great dollop for vegetable soup. It is the classic French pistou soup which is borrowed from the Italian word pesto.

- Sometimes a drizzle of olive oil and a spoonful of Parmesan is all a soup needs for garnish.

SOOTHING SOUPS

SMOKED OYSTER & CORN BISQUE
This soup is a bit advanced, but worth the effort

Oysters have been an important food source since the first early human smashed one open on a rock and ate it at the water's edge. The beauty of this is that whenever you eat a raw oyster, you taste a food product exactly as it tasted millennia ago. Oysters were first smoked to increase the shelf life of these very perishable shellfish. In Asia, oysters are often preserved by being dried in the sun. The sun-dried oysters are simply plumped in water before use. The smoked oysters available today come from Asia and are mostly tinned, packed in soybean oil. Find a brand you like and enjoy this soup. *Yield: 1 bowl of soup*

Ingredients

1 3-4 ounce can smoked oysters

2 tablespoons Wondra flour, a very finely-milled flour

1 cup milk

1 8-ounce can creamed corn

$1/2$ teaspoon dried parsley

Black pepper to taste

Smoked Oyster and Corn Bisque

- Drain the oysters and reserve the oil/juices in a microwave-safe bowl big enough to hold all the ingredients. Mix well with the flour and then slowly whisk in the milk.

- Microwave this mixture for 1 minute and then stir in the creamed corn. Micro-wave for 1 minute more.

- Stir in the oysters and parsley and then check the temperature of soup. You may have to heat the soup a bit more. Add black pepper to taste.

- Serve with oyster crackers or buttered toast.

The benefits of eating oysters have been touted for thousands of years—particularly the effect they have on the libido. It has been said that eating oysters, particularly raw oysters, increases the sex drive. Now there seems to be some research actually supporting this culinary myth. It seems that the high levels of zinc in the oysters may have an effect on libido. Enjoy your oysters!

YELLOW ● LIGHT

While the oysters in this soup are canned and have almost no possibility of causing food-borne illness, raw oysters are not so fortunate. If eating raw oysters, try to go somewhere that specializes in them and moves through them quickly so they're not sitting for a while. There is also the R rule, which states: Avoid raw shellfish in months that do not have an R in them, such as June. These are the warmer months, and shellfish are more prone to bacteria during warm months.

Do the Roux

- A roux (pronounced *roo*) is a blend of flour and fat used to thicken soups and sauces.

- The mixture of flour and oyster juice in this recipe is a simple roux and acts to thicken this soup.

- Some recipes call for a roux that is cooked for a time to give color and a nutty flavor to the roux.

- You can mix flour and water to thicken a soup. This is called a whitewash.

Born to Eat Corn

- Sweet corn is native to the Americas. It was brought to Europe in the 1400s and was widely adapted there.

- Corn is available canned, frozen, dried, and fresh in season. The season for corn is summer.

- White and yellow corn can be equally sweet. There are also hybrid corn breeds with white and yellow kernels on the same ear.

- Corn in the height of sweetness is excellent eaten raw. Don't be afraid to try it.

SPICY BLACK BEAN SOUP

This soup can double as a dip; your immersion blender will come in handy here

Black bean soup is a culinary staple in many Latin American countries. There are as many recipes for black bean soup as there are Latina grandmothers. And they are all correct! The black bean has been used as food for over five thousand years. In China, the beans are dried and fermented and used as an ingredient in chicken in black bean sauce recipes.

The beans have a blackish purplish skin and actually have a creamy white interior.

This recipe calls for pureeing half of the soup with a blender. This technique yields a very pleasing texture with a smooth backbone and pleasant chunks of veggies and whole beans floating through it. *Yield: 2 bowls of soup*

Ingredients

¹/₄ cup finely diced white onion

¹/₄ cup finely diced red bell pepper

3 tablespoons olive oil

1 tablespoon ground cumin

1 teaspoon dried oregano

1 teaspoon smoked paprika

¹/₄ teaspoon cayenne pepper

1 14-ounce can black beans

2 cups chicken broth

Salt and pepper to taste

2 tablespoons sour cream

¹/₄ cup fresh cilantro leaves

Lime wedge

Spicy Black Bean Soup

- Combine onion, red pepper, olive oil, and spices in a large microwavable bowl. Cover and microwave 1 minute.

- Add the beans and broth and mix well. Remove half the soup to another bowl and puree very fine with an immersion blender. Return

to the nonpureed soup.

- Microwave the soup 4 minutes, stirring halfway through. Season with salt and pepper.

- Divide soup between two serving bowls. Top with sour cream, cilantro leaves, and lime.

Spicy Pepperoni and Black Bean Soup: This soup uses smoked paprika to give it a smoky character. This is an excellent ingredient that really does the job well. Traditionally, chorizo sausage is used in this soup, which gives it a smoky and somewhat spicy flavor. If you cannot find chorizo sausage and want to try this dish, you can substitute pepperoni or bacon.

Beans are one of the most nutritious foods around. Adding beans to your diet has many benefits. Their high protein and fiber content make them an excellent addition to your pantry. Try adding them not only to soups, but pureeing them into dips, rolling them up into tacos and burritos, and making franks and beans for that childhood memory.

Semi-Sauté

The Magic Wand

SOOTHING SOUPS

- Cooking these veggies in the microwave first is mimicking the technique of sautéing.

- Sauté means "to jump" in French, which relates to the fact that things cooked quickly in a pan with a little bit of oil "jump" around over high heat.

- Sautéing brings out the flavors in aromatic foods by releasing their essential oils. Most soups start with some vegetables being sautéed.

- Adding spices to sautéing veggies brightens their flavor.

- The immersion blender is like a magic wand. It is an incredibly useful tool.

- When pureeing hot soups with the immersion blender, it is essential that you not lift the blender out of the soup while it is spinning. You can get burned.

- Always clean your blender when it is unplugged; the blade spins fast and is sharp.

- Try using the blender to make smoothies right in the glass and to make silky smooth dips and emulsified dressings.

LOADED BAKED POTATO SOUP
You could cheat on this one with instant-mashed potatoes—just make 'em watery

Many believe the potato is native to Europe, but it is actually native to Peru. There are hundreds of varieties of potatoes in all shapes and sizes. There are even bright purple potatoes. Columbus brought the potato back to Europe, and it was instantly brought into the fold of European cuisine. The potato has incredible culinary properties. It has many vital nutrients for humans, as well as a fiber-like starch that is said to help prevent colon cancer. The potato is the fourth largest crop in the world, and it is estimated that the average person eats fifty pounds of potatoes a year. This soup uses a baking potato; you could use Yukon gold or russet potatoes as well. *Yield: 1 large bowl of soup*

Ingredients

1 large baking potato

1/2 cup milk

2 cups chicken broth

Salt and pepper to taste

Instant potato buds, just in case

2 strips microwaved bacon, crumbled

1/4 cup shredded sharp cheddar cheese

2 tablespoons freshly snipped chives

2 tablespoons sour cream

Loaded Baked Potato Soup

- Prick the potato with a knife and microwave for 8 minutes. Cool for 2 minutes.

- Cut the potato in half and scoop out all the flesh; place in a microwave-safe bowl. Mix in the milk, broth, and salt and pepper.

- Microwave for 4 minutes, stirring halfway through. Carefully puree the soup with your immersion blender. If the soup is too thick, add some more hot milk or broth; if it's too thin, add a few tablespoons potato buds.

- Garnish with bacon, cheese, chives, and sour cream.

The old wives' tale that a sprouting potato is poisonous has truth to it. Almost all parts of the potato plant are poisonous except the tuber portion that we eat. In fact the sprouts of a potato are poisonous and should always be removed. Also, the green skin has the same toxins, and you should not eat green-skinned potatoes. Do not fear the humble potato; just keep your "eyes" open for sprouting or green ones.

RECIPE VARIATION

Forest Mushroom Soup: Potato soup is one of the world's great soups and is custom-made for variations. Try garnishing with canned mushrooms for a forest mushroom soup, or add $1/4$ cup crispy french- fried onions and 2 tablespoons crumbled blue cheese for a very sophisticated soup. Another beautiful variation is to wilt $1/2$ cup spinach directly into the soup.

You Say Potato

- Be careful when scooping out potato flesh. The game Hot Potato has that name for a reason. Potatoes retain their heat for a long time.

- There are many ways to cook a potato, and they come in a convenient "jacket" to keep the steam inside.

- Boiling potatoes in the skins yield dryer potatoes, which are better for mashed potatoes.

- Sweet potatoes can be cooked the same way as conventional potatoes.

Notes about Pureed Soups

- Pureed soups are some of the easiest to make, as you do not have to worry too much about cutting the veggies in uniform pieces.

- The key is to make sure the main item you are cooking is completely soft so when you puree you get a silky smooth soup.

- If your soup has some lumps, you can strain it through a fine sieve.

- If using a conventional blender for any pureed soup, make sure to cool the soup before pureeing.

SOOTHING SOUPS

OVER 21 CHEDDAR ALE SOUP
Check all state and campus rules before attempting this soup

Beer is probably the world's first alcoholic beverage. It started with wild yeast floating in the air, which accidentally fermented liquid that had some grain cooked in it. The people who gave this quasi-beer a try probably liked the effects. There is evidence that beer was being brewed as long ago as 3,000 BC. Beer and ales have found their way into many recipes, including this soup and beer batter, to name only two. The varieties of beer are staggering. To name a just a few, there are lagers, stouts, porters, lambics, ales, pale ales, and cream ales. Beer has been brewed in every culture and tends to pair well with local cuisine. *Yield: 1 large bowl*

Ingredients

¹/₄ cup finely minced white onion

1 clove garlic, minced

¹/₄ cup finely minced celery

¹/₄ cup butter

¹/₄ cup Wondra flour

1 cup half-and-half

¹/₂ cup dark ale

1¹/₂ cups chicken broth

³/₄ cup shredded sharp cheddar cheese

Dash Worcestershire sauce

Salt and pepper to taste

Over 21 Cheddar Ale Soup

- Place the onion, garlic, celery, and butter in a microwavable bowl; cover and microwave 1 minute.

- Stir in flour, half-and-half, ale, and broth. Microwave 4 minutes, stirring halfway through.

- Add the cheese and Worcestershire sauce and microwave 1 minute. Be careful not to overnuke this dish, as the cheese can "break" and the soup will be ruined. Stir well.

- Season with salt and pepper to taste. If too thin, shake a little Wondra into the soup while whisking.

Ale is a type of beer that is distinctly different from the popular lager-style beers mostly brewed in the United States. The main difference is that ales are made with malted barley, which tends to add a sweeter flavor to the ale, and the yeast that ferments it is a "top-fermenting" yeast. Lager beers are much lighter in flavor and color and utilize a "bottom-fermenting" yeast.

Underage Cheddar Soup: A very similar soup can be made without the ale. Make the soup the same way and substitute more chicken broth for the ale. To give the soup a complex flavor in order to make up for the ale, add 3 tablespoons each Parmesan and blue cheese at the very end of the process.

Thickening Agents

- The mixing of flour and fat together is one way to thicken a soup. There are many others, too.

- A slurry made with equal parts cornstarch and cold water is commonly used in Chinese foods to thicken soups and sauces.

- The French use ground arrowroot instead of cornstarch.

- Adding mashed potatoes to a soup, or even bread crumbs, can thicken the broth nicely.

The Break Dance

- Many times you will hear a chef speak of a sauce or soup "breaking." What is that?

- When something "breaks," the fat separates out of the solution and becomes a greasy and congealed mess.

- The cheese in this soup contains fat, and if it gets too hot it will break or separate.

- If your soup does break, there is no way to fix it; you must start again or go out to dinner!

LOW-FAT SPICY HUMMUS
Hummus is usually loaded with olive oil, but you can substitute some bean liquid for great results

Hummus is one of the most popular foods eaten in the Middle East. It is a humble food made from simple ingredients and is popular with all classes of people. The true origins of this dish are disputed, but the chickpea has been a human food item for over ten thousand years.

In Israel there are many small shops and restaurants devoted to hummus. They have a dedicated clientele who all believe their little neighborhood place makes the best in town. Some shops serve grilled meats and skewers to be eaten with the hummus. Some serve only the dip and warm pita bread to dip into the silky spread. The common thread in every recipe is the addition of tahini. *Yield: 2–3 servings*

Ingredients

1 14-ounce can chickpeas

2 tablespoons lemon juice

2 tablespoons extra-virgin olive oil

2 cloves garlic

$1/2$ teaspoon ground cumin

$1/4$ teaspoon cayenne pepper

2 tablespoons tahini paste or peanut butter

Salt and pepper to taste

Low-Fat Spicy Hummus

- Drain the chickpeas, saving the liquid in a bowl. Mix the liquid with the lemon juice and olive oil.

- Place the chickpeas, garlic, spices, and tahini or peanut butter in a food processor. Pulse until the mixture starts to blend. Scrape down the sides of the bowl.

- Continue processing. Then slowly drizzle in the liquid mixture until very smooth. Season with salt and pepper.

- Serve with pita chips and fresh veggies for dipping.

ZOOM

When visiting Israel, it is easy to believe that hummus is an Israeli invention. In fact hummus is a purely Arabic invention, and it is widely agreed that the Arabs in Israel have the best hummus shops. The fervor with which Israelis devour this silky dip verges on fanaticism. Hummus, along with falafel and baba ghanoush, are all Arabic inventions. Peace in the Middle East may start with hummus!

• • • • RECIPE VARIATION • • • •

Bean-Based Hummus: You can substitute almost any bean for this dish in place of chickpeas. Canned white beans, butter beans, and black beans all make wonderful hummus. You can also play around with the flavor and omit the tahini and add yogurt, hot sauce, basil, lime juice, or other seasonings. What is important is that the puree is smooth.

Garbanzo Beans, Chickpeas, Ceci

Emulsification

- Chickpeas go by many names including garbanzo beans and ceci beans. If you want to try to cook them from scratch, you can.

- Soak the chickpeas in cold water overnight.

- Very gently simmer the beans in water until they are very tender.

- Add a little salt to the water and cool the chickpeas in the water in the fridge for best results. Then drain and use in recipes. The cooking water is good for soups.

- Emulsifying is the process of gradually adding oil or other liquids to a protein in order to evenly distribute it.

- Mayonnaise is one of the most common emulsifications. It is oil emulsified into egg yolks.

- In order to be successful, the oil or liquid must be added very gradually.

- Some emulsions can be fixed if they break by adding a bit of hot or cold water or even reemulsifying with a bit more protein.

KILLER GARLIC TZATZIKI
This amazing garlicky dip is also used as a sauce for late-night gyros

Greece, as with many other Mediterranean countries, is famous for its assortment of small plates or appetizers called mezze. Many meals in Greece begin with lavish assortments of mezze, which are shared around the table, sometimes for hours before the main meal. Glasses of ouzo, the popular anise-flavored liquor, are copiously consumed during these lively meals. Warm breads, olive oil, platters of cheeses, marinated vegetables, small meatballs, and an assortment of dips adorn the table. One of the most famous and interesting dips is tzatziki, a garlicky yogurt dip that is also used as a sauce for gyros and roast lamb. Other well-known dips of Greece are taramasalata, skordalia, and hummus. *Yield: 3 cups*

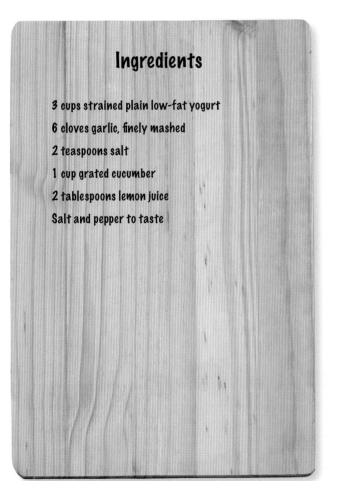

Ingredients

3 cups strained plain low-fat yogurt

6 cloves garlic, finely mashed

2 teaspoons salt

1 cup grated cucumber

2 tablespoons lemon juice

Salt and pepper to taste

Killer Garlic Tzatziki

- Strain yogurt as for Yogurt "Cheese," Sweet or Savory on page 52. Reserve.

- Mash the garlic with the salt by grinding it into a cutting board with a knife. Add to the yogurt.

- Squeeze the grated cucumber in a clean cloth to get out as much water as possible. Add cucumber to the yogurt mixture.

- Add the lemon juice and some pepper. Taste for salt and add if needed. Serve with warm pita or any type of chips.

ZOOM

Yogurt sauces are popular in many regions of the world and all serve the same purpose. They are meant to cool the palate, especially while eating grilled meats or spicy foods. This Greek sauce is similar to raita, the Indian sauce that is a mixture of yogurt, cucumbers, and mint, which is served with the spicy foods of the subcontinent. Sounds familiar, huh?

MAKE IT EASY

There are some supermarkets, especially in major cities, that carry strained Greek yogurt. One of the most popular brands is FAGE, which is excellent. The other option to find this type of yogurt is to seek out a Greek market or Greek neighborhood, where you may even find homemade Greek yogurt. Plus, shopping in ethnic markets is always an adventure. Go out and explore.

Garlic 101

- Garlic is one of the most widely used seasonings and is reputed to have medicinal qualities including great benefits to heart health.

- Always choose very firm heads of garlic that have no green sprouts. A little purple hue to the skin is a good sign.

- Store garlic at room temperature in a basket, much as you would onions and potatoes.

- Use garlic quickly after it has been cut, as the flavor degrades rapidly.

Lose the Liquid

- Removing the liquid from the cucumbers is strictly to ensure the proper consistency of the dip. If left intact, the dip would become diluted and watery.

- There may be occasions when you want a more "loose" dip based on personal preference. If so, simply do not squeeze out the cukes and your dip will be a bit more wet in texture. This works well if you are using it as a sauce for grilled fish.

DIPS FOR THOSE CHIPS

COOKED PICO DE GALLO

Using canned diced tomatoes takes the guesswork out of picking perfectly ripe tomatoes

Pico de gallo is a traditional term, which translates to "the rooster's beak" for what we in America typically refer to as salsa. The term may get its name from the shape of the peppers sometimes used to make the sauce, which resembles a chicken beak, but no one knows for sure. While most salsas are traditionally made with only fresh ingredients, the salsa

we buy in jars in supermarkets are always fully cooked and quite different from the traditional. This recipe blends the two techniques for a dorm-friendly version that you will surely enjoy while eating those nachos at midnight. You can always substitute other herbs such as fresh basil, parsley, or oregano for the cilantro if you do not care for it. *Yield: 4–6 servings*

Ingredients

2 14.5-ounce cans diced tomatoes

1 clove garlic, minced

1/2 cup finely diced red onion

1 small jalapeño pepper, seeded and minced

2 tablespoons vegetable oil

Juice of 1 lime

1/4 cup loosely packed cilantro leaves, chopped

Salt and pepper to taste

Cooked Pico de Gallo

- Rinse and drain the tomatoes, discard the juice.

- Place the garlic, onion, jalapeño, and oil in a small microwavable bowl; cover and microwave for 30 seconds. Cool in the fridge uncovered for 5 minutes.

- Mix together the cooled onion mixture, tomatoes, and lime juice.

- Toss in the cilantro leaves and season with salt and pepper. If you hate cilantro, substitute scallions or basil.

Traditional Mexican Style: Of course, you can go for it and make this salsa with all fresh ingredients in the traditional Mexican style. Use the same ingredients but substitute fresh tomatoes for the canned and do not cook anything. The key is to find very ripe and red tomatoes. Try making this salsa in the summer, when your chances of finding great tomatoes increases.

Fruit Salsas: Fruit salsas have become all the rage these days, especially as a garnish for grilled fish. You can't swing a dead cat in a big city restaurant without seeing a mango salsa on a piece of fish. These salsas are yummy and fun to make. You can substitute ripe mango, pineapple, peaches, nectarines, and others for all or part of the tomatoes.

Canned Tomatoes Are Wonderful

- The array of tomatoes that can be found in cans is amazing. Besides diced, there are whole, pureed, stewed, crushed, and many others.

- When using diced tomatoes, rinse and drain them to get rid of the stray sauce, especially if you are not using them in soups or stews.

- Diced canned tomatoes are also available with different herbs and flavors already mixed in.

- Rotel is a canned diced tomato with green chiles and is great.

Cook and Cool

- The step of cooking and cooling this mixture will give the salsa a longer shelf life in the fridge.

- Cooling hot foods quickly if they are going to be added to a cold dish is essential for food safety.

- Cooking the jalapeños mellows the heat a bit. If you like hot foods, leave the seeds in the peppers, as that's where most of the heat is.

- Remember to wear gloves and/or wash your hands well after touching hot peppers as they can burn sensitive parts.

STEAMIN' CHEESE CHILI DIP
This dip is so easy and so good; serve it with extra tortilla chips

While inspired by Americans, the nacho was actually invented in Mexico, unlike so many other Tex-Mex dishes. The story goes like this: In a little town in Mexico, very close to the Texas border, a group of wives of American soldiers stationed nearby needed something to eat. The restaurant they stopped into was closed, and they were hungry. After some begging and pleading from the hungry bunch, the maître d', a man nicknamed "Nacho," whipped something up with the only ingredients he had on hand, some tortillas, which he cut into triangles and fried, some cheddar cheese, and a few jalapeños. Viola! The nacho was born. May you find your own inspiration with this cheesy dip. *Yield: 6–8 portions*

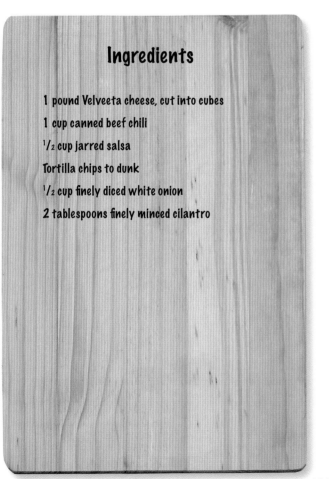

Ingredients

1 pound Velveeta cheese, cut into cubes

1 cup canned beef chili

1/2 cup jarred salsa

Tortilla chips to dunk

1/2 cup finely diced white onion

2 tablespoons finely minced cilantro

Steamin' Cheese Chili Dip

- Dice the Velveeta into large cubes, set aside. In a microwavable bowl, microwave the beef chili until very warm.

- Add the cheese and salsa to the chili and continue to microwave in 2-minute intervals, stirring in between, until very hot and gooey.

- Pour dip into a serving bowl and surround with tortilla chips.

- Mix together the onion and cilantro and sprinkle over the top of the dip.

Vegetarian Cheese Dip: You can easily make a vegetarian version of this dip. Replace the chili with an equal amount of salsa. You can also add 1 cup corn kernels or 1 can drained canned beans. Another excellent option is 1 cup cooked and chopped mushrooms, as they provide a "meaty" texture and flavor. You can use canned mushrooms; drain them and finely chop them.

ZOOM

We are using Velveeta here because processed cheese or cheese food has an amazing ability to not "break," or separate, during the heating process. The unique method for producing this cheese food (by adding emulsifiers and whey) makes this possible. The most popular cheese food is American cheese, which contrary to popular belief is not cheddar cheese.

Heat and Eat

Chili con Queso

DIPS FOR THOSE CHIPS

- This dish is ideally suited for microwave cooking, as the high and uneven heat will not break the cheese.

- It is important to stir occasionally to ensure even mixing and heating of this dip.

- If your bowl is taking too long to heat, you can split this into two or three batches and keep them warm while the other batch cooks. Or, just make batches as you need them.

- Do not try to use "real" cheese such as cheddar for this dish; it will break in the microwave.

- This dish is very similar to a dish called chili con queso, which translates to "chili with cheese."

- The traditional dish uses real cheddar or Monterey Jack cheese mixed with condensed milk, tomatoes, and chiles.

- It is served in the same way, as a dip or sauce.

- The condensed milk helps the dish to not break, but if cooked in a microwave it will break. Try chili con queso if you have a stove as opposed to a microwave.

SPINACH & ARTICHOKE DIP

A classic, this creamy dip is worth making; try adding it to an omelet

Spinach and artichoke dip has become a pub favorite across the globe, and there is no reason you should not be able to make this at home (or at your dorm). Traditionally baked in a crock in the oven, this microwave-friendly recipe does a great job of grabbing the flavors of the classic. Of course, you cannot get the deeply browned top that you would if you bake

this in the oven. When you graduate to an apartment with an oven, you can make this exact same recipe. Just mix the ingredients together, place in an ovenproof crock, and bake at 375°F until the top is brown and bubbly. Don't try to eat it right away—it's hot like lava! *Yield: About 4 cups*

Ingredients

1 pound cream cheese cut into large chunks (2, 8-ounce blocks)

$^1/_2$ cup sour cream

$^1/_2$ cup grated Parmesan cheese

1 cup chopped frozen spinach

1 cup canned artichoke hearts or bottoms, chopped

$^1/_2$ cup mayonnaise

2 garlic cloves, minced

Dash Worcestershire sauce

Dash Tabasco sauce

Salt and pepper to taste

Spinach and Artichoke Dip

- Place the cream cheese, sour cream, and Parmesan cheese in a microwavable bowl and microwave for 2 minutes. Stir well.

- Thaw the spinach under warm water and squeeze dry. Add to the warm cheese mixture and microwave 1 minute more.

- Add remaining ingredients and microwave in 2-minute intervals, stirring in between, until hot and bubbly. Pour into a serving crock.

- Adjust seasoning with Worcestershire and Tabasco sauces and salt and pepper. Serve with crusty bread or chips.

Crabmeat and Spinach Dip: One of the best variations to this dish is adding crabmeat. You can add about $1/2$ pound crabmeat with the spinach and proceed with the recipe as written. You can also add 1 teaspoon Old Bay seasoning for an extra-crabby taste. When choosing crab for this dish, do not waste money on jumbo lump. Just use regular lump or "special" crabmeat.

Mushroom and Artichoke Dip: Some folks hate spinach. No matter how many times I tell them how healthy it is or that Popeye got his trademark muscles by eating it, they just can't be swayed. For those people, you can do a few things. First, bump up the artichokes and lose the spinach. Or add chopped canned mushrooms instead of the spinach.

Fresh vs. Frozen

- There are some real differences between fresh and frozen spinach, and they are important to note.

- Frozen spinach has already been partially cooked and will basically keep its same volume.

- Fresh spinach, when cooked, will loose about 80 percent of its volume. A huge bag of raw spinach cooks down to just a couple of cups.

- Fresh spinach can be eaten raw in a salad, while frozen cannot. But fresh can be cooked to mimic frozen.

Timing Is Everything

- When microwave cooking, you really need to be patient and experiment to see what works. There are many variables, including the size and wattage of your microwave and the size and temperature of the food.

- Adding the spinach after the cheese has heated helps this dish heat more evenly and effectively.

- Thawing the spinach under warm water is key here, as it will not "shock" the hot cheese.

- Stir in 2-minute intervals to ensure even cooking.

CHEATERS' SKORDALIA

This is a Greek potato and garlic dip that is strangely addicting and great on anything

Skordalia is one of those magical Greek dips like tzatziki or taramasalata. Every good Greek restaurant has this killer garlic and potato dip on the menu. Traditionally it is served with fried fish as a sort of sauce, but in the United States it has turned into a dip for bread. Although almost always made with potatoes, the main player here is the garlic. Some old recipes use stale bread cubes moistened with lemon or vinegar and water or even ground nuts. All recipes use an emulsion of olive oil to give the sauce/dip its smooth and creamy character. It is also great on grilled vegetables and meats and makes an excellent sandwich spread. *Yield: About 6 cups*

Ingredients

1 1/2 cups water

1/2 cup milk

2 1/2 cups instant potato buds

8 cloves garlic

1 teaspoon salt

3/4 cup extra-virgin olive oil

1/4 cup white wine vinegar

Salt and pepper to taste

Cheaters' Skordalia

- Pour the water and milk into a microwavable bowl and heat in the microwave for 2 minutes.

- Stir in the potato buds and mix well. Cool in the fridge uncovered for 20 minutes.

- Grind the garlic and salt into a paste on a cutting board with a broad knife. Add to the potato mixture.

- Spoon the potato and garlic mixture into the bowl of a food processor and turn on. Slowly drizzle in the oil and vinegar until smooth. Season with salt and pepper.

Using Boiled Potatoes: Traditionally this dish is made with boiled potatoes, not instant. Of course, instant are easy and make more sense in a dorm room. When you move to a better kitchen, try this dish with boiled potatoes. Simply boil in the skin until tender, cool, and mash. Then mix all the ingredients except the oil. Slowly add the oil, stirring constantly to emulsify.

ZOOM

Instant mashed potatoes are an amazing product. Here's how they make 'em. First they make regular mashed potatoes, minus the butter. Then they spread the potatoes very thin and allow them to dry. They then flake the potatoes and pack them into boxes. This way, when you add hot water and/ or milk, you are basically just reconstituting dried mashed potatoes. They are great in a pinch.

Instant vs. Traditional Mashed

- Instant mashed potatoes are a great time-saver and substitute for traditional mashed, but there are differences from the "real" thing.

- Instant mashed potatoes do not have the same texture as traditional. You cannot get lumps with instant.

- Instant mashed potatoes can be kept, uncooked, in a box for years, while fresh potatoes will sprout and spoil.

- Instant potatoes also take 2 minutes as opposed to 30 minutes with real potatoes.

Why Olive Oil?

- This recipe uses extra-virgin olive oil as opposed to other oils for several reasons.

- Extra-virgin olive oil is traditional in this dish and to Greek cooking in general. It has a flavor that is essential to this dish.

- Extra-virgin olive oil is pressed without the addition of heat or pressure and is considered one of the most healthful oils to consume.

- The green color of extra-virgin olive oil helps add a golden hue to the finished spread.

RAMEN AS PAD THAI

Ramen is a typical Japanese comfort food; try this twist with a Thai flavor

Ramen is a cult in Japan. No food is more traditional for the workingman as ramen is. For college students, ramen is a convenience and instant food, but in Japan, countless ramen shops dot the cities. Hungry patrons line up, sometimes for over a half hour, to sit down at a little bar and slurp down a bowl of noodles in about 5 minutes.

Traditional ramen is made with a broth of pork bones boiled in water for up to 30 hours. Some ramen shops claim their pot of broth hasn't been turned off in over forty years. The pork broth is usually enhanced with items like miso, dried fish, chicken bones, and seaweed, among other seasonings. The best shops make their own noodles, too. *Yield: 1 bowl*

Ingredients

1 package ramen, noodles only

2¹/₂ cups water

¹/₄ cup thinly sliced white onion

¹/₄ cup shredded carrot

¹/₄ cup ketchup

1 teaspoon Thai fish sauce

2 teaspoon sriracha hot sauce

1 tablespoon sugar

1 tablespoon lime juice

¹/₄ cup fresh bean sprouts

¹/₄ cup sliced scallions

2 microwaved scrambled eggs, chopped

3 tablespoons crushed peanuts

Ramen as Pad Thai

- Place the ramen noodles and water in a large microwavable bowl and microwave, covered, for 3 minutes. Pull the noodles apart with a fork or chopsticks.

- Add the onion and carrot and microwave 1 minute more.

- In a separate bowl, mix together the ketchup, fish sauce, sriracha sauce, sugar, and lime juice and add to the noodles. Microwave 1 minute more.

- Add the bean sprouts, scallions, and eggs and mix well. Transfer to serving bowl. Top with peanuts.

Pad Thai may be the most well-known Thai noodle dish. The traditional recipe calls for noodles made from rice flour. Ramen, on the other hand, is made with wheat flour. Pad Thai noodles are translucent and have a very silky and slippery texture, while ramen noodles have a firmer texture and slightly better broth-soaking capability. The flavors and texture of pad Thai work well with the ramen noodles.

As ramen is considered such a traditional food in Japan, there are very few non-Japanese who would venture to open a ramen shop in Tokyo. Enter Ivan Orkin and his shop, Ivan Ramen. Orkin was born in New York and fell in love with all things Japanese. He eventually moved to Tokyo and did the unthinkable by opening a ramen shop and expecting people to take him seriously.

Use Your Noodle

- Noodles, it seems, were in fact first invented in China, but contrary to legend, it looks as though Marco Polo really did not introduce them to the Italians.

- Noodles can be made from any starch including wheat, rice, sweet potatoes, and bean starch, and some are even made with tofu.

- Most noodles can be cooked ahead of time and then chilled quickly in cold water.

- No one knows why the human brain is referred to as "your noodle."

Thai Fish Sauce

- Thai fish sauce has the incredible distinction of being the food product that smells most like old socks.

- This pungent sauce is used widely in Southeast Asian cuisine and adds a salty complexity to dishes.

- Thai fish sauce is made from fermented anchovies, salt, and water.

- Seek out this sauce; you may have to go to an Asian or specialty market. There are many brands to choose from.

RAMEN AS PHO

Pho is an incredible beef and noodle soup and the traditional breakfast in Vietnam

If you have never had a bowl of Pho (pronounced *fa*) you are missing out. This traditional breakfast soup from Vietnam is a culinary masterpiece. The broth is a slow-cooked beef stock infused with caramelized ginger, burnt onion, toasted cinnamon sticks, and star anise. It is brought to the table and then the diner garnishes it with a variety of aromatics. Thai basil leaves, lime, and bean sprouts are then added to the soup. The soup is typically eaten with sriracha and hoisin sauces. Diners loudly slurp the noodles and then pick up the bowl and drink the incredibly flavorful broth directly from it. Seek out a good pho joint. In the meantime, this recipe will do. *Yield: 1 bowl*

Ingredients

1 cup water

3 cups canned beef consommé

Pinch of cinnamon

Pinch of ground ginger

1 teaspoon hoisin sauce

1 teaspoon sriracha hot sauce

Dash fish sauce

1 package ramen, noodles only

$^1/_4$ pound very thinly sliced raw beef, any cut, but preferably eye round

1 cup fresh bean sprouts

12–15 leaves fresh Thai or sweet basil leaves

1 scallion, minced

1 tablespoon cilantro leaves

1 lime wedge

Salt to taste

Ramen as Pho

- Mix together the water, consommé, cinnamon, ginger, hoisin sauce, sriracha sauce, and fish sauce. Pour over the noodles in a microwavable bowl and microwave for 2 minutes.

- Break up the noodles with a fork or chopsticks and microwave 2 minutes more.

- Arrange the raw beef in the bottom of a deep soup bowl and carefully pour the noodles and broth over.

- Top with the sprouts, Thai or basil leaves, scallion, and cilantro. Squeeze the lime over the soup. Season with salt.

Chicken Pho: Chicken Pho is a common variation in Vietnam and is quite easy to make. Simply substitute chicken broth or consommé for the beef consommé and then use thinly sliced or pulled chicken meat. You do not use raw chicken meat as you do with the beef for both food safety and texture. Some add a little sesame oil at the very end in Chicken Pho.

ZOOM

In Vietnam almost every part of beef is used in pho. Typically the soup is adorned with slices of poached tripe (stomach lining), thin slivers of fat cut from the brisket, braised tendon, beef flank, and raw eye round, as we serve here. It may sound unappetizing to most in America, but an authentic pho place will have all these options, and the diversity of textures are really nice in the soup.

Seek Out the Sriracha

The Hot Pot

- Sriracha hot sauce is a condiment that is widely available. The most common brand is Wild Rooster.

- This sauce is actually an invention of an Asian-American man living in California and is not a traditional sauce.

- It has gained such popularity in this country that almost all Vietnamese restaurants have it on hand.

- This sauce is also great on eggs, burgers, pizza, and hot dogs. If you like hot sauce with flavor and not just heat, this is it.

- Pouring hot broth over raw meat is a very popular technique in Asia.

- More often, a pot of boiling broth sits on the table and diners dip vegetables and meats into it and eat as they go.

- The Chinese call this technique hot pot, and the Japanese call it nabe. We could call it a fondue of sorts.

- Be sure the broth is boiling when you use raw meat.

KICKED-UP TUNA CASSEROLE
Microwavable mac and cheese is a great base for this comforting dish

Ah, tuna casserole. This dish was made incredibly popular during the 1950s, when the casserole craze was in full swing. Many have memories of gummy or dry casseroles being brought to the table in a huge and horrifying dish. The leftovers would be around in the fridge for days, and the crust forming on it became its own life-form.

This incarnation, fortunately, is not Grandma's 1950s casserole. First of all, this dish is a quick dish, not requiring a long and slow bake in the oven. Second, the use of store-bought mac and cheese tends to be a crowd-pleaser, as everyone has fond memories of this dish from childhood. Give this one a shot. *Yield: Enough for 1 hungry student*

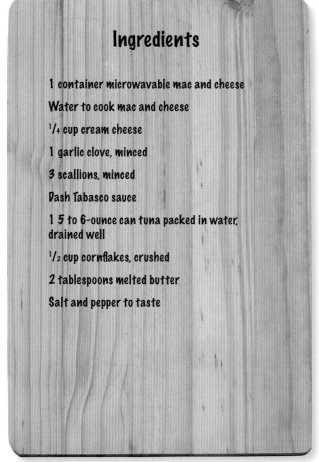

Ingredients

1 container microwavable mac and cheese

Water to cook mac and cheese

$1/4$ cup cream cheese

1 garlic clove, minced

3 scallions, minced

Dash Tabasco sauce

1 5 to 6-ounce can tuna packed in water, drained well

$1/2$ cup cornflakes, crushed

2 tablespoons melted butter

Salt and pepper to taste

Kicked-Up Tuna Casserole

- Prepare the mac and cheese according to package directions.

- Scoop into a bowl and add the cream cheese and garlic and microwave another 30 seconds.

- Add the scallions, Tabasco, and tuna; mix well. Scoop into a shallow baking dish and top with the crushed cornflakes and melted butter. Add salt and pepper to taste.

- Microwave another minute and serve.

112

Leftovers in Casserole: This casserole is ripe for variation. Tuna is just one protein that you can add to this recipe. Leftovers fare very well in this dish. Shredding leftover rotisserie chicken into this dish is excellent, as is some chopped leftover steak or even meatloaf or hamburger. Be creative. See what's going on in the fridge and cupboard, mix it up, and make a casserole out if it.

ZOOM

Macaroni and cheese has a long history in the United States. It is reputed that Thomas Jefferson first served it in the White House in 1802. The recipe was popular in England and was called baked macaroni with cream and cheese and was surely different from the boxed versions we enjoy today. It gained a resurgence during World War I, when meat was rationed and at a premium.

The Secret Ingredient

Not Just for Breakfast

- Cream cheese has some fantastic characteristics, which makes it ideal for this dish.

- Cream cheese has a unique ability to melt into dishes and provide fantastically creamy and luxurious textures.

- Cream cheese is often used in baking and makes very moist cakes as well as killer icing for carrot cake.

- Try melting 1 tablespoon into 2 scrambled eggs for an amazing treat. Or use in place of butter in mashed potatoes. It really is a secret ingredient.

- Cornflakes are another secret ingredient for your arsenal. They can make a great topping for almost any casserole.

- If you are baking this dish in an oven, drizzle with 3 tablespoons melted butter before placing in the oven.

- Bread chicken cutlets with crushed cornflakes for an ultracrunchy topping. Just put in a bag and smash with a rolling pin.

- You can also grind them into a fine powder and use them to thicken a sauce for pot roast; this adds a little sweetness.

THIRSTY POPCORN

Perfect for a night of libation, this spicy popcorn is complemented by frosty beverages

Popcorn was first discovered by the Native Americans, who believed the popping corn was a sign from an angry god. Corn pops because a small amount of moisture and oil is trapped inside the dried corn kernel and the outer skin of the kernel is virtually airtight. When the corn is heated, the water and oil expand and the kernel basically explodes, causing the corn to pop. There are a few species of corn that yield popcorn and they are specifically cultivated for this purpose. There are also two distinct types of popped kernels: mushroom shaped and butterfly shaped. The mushroom-shaped popped corn is less fragile than the butterfly corn, but it is less tender. *Yield: 1 bag*

Ingredients

1 bag microwave popcorn

1 stick butter

1 teaspoon paprika

1 teaspoon chili powder

1 teaspoon garlic powder

1 teaspoon granulated onion

1 teaspoon dry mustard

1 teaspoon sugar

1 tablespoon fresh parsley leaves, chopped fine

2 scallions, minced fine

1 teaspoon fresh thyme leaves, chopped

Thirsty Popcorn

- Pop corn according to package directions.

- Cut butter into 6 pieces, place in a microwavable bowl, and melt in the microwave. Add all the dry spices and sugar and microwave for 30 seconds; mix well.

- Mix the popcorn with the spiced butter and fresh herbs.

- Serve in a big bowl with plenty of napkins and frosty drinks.

ZOOM

Once popcorn became popular in the United States, street vendors began setting up stands in front of movie theaters to provide a snack to moviegoers. As this became more and more popular, the theater owners realized they could grab that extra money by installing their own poppers inside the theaters, and they soon capitalized on this emerging trend.

• • • • RECIPE VARIATION • • • •

Popcorn, Savory or Sweet: Popcorn is yummy both savory and sweet, and there are many popcorn seasonings that include a sweet component. A very simple recipe is to melt 1 stick of butter in the microwave with $1/4$ cup honey or maple syrup. When the popcorn is popped, toss it with this sweet seasoning for an unusual treat. Try adding a pinch of cayenne pepper.

Toasty Goodness

- Spices contain essential oils, which are enhanced when heated, especially in a solution of fat like oil or butter.

- Not only do the spices improve in flavor, they infuse the surrounding fat with their flavor to make the entire dish more intense.

- You can also toast spices in a dry pan, but be careful, as burning is a real possibility.

- Toasting spices can bring up the flavor of old spices, but it is recommended that you replace spices every two years.

Fresh Herbs

- Fresh herbs add a dimension of "brightness" to this popcorn. You should not substitute dried herbs; they are too strong in flavor.

- If you cannot find fresh herbs, go ahead and make the popcorn without the herbs.

- Other great herbs you could add to this dish include basil, cilantro, oregano, chervil, and chives.

- Herb purees such as pesto can also be added to the popcorn. Add a little Parmesan, too!

TWISTED DORM CLASSICS

BURRITO BITES WITH THREE SALSAS
Use flour and not corn tortillas for these tasty treats

Tortillas are a staple food source in Mexico. The word is derived from the Spanish *torta,* which literally translates to "round cake." When the Spaniards arrived in Mexico, they saw the small flatbreads being made by the native Indians and called them tortillas, which means "little round cakes."

Small independent tortilla shops dot every neighborhood, and many are made by hand, although mechanized production is very common. There are two main types of tortillas: flour and corn. Corn tortillas are made from a less finely ground meal and can be crumbly, while flour tortillas are made from finely milled wheat flour and are ideal for wrapping these yummy burritos. Do not attempt these with corn tortillas. *Yield: 8 burritos*

Ingredients

1 14-ounce can refried beans

1 cup shredded Monterey Jack cheese

1/4 cup canned diced green chiles, drained

1/4 cup grated onion

8 6-inch flour tortillas at room temperature

1/2 cup minced cilantro

1 8-ounce jar chunky salsa

1 4-ounce can salsa verde

1 cup sour cream

1 ripe avocado

Juice of 1 lime

Salt and pepper to taste

Burrito Bites with Three Salsas

- Combine the refried beans, cheese, green chiles, and onion; microwave for about 2 minutes.

- Divide mixture among the 8 tortillas and roll into burritos. Reserve on a plate to reheat.

- Mix together the cilantro and salsa for sauce one. Use the salsa verde for sauce two. For sauce three, combine the sour cream, avocado, and lime juice and puree with an immersion blender until very smooth. Season with salt and pepper.

- Reheat in microwave for 1 to 2 minutes.

In Spain, a tortilla is not a tortilla. The recipe most associated with the word tortilla in Spain is actually a type of omelet. It is commonly referred to as tortilla Española and is a fantastic mixture of onions, potatoes, and eggs. It is a common dish served in tapas bars and is eaten hot or most often at room temperature with a glass of wine or sherry.

• • • • RECIPE VARIATION • • • •

Shrimp Burritos: These burritos use all vegetarian ingredients. The beauty of the burrito is that it invites all manner of fillings. A great option is adding 1 cup cooked diced shrimp to this recipe. Of course, ground meat and rice is a classic filling; use 1 cup of each, cooked. Burritos are a great way to clean out the fridge and use some leftovers.

Roll or No Roll?

Cool It Down

- When ingredients are rolled into a flour tortilla, the creation is called a burrito. There are, however, many options for eating a tortilla.

- Filled, folded in half, and griddled, a flour tortilla is referred to as a quesadilla. This is the most popular use of flour tortillas in Mexico.

- If fried crisp and layered with ingredients, the tortilla concoction is referred to as a tostada.

- Tortillas can be used as a pasta substitute to make a Mexican lasagna.

- Sour cream is typically used in Mexican dishes as a cooling agent to counteract the hot and spicy condiments.

- Adding avocado adds another layer of richness and complexity to this cooling sauce.

- Another common sauce is lime juice, fresh cilantro, and sour cream.

- In Mexico, the sour cream is called crema and is slightly thicker and more tangy than American sour cream. Look for it in Latino markets.

ELEVATED FRANKS & BEANS

Like a hearty, homey stew, this is not your mom's lunchtime standard

Hot dogs are as American as apple pie, right? Not really. The hot dog's provenance is hotly debated (no pun intended). The German town of Frankfurt lays claim to them, citing one of the hot dog's other names, frankfurter. The Austrian city of Vienna claims the invention based on the German word wiener, which refers to the city of Vienna (Wien in German).

There is also a connection to the good ol' USA. Supposedly in 1880, hot dogs were first served on a bun on the streets of St. Louis, Missouri. Whichever is true, the hot dog is a favorite among children and adults around the world. Typically made with a blend of pork and beef, most hot dogs are smoked and have a garlicky flavor. *Yield: 2 servings*

Ingredients

1 14-ounce can premium baked beans, such as Bush's

2 high-quality natural-casing hot dogs cut into 4 pieces each

1 tablespoon brown mustard

2 teaspoons ketchup

1 tablespoon maple syrup

1 teaspoon curry powder

³/₄ cup french-fried onions, such as French's, divided

1 small can Boston brown bread with raisins (found in the supermarket next to the baked beans), divided

Elevated Franks and Beans

- In a microwavable bowl, mix together the beans, hot dog pieces, mustard, ketchup, maple syrup, and curry powder. Microwave in 2-minute increments, stirring in between, until piping hot.

- Place half the onions in the bottom of a serving bowl.

- Remove the brown bread from the can by opening both sides of the can and sliding the bread out. Slice into 6 slices.

- Top with the franks and beans and serve with the remaining bread.

ZOOM

Nathan Handwerker was an employee of a hot dog seller in Coney Island, New York. He decided to go into business for himself. To set himself apart from his former employer, he charged half of the ten cents his old boss charged for a dog, and, he put his workers in pristine white smocks to appear hygienic. Nathan's famous hot dogs were born.

• • • • RECIPE VARIATION • • • •

Feijoada: For a total about-face on this recipe, you can substitute sausage and black beans for the hot dogs and the beans. Try a can of black beans with its liquid, and add about 4 ounces sliced cooked smoked sausage or chorizo sausage. Heat the mixture, add a little cilantro and lime, and you have a loose representation of feijoada, the national dish of Brazil.

Boston Baked Beans

- It wasn't long ago when what we now call baked beans were commonly referred to as Boston baked beans.

- The traditional method for slow simmering in a molasses-based sauce originated in Boston.

- Boston was awash in molasses from the rum trade, and it was used in many recipes.

- Try making your own Boston baked beans from scratch someday.

Crispy Toppings

- You can make the french-fried onions if you have a tabletop-fryer (not in a dorm room).

- Slice onions as thinly as possible and gently separate the rings.

- Dust them in flour seasoned with salt and pepper and fry in 350°F peanut or canola oil for about 2 minutes or until very crispy.

- Drain the onions on paper towels and, if storing for a later use, wait until completely cool before storing in an airtight container.

TUNA STEAK PROVENÇAL

Look in the canned tuna section for these great tuna steaks in the foil pouch

There are many types of tuna that swim in the sea. Interestingly enough, the tuna is the largest member of the mackerel family. Tunas range in size from the mighty Bluefin, which can reach well over a thousand pounds, to the petite "little tunny," or false albacore, which weighs about ten pounds. All tuna are edible, but not all have the red flesh that is prized by so many sushi connoisseurs. The tuna most widely canned is albacore or "white" tuna, which is considered the best species for this purpose due to its pure white flesh and non-oily flavor. The tuna steaks in this recipe are found in the supermarket in pouches near the canned tuna and are usually from the albacore. *Yield: 1 serving*

Ingredients

1 pouch tuna steak, any flavor

1/2 cup fresh tomato dices

1 teaspoon capers, rinsed

1 tablespoon extra-virgin olive oil

1 garlic clove, minced

4 kalamata olives, pitted and minced

6 fresh basil leaves, chiffonade cut, divided

Pinch of red pepper flakes

Salt and pepper to taste

1 pouch instant or "minute" rice

1 tablespoon butter

Tuna Steak Provençal

- Remove the tuna steak from the pouch and put in microwavable dish, covered. Set aside.

- Mix together the tomato, capers, olive oil, garlic, olives, half the basil, and red pepper flakes. Season with salt and pepper.

- Prepare the instant rice according to directions for the microwave. Toss rice with butter. While rice is resting, place tuna in the microwave for 2 minutes.

- Layer rice, then tuna, and top with tomato relish. Garnish with basil.

ZOOM

The tuna is one of the world's few warm-blooded fish. They are actually able to raise their body temperature above water temperature by swimming at increased speeds. This allows them to survive in colder waters. This may also explain their tremendously strong muscles. The tuna is one of the fastest fish in the sea, curising at over fifty miles per hour!

• • • • RECIPE VARIATION • • • •

Tuna a la Mexicana: The flavor profile of this dish is clearly Provençal or Mediterranean. A few changes and this recipe completely transforms the flavor. Try substituting 1 jar of salsa for all the tomato mixture. Substitute cilantro for the basil. Add 1 can of drained corn and a pinch of cumin to the rice and top with ¼ cup shredded Monterey Jack cheese.

Fully Cooked Fish

Fast and Tart

- The tuna steak used in this recipe is already fully cooked and completely safe to eat as is.

- This tuna steak is also great eaten cold on a salad or even as a sandwich with some lettuce, tomato, and mayo.

- It is possible to dry this steak out by over-microwaving it, forcing the moisture out of it. Cook until just heated through.

- You can also use a more fully cooked fish steak, found in the fish section of the supermarket.

- This quick tomato relish bears a striking resemblance to the Italian puttanesca sauce.

- Puttanesca sauce gets its name from the Italian word for prostitute and is known as a "working girl's" sauce.

- Supposedly this is because the sauce requires little or no cooking, so the girls could prepare it quickly between clients.

- Puttanesca sauce is usually a bit spicier than this relish and utilizes a good measure of red pepper flakes for an added punch.

MICROWAVE SHRIMP SCAMPI

Cooked, frozen, peeled, and deveined shrimp are a time-saver in this great recipe

Shrimp are the most popular seafood consumed in America. Shrimp are typically sold frozen or thawed after being frozen. It is rare to see fresh shrimp in the market and even rarer to see live shrimp. Shrimp are sold by count. For instance, if shrimp are labeled 16–20, that means there are between 16 and 20 shrimp per pound. There are tiny shrimp as small as

51–60 and huge shrimp such as U4, which means there are under 4 shrimp per pound.

The other way shrimp are sold is by species. Many shrimp these days are called tiger shrimp. These freshwater shrimp are farmed in Southeast Asia and have an inferior texture and flavor to wild-caught white, brown, or pink shrimp. *Yield: 2 servings*

Ingredients

12 16–20 cooked, frozen shrimp thawed under cold water and dried

1 tablespoon butter

1 tablespoon extra-virgin olive oil

2 cloves garlic, minced

1 tablespoon white wine or lemon juice

1/2 teaspoon fresh thyme leaves

Salt and pepper to taste

1 tablespoon Italian bread crumbs

1 1/2 cups frozen broccoli, thawed under cold water

Microwave Shrimp Scampi

- If tail shell section of shrimp is still on, it is okay to leave it intact.

- Combine the butter, olive oil, garlic, wine or lemon juice, thyme, and salt and pepper in a microwavable bowl and microwave for 30 seconds to combine and melt.

- Toss the shrimp and bread crumbs in with the butter mixture and microwave for about 3 minutes, stirring halfway through. Set aside.

- Microwave the broccoli with a little salt and pepper for 2 minutes and place on a serving plate. Pour shrimp mixture over the broccoli.

ZOOM

Scampi is actually a name for a species of lobster and not a preparation method, as many people think. Shrimp are referred to as langoustine in France, or langostinos in Italian. In the United States, Italian-American immigrants invented a dish of shrimp cooked with garlic and white wine and sometimes bread crumbs. It became wildly popular.

•••• RECIPE VARIATION ••••

Scallops in the Same Style: Try making this dish with scallops. Fresh "dry" scallops are best, but frozen scallops, thawed and patted with paper towels to get rid of excess moisture, will also work. The great thing about scallops is that they are sold the same way as shrimp, that is, by count. You can easily find 16–20 scallops in the market.

Oil Plus Butter

- Olive oil and other oils are often mixed with butter for broiling, sautéing, and frying, and in this case microwaving.

- Butter has a wonderful flavor but tends to burn during high-heat cooking.

- Adding the oil to the butter will prevent the butter from burning, while preserving the flavor of the butter.

- The mixture of extra-virgin olive oil and butter has the best of both worlds, as the oil has a wonderful flavor of its own.

Broccoli Options

- This recipe uses frozen broccoli, but fresh has a much firmer texture and better flavor.

- You can cook fresh broccoli in the microwave. Put it in a microwavable dish, add ¼ inch water, tightly cover the dish, and microwave for about 2 minutes.

- If you have a stove, boil the broccoli in plenty of salted boiling water for about 4 minutes.

- Broccoli, dressed with a little oil and salt and pepper, can also be roasted in a very hot oven.

HEALTHY SAUSAGE STEW

Beans, light kielbasa, and healthy kale make this soup both satisfying and good for you

This soup is loosely based on the national dish of Portugal, *caldo verde*, which literally means "green soup." The Portuguese version uses collard greens or turnip greens but many cooks in the United States use kale. The Portuguese use potatoes in place of the beans and use a sausage known as linguica, which is a slightly spicy pork sausage. At the markets in Portugal, women use special hand-cranked shredders to finely shred the collards or kale into huge green piles onto wooden tables. Local housewives will then come to the market and fill bags with these freshly shredded greens. The soup is so common that it is served in virtually every home at least once a week and is very common in restaurants. *Yield: 1 bowl*

Ingredients

1 tablespoon extra-virgin olive oil

2 cloves garlic, minced

¼ cup minced white onion

1 cup frozen, chopped kale, defrosted and squeezed dry

1 cup chicken broth

1 14-ounce can small white beans, undrained

4 ounces light or turkey kielbasa, sliced into ¼-inch rings

Salt and pepper to taste

3 tablespoons grated Parmesan cheese

Healthy Sausage Stew

- Place the oil, garlic, onion, kale, and broth in a microwavable bowl and microwave for 4 minutes, stirring halfway through.

- Add the beans with their liquid and the sausage; stir well.

- Microwave for 3 minutes, stirring halfway through. Season with salt and pepper.

- Place in a serving bowl and top with Parmesan cheese.

ZOOM

Kale is a member of the cabbage family and is related to broccoli and cauliflower. It is extremely good for you, with high levels of beta-carotene, vitamin C, and calcium. It is also very rich in fiber and aids in digestion. Kale is eaten around the world. In Africa it is slowly simmered with coconut milk and peanuts. The Irish have a dish of mashed potatoes mixed with kale called colcannon.

• • • • RECIPE VARIATION • • • •

Southern "Soul Food" Style: For an interesting twist on this recipe, substitute equal parts frozen chopped collard greens for the kale and black-eyed peas for the white beans. You can also substitute "red hot" sausages for the kielbasa if you like it hot. Omit the cheese and make the recipe in the same way. This would be a great side dish for some fried pork chops or catfish.

Cooking Kale

- Kale, unlike other leafy, more delicate greens, usually needs to be cooked for at least 20 minutes in boiling water to become tender.

- Frozen kale has been precooked, so this recipe takes less time than if using fresh kale.

- Steaming together with the onions, oil, and garlic perfumes the kale with their flavors.

- If cooking fresh kale, remove the broad stem, or "rib," and boil in salted water for about 20 minutes. In winter, kale may take a bit longer to cook.

Classic Combo

- Cooking beans with sausage is a very old culinary technique. It is practiced all over the world.

- In Brazil, black bean and chorizo feijoada uses blood sausage and chunks of pork.

- In Italy, small white beans are cooked with fennel sausage and plum tomatoes.

- In the United States, franks and beans are a classic lunchtime dish.

- Try all these classics or make your own combo.

MOROCCAN COUSCOUS

This is an excellent vegetarian dish and can be eaten as a main course or side dish

If you have not eaten or cooked couscous, you are missing out. The fluffy and grainy texture is amazing, especially when soaked with some delicious sauce or gravy. Couscous can be eaten cold as a salad, mixed with oil and vinegar and garnished with dried fruits and nuts. In Morocco, where couscous is omnipresent, it is often paired with the amazing stews of Morocco, called tangine.

Most people think couscous is a type of grain and are surprised to learn that it is actually pasta made from semolina flour. Traditionally women made the couscous by moistening the semolina flour with water and rubbing it between their hands, creating the granular pasta. *Yield: About 2 cups*

Ingredients

1 cup instant couscous

2 tablespoons extra-virgin olive oil, divided

1 cup water

¼ cup minced onion

1 teaspoon ground cumin

1 teaspoon ground coriander

Pinch of ground cardamom

Pinch of ground cinnamon

Pinch of ground ginger

1 tablespoon raisins

½ teaspoon salt

1 14-ounce can chickpeas, drained, reserving 3 tablespoons liquid

Salt and pepper to taste

2 tablespoons chopped fresh parsley

2 tablespoons slivered almonds

Harissa for a condiment

Moroccan Couscous

- In a bowl, combine the couscous with 1 tablespoon oil. Set aside.

- In a microwavable bowl, combine the water with the onion, dried spices, raisins, and salt. Microwave for 2 minutes and stir well. Pour over the couscous and cover with plastic wrap. Let sit 5 minutes.

- Meanwhile, combine the remaining oil, chickpeas, and liquid. Season with salt and pepper and microwave for 2 minutes.

- Combine the cooked couscous, chickpeas, parsley, and almonds.

ZOOM

Many people have eaten what is referred to as Israeli couscous. These little round pasta balls bear little resemblance to their Moroccan relative. They must be boiled, as opposed to steamed, and are usually added to soups and stews, as opposed to served as a main component. Some chefs cook Israeli couscous like risotto, slowly adding boiling stock and finishing with butter and Parmesan.

• • • • RECIPE VARIATION • • • •

Beef Stew and Couscous: Couscous is traditionally served with the fragrant tagine stews of North Africa. For a twist, empty 1 can of beef stew into a microwavable bowl and add to it all the ingredients used in this couscous recipe. Microwave for 4 minutes. Then make plain couscous and pour the stew over the couscous. Any leftover stew would work well for this.

Screamin' for Steamin'

- The couscous gently steams in the hot liquid until all the water is absorbed. It is important not to disturb it as it steams.

- The oil added to the couscous helps keep the grains of pasta separated and fluffy.

- When it is done steaming, fluff the couscous with a fork until the grains separate and it becomes very fluffy and well mixed.

- Couscous can be reheated in the microwave. Just add a few tablespoons of water and cover.

Garnishing Couscous

- Traditionally couscous is served plain and gets most of its flavor and other textures from the stews it is served with.

- Garnishing with the fruits and nuts evokes these traditional Moroccan flavors. They pair naturally with the couscous.

- Other great garnishes include minced scallions, diced apricots, toasted pecan pieces, and chopped olives.

- Chickpeas are very traditional in Moroccan cooking and are found throughout the culture in soups, stews, dips, and even sweets.

MUSHROOM & PEPPER STEAK
Almost like a mock stir-fry, this dish has countless variations

Bell peppers are the sweetest member of the chili family. Red, yellow, orange, and purple peppers all have basically the same flavor. Green peppers are the unripened version of any and all of these.

Many bell peppers are grown in the United States, but the peppers grown in Holland are reputed to be some of the best. They tend to be very thick walled, very sweet, and uniform in color, which helps when trying to make attractive, uniform slices or dice. This recipe uses red bell pepper, but any color or blend would work well. *Yield: 1 large portion*

Ingredients

1 red bell pepper, cut into thin strips

$\frac{1}{2}$ cup white onion, sliced thinly

$\frac{1}{2}$ cup large white mushrooms, sliced thinly

2 tablespoons extra-virgin olive oil

3 tablespoons water

1 tablespoon Worcestershire sauce

Pinch of dried thyme

1 tablespoon instant gravy mix (from packet)

6 ounces cube steak cut into 4 x $\frac{1}{4}$-inch strips

2 tablespoons vegetable oil

Salt and pepper to taste

2 tablespoons minced fresh parsley

Mushroom and Pepper Steak

- Place the peppers, onion, mushrooms, and olive oil in a microwavable bowl; cover and microwave for 1 minute. In a separate bowl, mix the water, Worcestershire, thyme, and gravy mix together; add to the pepper mixture.

- On a microwavable plate, toss the steak with vegetable oil and salt and pepper. Microwave for 2 minutes, stirring halfway through. Add the meat to the pepper mixture, including any juices.

- Microwave the entire mixture for 2 minutes; Top with parsley.

• • • • RECIPE VARIATIONS • • • •

Stir-Fried Beef with Peppers and Mushrooms: This dish is similiar to stir fry in nature. It is quite easy to create a Chinese spin on it. Substitute peanut oil for the olive oil. Substitute 1 teaspoon of each fresh minced garlic and ginger for the thyme. Substitute soy sauce for the Worcestershire sauce, and substitute scallions for the parsley. Drizzle with a little sesame oil when finished.

Fajitas: This dish can also be transformed into fajitas in no time. In place of the thyme add 1 teaspoon of each: ground cumin, ground coriander, and ground chili powder. In place of the Worcestershire sauce add lime juice, and substitute cilantro for the parsley. You may want to omit the gravy packet if you like your fajitas dry. Serve with some warm tortillas, guacamole, and salsa.

Cuts of Beef

- Cube steak can be used for this recipe, since it can be cut from almost any muscle and is passed through a series of tenderizing blades.

- In this example, we used flank steak, which can be used as long as it is cut very thinly across the visible grain running through the meat.

- When choosing cuts of meat for this dish, it is important to avoid cuts from the shoulder, as these cuts tend to be tough.

- If you do use shoulder meat, it must be well pounded to tenderize.

Microwave Deconstruction

- Cooking these types of semi-complex dishes in the microwave requires several steps and a bit of preplanning.

- Because you do not have the luxury of a sauté pan or wok in a dorm room, the meats and veggies need to be cooked in batches.

- You can keep the first cooked batch warm while the other is cooking by covering with foil.

- Always remember to stir frequently when using the microwave to ensure even heating.

129

CHEATERS' PARMESAN RISOTTO

True risotto takes time and constant stirring; this is a great shortcut

Risotto is considered one of the great culinary treasures brought to us from Italy. The secret to the preparation of true risotto is twofold. First, one must use the correct rice. There are several rice varieties that can be used, but Arborio is the most popular and readily available in supermarkets. Some Arborio rice is even grown in California. All risotto rice is short grained and has a very high starch content. This accounts for the creaminess of the resulting sauce if cooked properly.

Second, one must add hot stock to the cooking rice in batches, typically thirds, and stir constantly. This is time-consuming, but worth it. When you move into a real kitchen space, try making risotto the traditional way; you won't be disappointed. *Yield: 1 serving*

Ingredients

2 tablespoons extra-virgin olive oil

1 clove garlic, minced

1 cup finely diced white onion

1 1/2 cups chicken or vegetable broth

1/4 cup white wine, or 1 teaspoon white vinegar.

3/4 cup Arborio rice

1/2 cup freshly grated Parmesan cheese

1 tablespoon butter

1/4 cup half-and-half

2 tablespoons fresh minced chives

Salt and pepper to taste

Cheaters' Parmesan Risotto

- In a microwavable bowl, combine the oil, garlic, and onion; microwave for 2 minutes, stirring halfway through. Add the broth and wine and microwave for 2 minutes.

- Stir in the rice and pour into a shallow microwavable baking dish. Cover very tightly and microwave for 5 minutes. Stir and re-cover; cook for 5 more minutes.

- Remove the cover and stir in the cheese, butter, and half-and-half. Cook 5 more minutes. Gently stir in the chives and season with salt and pepper.

• • • • RECIPE VARIATION • • • •

Risotto Milanese: Perhaps the most famous risotto dish is Risotto Milanese, or risotto from the city of Milan. And, as Milan is always recognized for being the height of expensive fashion, the risotto attributed to this city is also highbrow. The key ingredient is saffron, which is the world's most expensive spice. If you can get a few threads, add about ¹/₂ teaspoon.

YELLOW ● LIGHT

Risotto is notorious for getting gummy and pasty if over-cooked, and it is very easy to overcook this dish in the microwave. The key to a proper risotto texture is to cook the rice to al dente, like firm pasta. Also, there should be a bit of creamy sauce surrounding the rice grains. If it is too dry, add a little more hot stock, but avoid cooking too much longer if the rice seems cooked.

Parmesan Cheese

- Known as the king of cheeses, Parmesan, or Parmigiana Reggiano, is produced under the strictest rules.

- Only cows from certain areas of Parma may give milk for this ancient artisanal product.

- In order to have the official Parmigiana stamp, the cheese must be certified by a government agency.

- The leftover whey from the cheese-making process is fed to pigs, which are used for prosciutto di Parma, which is considered the king of hams. Coincidence?

Untraditional Works Sometimes

- As discussed, traditional preparation of this dish is much different than the method used here.

- It is key to lift the cover off of the risotto for the last few minutes of cooking in order to achieve the proper texture.

- Usually the cheese is added at the very last second, but the method used in this preparation works best.

- In Italy, they would faint if they knew you made risotto in a microwave! Don't tell any Italians you know.

131

CRAZY PEANUT BUTTER SUNDAE

When the coffeepot is empty, you may need some sugar to keep you awake for studying

Peanut butter is one of those ingredients that has almost mystical properties. It can be sweet or savory and used in desserts, sauces for grilled meats, or eaten out of the jar at three in the morning. Of course the classic sandwiches, such as peanut butter and jelly; peanut butter and banana; and, for those who don't know, peanut butter and bacon, are among the greatest culinary creations ever. This ice-cream sundae borrows the flavors of the PB&J and hits it out of the park with a smattering of Nutella, the ridiculously incredible chocolate hazelnut spread that many people cannot keep in the house, as they eat the whole thing with a spoon at the drop of a hat. *Yield: 1 shareable sundae*

Ingredients

- 1 scoop chocolate ice cream
- 1 scoop coffee ice cream
- 1 scoop vanilla ice cream
- 2 tablespoons premium raspberry preserves
- 2 tablespoons peanut butter
- 2 tablespoons Nutella
- 4 strawberries, sliced thinly
- 3 tablespoons crushed pecans

Crazy Peanut Butter Sundae

- Arrange three scoops of ice cream in a dish or shallow bowl. Dip the scooper into very hot water before and after each scoop.

- Place a dollop of raspberry preserves on each scoop.

- Combine the peanut butter and Nutella in a microwavable bowl and microwave for 10 seconds. Mix again and pour over ice cream.

- Top with the sliced berries and the pecans. Prepare for the sugar buzz.

Peanuts probably originated in South America and then made their way to the United States. It was a doctor in the 1800s that invented peanut butter. He was looking for a high-protein food source for his patients who had bad teeth and could not chew well. But is wasn't until 1904 at the St. Louis World Fair when peanut butter really made its public debut, and it was a hit.

Nutella is wildly popular in Europe, where it is usually spread on bread and eaten for breakfast with a good cup of coffee. (Note to self: Try this!) Nutella was a 1940s invention of Pietro Ferrero, who owned a pastry business in Italy. Because cocoa was rationed and chocolate was hard to produce, he added hazelnuts to his chocolate, and that was it. Go get a jar!

Tricks of the Trade

- Keeping the scooper in hot water is an old trick to make nice uniform scoops of ice cream.

- Keeping a knife in hot water is an excellent way to make nice clean slices of cakes and ice-cream cakes.

- If you do not have an ice-cream scoop, a large spoon, dipped in hot water and pulled through slightly warmed ice cream works very well.

- Ice cream can be thawed for 30 seconds in the microwave.

Take Care When Melting

- Melting Nutella and peanut butter together results in an incredible mixture that is amazing on ice cream or even bread.

- When melting things in the microwave, be aware that things sometimes "pop" and can burn you.

- Do not allow any water to make it into the mixture, as the water will cause the chocolate to "seize" by becoming lumpy and inedible.

- Peanut butter all by itself will also work well in this recipe.

MINTY STRAWBERRY SHORTCAKES

Fresh mint adds an amazing touch to this classic and easy dessert

This recipe takes a nice, simple shortcut to shortcake and uses premade biscuits. Although very similar in nature, biscuits differ slightly from true shortcake. In Britain, shortcakes are referred to as scones, which are similar to American biscuits. Many older recipes from the 1800s called for crumbled piecrust as a base instead of the actual shortcake or biscuits. Versions of this dish are still served in the South. The basic

gist remains the same: A rich and crumbly base is topped with fresh strawberries and freshly whipped cream. This dish is best made in the summer, when strawberries are at the height of the season. *Yield: 2 servings*

Ingredients

2 large biscuits

1 cup sliced fresh strawberries

1 tablespoon orange juice

1 tablespoon granulated sugar

6 mint leaves, cut in chiffonade, plus 2 sprigs for garnish

$1/2$ cup whipping cream

2 teaspoons confectioners' sugar

$1/2$ teaspoon ground cinnamon, plus some to dust

Minty Strawberry Shortcakes

- Cut the biscuits in half. Marinate the strawberries with orange juice, granulated sugar, and mint.

- Place the cream in a cold, clean bowl and whip with the confectioners' sugar and cinnamon until soft peaks form. Do not overwhip.

- Divide the strawberries and juice between the biscuit bottoms and top each with a fourth of the whipped cream.

- Place the other biscuit halves on top and scoop on the remaining whipped cream. Top with a dusting of cinnamon and mint sprig.

• • • • RECIPE VARIATION • • • •

Easy Minty Strawberry Pound Cake: The pound cake version of this dish, which is close to many people's heart, is a wonderful change to the biscuit classic. Simply slice off a nice piece of pound cake and top as you would the biscuit. Rich and dense pound cake does an amazing job of soaking up the strawberry juices.

ZOOM

Mint plays a nice role in this dessert by brightening the flavors. Mint is an amazing herb. It has been cultivated for over one thousand years and has many uses, mostly sweet and in desserts. Some cultures dry the leaves and make tea from them. Other cultures, most notably in Southern Italy, use the mint as they would basil, adding it to salads of tomatoes and vegetables.

Working with Mint

- A great way to slice mint leaves is to stack and chiffonade them by cutting superthin ribbons with a sharp knife.

- Some people prefer to tear the leaves into uneven slices.

- You can also briefly boil the mint leaves in sugar and water and use this syrup in place of fresh leaves if you do not want the green in the recipe.

- Picking the tiny mint tops and using them in place of leaves is a wonderful way to crown a dessert.

Real Whipped Cream

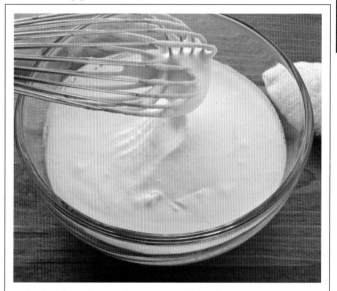

- Real whipped cream is an amazing thing and can be made easily in any kitchen—including dorm kitchens.

- Be sure the cream is cold and that there is no residual fat or oil in the bowl or on the whisk. If there is, the cream will not whip.

- If the dessert you are serving is very sweet, try omitting the sugar in the whipped cream for a nice contrast.

- Unsweetened whipped cream is also used in many French savory sauces.

135

CHOCOLATE MICROWAVE FUDGE
The microwave almost makes fudge easier to make

Chocolate is a truly universal food these days, and its comforting and complex richness has reached all corners of the globe. When the Spaniards first came to Mexico and tasted the chocolate drink presented to them by the infamous Montezuma, there was absolutely no sugar in the drink. In fact the beverage was spicy. It contained chili peppers, almonds, and cinnamon and was bitter and complex. Nonetheless, the Spaniards were so impressed that they brought chocolate to Europe, and it became a huge phenomenon. *Yield: About a pound of fudge*

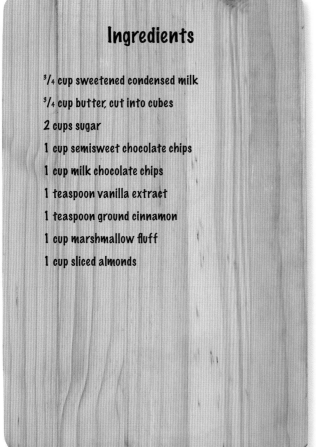

Ingredients

- ³/₄ cup sweetened condensed milk
- ³/₄ cup butter, cut into cubes
- 2 cups sugar
- 1 cup semisweet chocolate chips
- 1 cup milk chocolate chips
- 1 teaspoon vanilla extract
- 1 teaspoon ground cinnamon
- 1 cup marshmallow fluff
- 1 cup sliced almonds

Chocolate Microwave Fudge

- In a microwavable bowl, combine the milk, butter, and sugar and microwave for 10 minutes, stirring and scraping the bowl every 2 minutes.

- Add the chocolate chips and stir well to combine.

- Add the vanilla, cinnamon, fluff, and nuts and continue to stir until well incorporated.

- Pour into an 8-inch square baking pan that has been lightly sprayed with cooking spray. Allow to cool at room temperature for at least 2 hours. Cut into cubes.

There is so much to know about chocolate that entire books have been written about it. One thing that makes chocolate so addicting and wonderful to eat is that milk and dark chocolate have a melting point of just about 98.6°F. This is an amazing coincidence, as the human body is the same temperature, and that is why chocolate gets so nice and melted when you eat it.

Switch Up the Fudge: The beauty of this simple recipe is that making variations is supereasy. First of all, any nuts can be used in place of the almonds. Another nice variation is adding about $1/2$ cup shredded toasted coconut when you would add the nuts to the original recipe. You can also add $1/4$ cup chopped dried fruits, minimarshmallows, or peanut butter chips.

Mixing, Folding, and Scraping

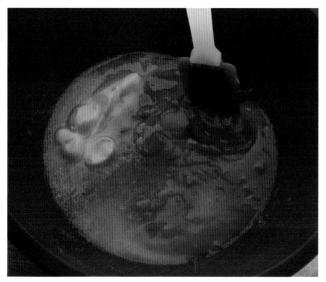

- Whenever making fudge, it is critical that all the ingredients be very well combined.

- Scraping down the bowl during the process ensures that no goodies get left on the bowl.

- Folding is a technique used to bring ingredients from the middle of the bowl out to the edge and back.

- You really need a good rubber spatula to do both of these techniques. Invest in a heatproof one; it does double duty.

Grease or No Grease?

- Many recipes call for lightly greasing a pan before pouring a mixture into it to avoid sticking and promote easy removal of the item.

- Items with a high fat content rarely need a greased pan, as the fat in the item will act as the grease.

- You can line pans with parchment paper or plastic wrap if you do not want to grease.

- If in doubt, lightly spray or grease the pan with vegetable oil. Better safe than sorry.

MAGIC MICROWAVE POACHED PEARS

You'll be amazed that you can make this truly elegant dessert in a dorm room

Poached pears have been a staple of French cooking for at least two hundred years. There are countless recipes with all manner of flavorings added to the poaching liquid, from cinnamon to black pepper and bay leaves. The common ingredient is always sugar. The sugar is essential to provide the flavor as well as to create the final syrup that is served with the pears. Look for firm, almost ripe pears to poach, as very ripe pears will fall apart. Any variety of pear can be poached except for the Asian round pears, which are a little tricky, as they have a more watery flesh and can easily turn to mush. Poaching is a gentle process, and the microwave hurries this along a bit. Check your pears frequently *Yield: 2 servings*

Ingredients

2 cups dry red wine

1 cup sugar

Pinch of ground cloves

Pinch of ground ginger

Pinch of ground cinnamon

1 bay leaf

4 black peppercorns

2 firm pears

4 small scoops vanilla ice cream

Magic Microwave Poached Pears

- In a microwavable bowl, mix together the wine, sugar, and spices; microwave for 4 minutes.

- Peel the pears and cut in half lengthwise. Carefully remove the cores with a melon baller. Place in the wine.

- Cover and microwave the pears for 6 minutes, flipping them halfway through.

- Remove the pears and cook the liquid for 3 minutes. Cool the pears and liquid.

- Top pear with syrup and add top with scoop of ice cream.

Poaching pears has always been seen as cooking pears slowly in liquid. Recently, a few chefs have discovered an amazing way to get this job done. The pears are left unpeeled and completely buried in coarse kosher salt (yes, salt). The salt-covered pears are then placed in a 300°F oven for about 40 minutes, and the results are amazing. The salt is an excellent heat conductor.

• • • • RECIPE VARIATION • • • •

Conventional Poached Pears: Once you escape the dorms and move to an apartment with a real kitchen, try poaching pears the conventional way: Completely cover the pears in the wine mixture and simmer very gently until a small pairing knife inserted into the deepest part of the pear comes free with no resistance. Cool the pears and reduce the liquid to a nice syrup.

Options for Pear Prep

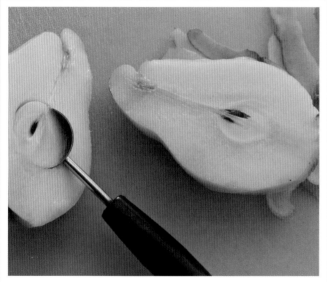

- Pears can be poached intact with the core and skin on, to be cleaned after cooking and cooling.

- Another fun option is to peel the pears, leave them whole, and push the melon baller in from the bottom and hollow out the pear. Poach whole.

- This cavity can be stuffed after cooking with all manner of creams and sauces.

- Some consider the pairing of pears and blue cheese amazing, and you can stuff the cavities with a blue cheese mousse.

Poaching 101

- Poaching is classically defined as cooking foods either fully or partially submerged in a flavored liquid.

- You can poach fish, meat, fruits, or vegetables. The liquid is typically transformed into a sauce, many times by reducing or adding butter or both.

- The microwave technique blends poaching and steaming.

- Sometimes when poaching a food fully submerged, the food will poke out and float. You can use a clean dish towel to keep the food covered while poaching.

LIME MARGARITA FRUIT SALAD

This is definitely a recipe for those of legal drinking age; use good tequila

Tequila! This interesting spirit is named after the town of Tequila in Mexico. It is made from the blue agave plant, which resembles a type of cactus. When trimmed of its leaves, the agave resembles a huge pineapple. The pinas, as they are called, can weigh upward of seventy pounds. They are then crushed and the juices fermented.

This liquid is also consumed in an ancient drink called pulque. These fermented juices are distilled into a clear white or silver tequila. Some producers then age the tequila in oak or other wood casks to mellow and add complexity to their specific batch. *Yield: About 4 cups*

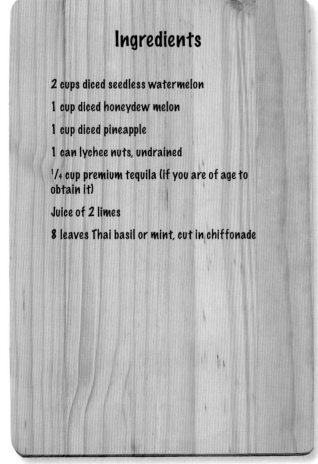

Ingredients

2 cups diced seedless watermelon

1 cup diced honeydew melon

1 cup diced pineapple

1 can lychee nuts, undrained

$1/4$ cup premium tequila (if you are of age to obtain it)

Juice of 2 limes

8 leaves Thai basil or mint, cut in chiffonade

Lime Margarita Fruit Salad

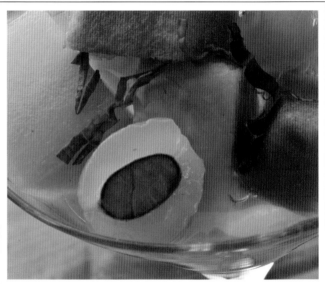

- Dice all the fruit into 1-inch chunks. Place in a large bowl.

- Drain the lychee nuts, saving the juice, and cut them in half. Combine the lychee juice with the tequila, lime juice, and Thai basil or mint.

- Combine all ingredients and allow to macerate for half an hour.

- Serve in margarita glasses garnished with some basil or mint leaves and a wedge of lime.

Lychee nuts are a great secret ingredient in this dish. They are actually not a nut but a fruit from a type of evergreen tree native to Asia. The type of fruit is called a drupe, which has an interesting pink nubby skin on the outside and an inedible large nutlike seed in the center. These are commonly available canned in syrup as used in this recipe, but fresh fruits do occasionally show up.

• • • • RECIPE VARIATION • • • •

Minty Melon Medley: Summer is the best time to eat melons, as they are in season and at their peak. Look for melons such as Crenshaw, Santa Claus, orange fleshed, Galia, or Cavaillon. Substitute any of these melons for the pineapple and watermelon and omit the tequila. Add ¼ cup shredded mint leaves and toss the ingredients together with the lime juice and lychee nuts.

Picking Good Fruit

- This fruit salad, as in all fruit salads, depends on great fruit to be successful. Picking fruit can be a real crapshoot.

- Always look for fruit in season. For melons, this means late spring until early fall.

- Another trick for melons is to make sure they are a bit soft when pushed at the stem end.

- Also, pick them up and shake them. If you can hear the seeds moving inside, they are probably ripe.

Lychee Juice

- The flavor of lychee is hard to describe, but after tasting it, you will understand why it is so prized.

- The juice from canned lychees can be used in soft drinks, mixed with alcohol for sweet cocktails, or used in poaching liquid for fruit.

- Lychee nectar is sold in boxes at supermarkets. Look for it in the ethnic section.

- If you cannot find either canned lychees or lychee nectar, make the salad without.

CHEESECAKE WITH RASPBERRIES

The magic of no-bake cheesecake is appreciated with this dessert; invite friends to share this

There are cheesecakes and then there are *cheesecakes,* and everyone seems to have an opinion. The New York-style or Jewish-style cheesecake always uses cream cheese for an intensely dense and rich cheesecake. The Italian-style cheesecakes are made with ricotta cheese and have a lighter and almost coarse texture that is a little less dense than the cream cheese version.

Whichever version you prefer, cheesecakes remain a favorite dessert. Whole companies and even restaurant chains have mushroomed out of making a good cheesecake. This recipe is an unbaked version, which is quite good, especially for being made without a true kitchen. *Yield: 4 servings*

Ingredients

- ¹/₂ cup raspberry preserves
- 1 large graham cracker piecrust
- 8 ounces cream cheese, room temperature
- 1 cup evaporated milk
- ¹/₂ cup sour cream
- 1 teaspoon grated lemon zest
- ¹/₂ teaspoon vanilla extract
- ¹/₂ pint raspberries
- 1 can instant whipped cream

Cheesecake with Raspberries

- Spread the raspberry preserves evenly over the bottom of the crust. Set aside.

- Beat the cream cheese in a bowl with a wooden spoon for about 3 minutes until fluffy. Slowly whip in the milk and sour cream.

- Add the lemon zest and vanilla and mix well. Fill piecrust with this mixture and smooth the top. Chill for at least 2 hours.

- Top with raspberries and whipped cream.

Perhaps the most famous cheesecake is the classic New York cheesecake. Legend has it that the owner of the famous Reuben's restaurant (from where the sandwich gets its name) ate a cheese "pie" at a friend's party. He took the recipe, adapted it, and placed it on his restaurant's menu. It was such a hit that this became the base recipe for all New York cheesecakes. Thank you, Reuben!

Apple Pie or Blueberry Pie Cheesecake: Try adding some internal garnishes to this cheesecake. Add 1 can apple pie filling or blueberry pie filling to the bottom of the crust instead of the jam before pouring the cheese mixture over it. It may be a little runny or saucy, but this is still a great way to enjoy this cake. You can also add crushed nuts to the cheese mixture.

Crust Options

- This recipe calls for a readymade graham cracker crust, which is a wonderful convenience.

- You could easily make a graham cracker crust in a food processor if you want a more homemade version.

- Another option is to take thin slices of pound cake and lay them in a pie plate, compress them slightly, and proceed as directed.

- If you have an oven, "blind baking" or pre-cooking a real piecrust and then filling it after cooling is a wonderful option.

Fill 'er Up

- "No-cook" pies and cakes are an excellent way to make homemade desserts without turning on the oven and are well suited for college living.

- There are many types of no-cook pies. Many use gelatin as a thickener. Although not baked in an oven, the gelatin does need to be heated in order for it to be able to thicken the main ingredient of the pie. This can be done in a microwave.

- A nice cheaters' method is to take some canned fruit such as cherries or peaches, drain them and fill a crust. Top with some whipped cream.

143

SPINACH & EGG WHITE OMELET

This is a nice, healthy alternative to diner breakfast; having a good nonstick skillet is key

Egg whites are a great no-fat protein source. They have tons of high-quality proteins and none of the fat associated with whole eggs. However, it is the egg yolk that contains the omega-3s. Remember: Every diet needs some fat, as it helps the skin and hair and helps the body with certain nutrient absorption. Egg whites are now conveniently available in cartons at the supermarket. They are pasteurized and have a very long shelf life, so they are easy to keep around. If you miss the yolks but are still trying to keep a low-fat diet, try adding a whole egg to a few ounces of egg whites to make the dish a little lighter. *Yield: 1 omelet*

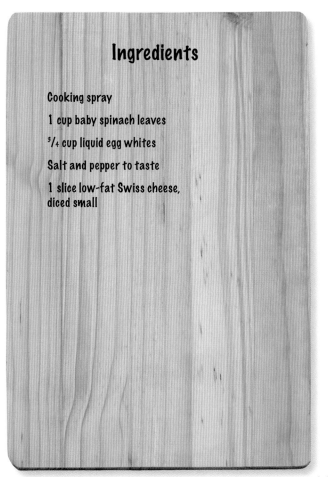

Ingredients

Cooking spray

1 cup baby spinach leaves

³/₄ cup liquid egg whites

Salt and pepper to taste

1 slice low-fat Swiss cheese, diced small

Spinach and Egg White Omelet

- Spray a 6-inch nonstick pan with cooking spray and sauté the spinach until completely wilted (about 3 minutes); set aside on paper towels to drain well.

- Wipe out the pan and re-spray. Add the egg whites and salt and pepper. Cook, stirring constantly and shaking the pan over medium heat, until the whites have completely set but are still moist.

- Add the cheese and spinach and fold the omelet in thirds to make a rolled shape.

- Serve on a warm plate.

Sautéed Mushrooms: A classic match to eggs has always been sautéed mushrooms. In fact, mushroom foragers often eat a wild mushroom omelet for dinner after a hard day's romp through the woods in search of their treasure. When sautéing mushrooms, cook them over high heat in a little oil or butter until all the moisture that escapes from them has evaporated.

Frittatas: In Italy the frittata often replaces the omelet. Classic frittatas often contain potatoes and are very hearty. Try making your own egg-white frittata by adding ¾ cup cooked, cubed, or sliced potatoes to this spinach omelet and, instead of folding, place under the broiler with 3 tablespoons Parmesan cheese on top. Cook like a "cake" until firm and piping hot in the center.

Water, Water Everywhere

Omelet Options

- Too much water in your omelet will make it, well, watery. It is important to rid the spinach of as much water as possible for this dish.

- The longer you cook the spinach, the more water will be removed.

- You can also squeeze the spinach in the paper towels to remove even more water than just draining.

- If preblanching spinach in boiling water, make sure to squeeze all the water from it before using in this omelet.

- There are several techniques for enclosing the fillings in an omelet. The most common is just to fold it in half over the fillings.

- A French or rolled omelet is folded in thirds and forms a neat roll around the fillings.

- To make a country-style omelet, simply mix the fillings into the eggs and make a sort of scrambled egg "cake."

- To create a flat-top omelet, spread the eggs out very thin on a griddle and roll up the fillings inside.

145

BACON, EGG & AVOCADO SANDWICH
Rich and satisfying, this breakfast will keep you fueled for an active day

The combination of avocado and bacon can make an old shoe taste good, and it works brilliantly with eggs. It is really nice if the yolks are a bit runny to ooze over the avocado and bacon slices. This almost becomes a sauce of sorts and really enhances the sandwich. The hot sauce adds a fantastic dimension to this dish, and a nice vinegar-based sauce like

Tabasco or Crystal seem to work very well with this sandwich, as the vinegar enhances, not overpowers, the flavors of the components. Be sure to use nice and ripe Haas avocados, as the larger Bacon or Caribbean avocados are a bit watery. Make this sandwich for others, and you will make friends. *Yield: 1 killer sandwich*

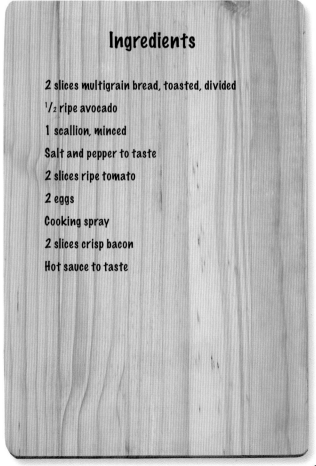

Ingredients

2 slices multigrain bread, toasted, divided

$^1/_2$ ripe avocado

1 scallion, minced

Salt and pepper to taste

2 slices ripe tomato

2 eggs

Cooking spray

2 slices crisp bacon

Hot sauce to taste

Bacon, Egg, and Avocado Sandwich

- Spread one piece of toast with the avocado and sprinkle with the scallion and salt and pepper. Top with the tomato slices and season them with salt and pepper.

- Fry the eggs in a little cooking spray in a 6-inch

nonstick pan; cook to over medium. Season with salt and pepper. Lay on top of the tomato slices and top with the crisp bacon.

- Splash a little hot sauce and top with the remaining toast.

MAKE IT EASY

If you want to simplify the building of this sandwich, you can crumble the bacon, dice the tomatoes, mix them both with the egg, and cook it omelet style. Simply place on the bread with the other ingredients and enjoy. Of course, you will miss the runny yolks of the over-medium eggs in the other version, but the sandwich will still be quite yummy.

YELLOW LIGHT

Remember that eating undercooked eggs carries a risk of salmonella or other food-borne illnesses. The very young, the very old, and people with suppressed immune systems should not eat undercooked or runny eggs. This is not to scare you; just be aware when you are cooking eggs and, if you have any doubts about freshness, discard the eggs immediately.

Flavor Country

- Topping the avocado with savory items such as black pepper and scallions adds incredible dimension to the avocado.

- Try a simple breakfast of avocado on toast with salt, pepper, and some kind of onion. It is amazing.

- You can also make an avocado "mash" with all manner of garnish and then spread it on toast.

- Smaller, purplish-skinned avocados seem to yield the richest flesh.

Thank Goodness for Nonstick

- Nonstick pans have been around for a long time, and they continue to get better each year.

- Look for heavy pans with high-quality coatings. You may spend more, but they are well worth it in the long run.

- Never use metal implements with nonstick pans and discard any pans that show visible peeling of the coating.

- A cast-iron skillet, properly seasoned, will be as good as any nonstick pan. Never wash it in the dishwasher!

SMOKED SALMON EGGS BENEDICT

An elegant twist on a classic, this dish is a must for the bagel-and-lox crowd

As with many famous recipes, eggs Benedict has its share of legends related to its inception. Some attribute it to an English recipe, while others attribute it to Lemuel Benedict, a retired stockbroker who claimed to have asked for buttered English muffins with poached eggs and hollandaise sauce. There are other claims to this dish, but whatever the origins, eggs Benedict has become a brunch favorite all over the world. The classic recipe was a toasted split English muffin, buttered and topped with two slices of ham or Canadian bacon and then two poached eggs. The whole affair was topped with luxurious hollandaise sauce and then a few slices of truffle to really crown the dish. *Yield: 1 serving*

Ingredients

1 whole grain English muffin, toasted

2 ounces smoked salmon

1 tablespoon vinegar

Pinch of salt

2 quarts simmering water

2 eggs

1 package instant Hollandaise sauce, prepared and kept warm

Tabasco sauce

1 teaspoon freshly minced chives

Smoked Salmon Eggs Benedict

- Top each muffin half with smoked salmon.

- Add the vinegar and a pinch of salt to the simmering water. Using a large spoon, stir the water along the edges of the pot to form a strong whirlpool effect. Break the eggs directly into the center of the whirlpool. Lower heat and cook 3 minutes.

- Remove eggs with a slotted spoon; blot, and place 1 egg on each muffin half.

- Top each egg with 2 tablespoons hollandaise sauce, a drop of Tabasco, and the chives.

Broiled Tomato Bottoms: The variations of this dish are endless, as you could put just about anything under a poached egg on top of a buttered muffin. A simple and easy option is to take 2 thick slices of beefsteak tomato, briefly sauté them in butter, and use them as a base for the eggs. You can also grill or broil the slices of tomato. This adds a British touch.

Rosy Hollandaise: Adding goodies to hollandaise sauce is a classic French technique. As a matter of fact, hollandaise was considered a "mother sauce," meaning it can be tweaked to make many other sauces. Try mixing a little bit of ketchup or tomato paste into the sauce with some fresh tarragon for a wonderful twist.

Poaching Eggs 101

- The "whirlpool" method is really one of the best methods for poaching eggs, but there are some others if you can't get the hang of it.

- You can simply crack eggs into a gently simmering skillet filled with about 2 inches of water.

- You can buy special egg poacher pans that keep the eggs in a nice shape.

- After poaching eggs you can actually drop them in ice water for later use. Simply reheat for 30 seconds in simmering water.

Is It Done?

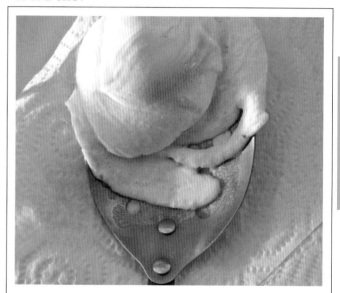

- When poaching eggs it is easy to either under- or overcook the eggs. Here is how to check.

- Gently pull the egg up with the slotted spoon. If you can see transparent white still jiggling, the egg is undercooked.

- You can gently touch the egg with your finger and make sure it is just firm enough to come out of the water without falling apart.

- Poached eggs should be runny, as the yolk becomes a sauce for the rest of the dish.

OVEN OMELET WITH JAM
This is an old-fashioned recipe that requires patience, but the results are worth it

Separated omelets are an "old school" dish rarely made these days in the United States. They are still eaten more frequently in Europe and can be topped with either sweet or savory ingredients. The key here is to make sure your pan has an oven-safe handle that will allow it to be in the oven without melting or burning. When whipping the egg whites for this dish, it is critical that the whites have no bits of yolk in them. If there is even the tiniest bit of yolk in the whites, they will not whip up no matter how hard you work. This is chemistry at work, and you cannot fight it. You chem majors can figure it out. *Yield: 1 omelet*

Ingredients

2 eggs

Pinch of salt

1 tablespoon butter

2 tablespoons strawberry jam

Powdered sugar to dust

Oven Omelet with Jam

- Preheat oven to 325°F. Separate the egg whites and yolks.

- Beat the whites to stiff peaks. Beat the yolks smooth with the salt. Gently fold the yolks into the whites.

- In an 8-inch nonstick pan, heat the butter over medium heat until it stops bubbling. Add the egg mixture and cook over medium-low heat for 2 minutes.

- Place the entire pan in the oven and cook for 6 minutes. Invert onto a plate and top with jam and sugar.

Oven Omelet with Grated Cheese: Instead of topping with sweet jam, try topping this omelet with ¼ cup grated cheese and then putting it back into the oven to melt. Another great twist is to top the omelet with ¼ cup chopped sausage or bacon and then serve with maple syrup. This becomes an egg/pancake hybrid and is a crowd-pleaser.

ZOOM

Whipping egg whites places molecules of air between the protein molecules of the egg whites. Egg whites whipped and mixed with sugar are called meringue. There are countless uses for this, including pies, and even little meringue puffs baked in the oven can be eaten as cookies. There are also advanced, so-called "Swiss" meringues, when the sugar is melted and added.

Fold Carefully

Keep It Hot

- When folding anything into whipped egg whites, it is important to work carefully and deliberately.

- The important point is to not lose the volume of the whites when adding the yolks to it.

- Work from the middle of the bowl outward while turning the bowl and scraping down the sides. Always be careful to keep the volume of the whites as high as possible.

- The same technique is used when folding items such as chocolate into whipped cream.

- It is a nice touch to warm the plate or platter before placing the omelet onto it. This keeps it warm on the table.

- If the plate is oven-safe, you can place it in the oven with the omelet for the last 2 minutes of cooking.

- You can also microwave the plate with a moist towel on it for 2 minutes. Just make sure to wipe the moisture off the plate.

- Some kitchens have special plate-warmer drawers built in to islands or ovens.

THE REAL-DEAL FRENCH TOAST

In French, the name of this dish is *pain perdu*, which means "lost bread"—you'll understand why

This is it. This is the French toast to beat all French toasts. Back in the olden days, nothing was left to waste. When bread went stale and hard, something was made with it. It could be ground into bread crumbs, soaked with milk, and used in meat loaves or meatballs. It was also soaked overnight in milk and eggs and fried in butter in the morning for breakfast. The fact that this bread is superstale before soaking and frying makes for its amazing texture. The empty pockets in the bread, which once contained moisture, are filled with the eggs and milk, and the toast gains an almost custardlike texture. This is worth all the effort. *Yield: 2 servings*

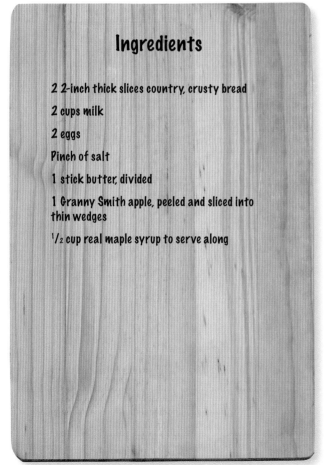

Ingredients

2 2-inch thick slices country, crusty bread

2 cups milk

2 eggs

Pinch of salt

1 stick butter, divided

1 Granny Smith apple, peeled and sliced into thin wedges

$^1/_2$ cup real maple syrup to serve along

The Real-Deal French Toast

- Leave bread out for 2 days until very stale. Mix together milk, eggs, and salt and pour into a shallow dish.

- Add the bread and soak for 6 hours, turning halfway through.

- Heat 2 tablespoons butter in a skillet and cook the apples over medium-high heat until caramelized. Add the maple syrup and keep warm.

- Fry the bread in the remaining butter over medium heat for about 5 minutes per side. Pour apple mixture over the top.

•••• RECIPE VARIATION ••••

French Toast Dessert: An amazing adaptation of this dish is to serve it for dessert. Simply make the exact same dish, place the toast on a plate, and top with a big scoop of vanilla ice cream and the apple syrup. You can also take it to the next level by making homemade apple and maple ice cream and top the toast with your own homemade ice cream. Simply decadent!

YELLOW ● LIGHT

Because the bread is hard and stale when you place it to soak, it can break apart when you remove it in the morning to fry,. Have no fear. If it breaks, simply reassemble it in the pan. The cooking of the protein in the eggs will act as a sort of glue and bring the toast back together. Flip gently!

Stale Bread Rocks!

- It is critical that the bread is very stale for this dish. While that may scare people, you must trust the recipe.

- The type of bread used is also key. Avoid standard white breads that have a dense crumb texture.

- Look for true artisan country-style bread with big bubbles in the interior and a hard crust on the outside.

- The large air bubbles in the bread will allow for better absorption of the custard and a creamier texture to the finished product.

Technique Is Everything

- Cook this toast over medium heat in plenty of butter. Be careful not to burn the butter.

- Before flipping, make sure the other side is well browned, as this is an important flavor component.

- Another trick is to place a dollop of butter on the "raw" side right before flipping to ensure good butter placement.

- If the bread is very thick, you can finish it in a 350°F oven to make sure the interior fully cooks.

OATMEAL BUTTERMILK PANCAKES

Real, long-cooking oatmeal is the key to these hearty pancakes, so seek it out

Pancakes are a crowd-pleaser, no matter how or when you make them. There are so many varieties of pancakes, it is staggering to think about. Almost any flour can be used to make them, too, from wheat flour to chickpea flour to chestnut flour. People make pancakes out of corn, barley, and rye. Some pancakes contain almost no flour and are made from sour cream or crème fraîche. Pancakes are also made savory with garnishes as varied as mushrooms to omelets, and don't forget the famous Jewish latkes, or potato pancakes, served with applesauce and sour cream. *Yield: A nice stack for 1*

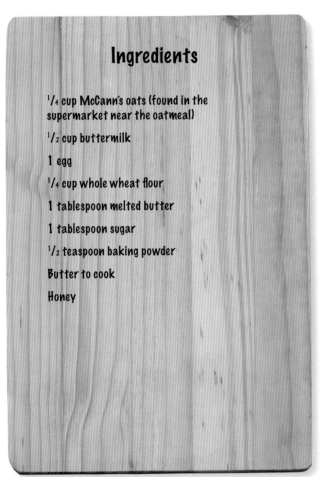

Ingredients

¹/₄ cup McCann's oats (found in the supermarket near the oatmeal)

¹/₂ cup buttermilk

1 egg

¹/₄ cup whole wheat flour

1 tablespoon melted butter

1 tablespoon sugar

¹/₂ teaspoon baking powder

Butter to cook

Honey

Oatmeal Buttermilk Pancakes

- Soak the oats in the buttermilk overnight.

- Beat the egg and mix with the oats, flour, melted butter, sugar, and baking powder; allow to rest for 10 minutes.

- Melt some butter in a non-stick skillet over medium-low heat and pour 3 ounces of batter into the pan. Flip when the pancake is well dotted with small holes.

- Add more butter if necessary.

- Repeat until all the pancakes are finished. Drizzle with honey.

ZOOM

Oatmeal is an extremely healthy food. Some studies have shown that a diet rich in oatmeal (not loaded with butter and sugar, of course) can help lower "bad" cholesterol and raise "good" cholesterol. Oatmeal also contains valuable fiber, which aids in digestion. Look for McCann's Irish oatmeal oats in your supermarket and try to use them instead of the quick or instant oats.

• • • • RECIPE VARIATION • • • •

Shredded Coconut Buttermilk Pancakes: Instead of oatmeal in this dish, try using toasted shredded coconut. Add 1 cup coconut and cook as directed in the recipe. A nice touch is to also substitute coconut milk for the buttermilk. Serve with a warm dish of pineapple preserves, mixed with a little maple syrup, and you'll have a tropical treat reminiscent of the islands.

Give 'em a Bath

- Oatmeal that it not of the instant variety requires long cooking or prior soaking in order to cook.

- Soaking the oats in buttermilk overnight allows them to absorb moisture as though they have been cooked.

- You can substitute instant oats for this dish and not soak overnight; you have to cut the buttermilk in half, too.

- Try the long-cooked oats as traditional oatmeal; it is a totally different experience from instant.

Timing Is Everything

- Be sure that the pancakes are evenly dotted with small holes before flipping. Otherwise you will have a mess when you flip.

- If the batter is too thick, the pancakes will burn before the holes appear. Adjust your batter with a little water or buttermilk if you have to.

- If the batter is too thin and spreading all over the pan, add a small amount of flour to thicken.

- Use your first pancake as a test and then adjust as necessary.

ASIAN TUNA & MANGO SALAD
Look for bright red tuna; there are many good frozen tuna options

Eating raw or rare fish is very popular these days, with sushi bars and trendy spots offering fish tartares, sashimi, sushi, and carpaccio. This recipe uses a very rare tuna steak.

It is important to understand how to judge freshness and safety when eating undercooked or raw fish. First, always buy your fish at a busy and reputable market or fish market. The busier the place is, the quicker they turn their inventory,

so their fish will be fresher. Second, frozen fish is inherently safer than fresh fish, as the freezing process does a great job in inhibiting bacteria from growing. In fact, most sushi restaurants use prefrozen fish in order to comply with certain health codes as well as to safeguard the health of their patrons. *Yield: 1 portion*

Ingredients

1 4- to 5-ounce tuna steak

1 teaspoon vegetable oil

Salt and pepper to taste

1 head frisée lettuce, washed and torn

1/2 cup roughly chopped romaine lettuce

1 small ripe mango, peeled and diced

1/4 cup diced red bell pepper

1/4 cup cilantro leaves

1/4 cup chopped water chestnuts

2 scallions, finely minced

2 teaspoons sesame oil

2 teaspoons soy sauce

1 teaspoon fresh ginger, minced

1 teaspoon peanut butter

2 tablespoons water

Asian Tuna and Mango Salad

- Rub the tuna with vegetable oil and salt and pepper. In a nonstick skillet over high heat, sear the tuna for 45 seconds per side; set aside.

- In a bowl, mix together the frisée, romaine, mango, bell pepper, cilantro, water chestnuts, and scallions.

- Place the sesame oil, soy sauce, ginger, peanut butter, and water in a small cup and blend well with an immersion blender.

- Toss all ingredients except the tuna in the dressing. Mound in a bowl. Top with sliced tuna.

ZOOM

Tuna is naturally bright red, but after being cut, it quickly discolors to a dingy brown. This is not a sign of the fish being spoiled. This chocolating, as the industry refers to it, is pretty unpopular, as the color is not as appealing as bright red tuna. The fishing industry has figured out that if you place the tuna in a smoke box filled with carbon monoxide (yes, the deadly gas), it will remain bright red.

• • • • RECIPE VARIATION • • • •

Shrimp and Mango Salad: This same salad can be made with almost any other protein if you do not like or are not brave enough to try the rare fish. A nice change for this dish is to use shrimp. Just use about 6 to 8 large peeled and deveined shrimp and cook the same way. Season with salt and pepper and sauté briefly until just cooked. Prepare the salad as directed.

How to Sear

- Searing is an important technique that serves more than one purpose. It provides a caramelized exterior for great flavor and also helps to seal in the meat's juices.

- Be sure the pan is very hot before you add the oil.

- There should be only a thin film of oil in the pan, and it should be barely smoking.

- Do not crowd the pan when searing, or your product will steam instead of sear.

Slice, Don't Tear

- Slicing something as delicate as tuna requires some finesse in order to make nice slices.

- Be sure your knife is sharp. A long thin blade works best.

- Draw the knife across the flesh instead of trying to

push down on it. Use gentle sawing motions with very little downward pressure.

- Be sure your cutting board is secure and not moving around your countertop. A wet paper towel or dish towel between the board and countertop works well.

ENTREE SALADS

157

CHIPOTLE CHICKEN CAESAR SALAD

Spicy and smoky, chipotle peppers add a wonderful note to a classic Caesar salad

These days most people think that chipotle is a restaurant chain, when in fact it is a great food product of Mexico. A chipotle is a dried and smoked jalapeño pepper. Often it is sold canned and packed in a tomato-based sauce called adobo. Chipotle peppers are also sold dried in bags in Mexican markets and can be easily rehydrated in water to be used

in many dishes. The characteristics of these peppers are that they are quite hot, but more important, smoked. The smoky flavor is the magical component that makes these peppers so desirable. They are excellent in stews and sauces and especially great in chili con carne. *Yield: 1 salad*

Ingredients

1 cup pulled chicken meat, preferably from a rotisserie chicken

3 cups chopped romaine lettuce

$1/2$ cup croutons

$1/3$ cup Caesar dressing

Juice of half a lime

$1/2$ teaspoon cumin

$1/2$ chipotle pepper packed in adobo sauce (caution: hot!), minced

$1/2$ cup grated aged Monterey Jack cheese, or Parmesan, divided

Salt and pepper to taste

Chipotle Chicken Caesar Salad

- Mix together the chicken, lettuce, and croutons in a large bowl.

- In a separate bowl, combine the dressing, lime juice, cumin, and chipotle pepper and mix well.

- Pour the dressing over the chicken mixture; add half the cheese and season with salt and pepper. Toss.

- Place salad in a serving bowl and top with remaining cheese.

ZOOM

Producing chipotles is no easy task. Typically, the last jalapeños of the harvest are allowed to stay on the vine until they turn bright red and begin to shrivel lightly. They are then picked and placed in a smoke box and slowly smoked with wood for several days. They have to be stirred frequently until they finally appear totally dried and ready to be packed and sold.

YELLOW LIGHT

The active ingredient that makes peppers hot is called capsaicin, a chemical that is extremely powerful. Peppers are rated on a scale of heat measured in Scoville units. The scale ranges from zero to sixteen million! The jalapeño rates about five thousand units, while the habañero rates about two hundred thousand units! Always wash your hands after working with hot peppers to avoid any capsaicin getting into your eyes or other sensitive areas.

Roast Your Own

- Market rotisserie chickens are very convenient, but roasting your own bird is satisfying and much cheaper.

- Be sure to remove the giblet bag from the cavity. Rinse the chicken under cold water and dry well.

- Rub with a little room temperature butter and season well with salt and pepper.

- Roast at 375°F until the deepest part of the thigh registers 165°F and the juices run clear. Let rest for 15 minutes before carving.

Chipotle Care and Storage

- Since you will only be using a small amount of the can of chipotles for this recipe, you will need to do something with the remainder.

- Never store food in cans in the fridge. This is dangerous and can cause food-borne illness.

- Place the remaining peppers in a small airtight container and store in the fridge. They will last for months.

- You can also puree the whole can with your immersion blender and then use a spoonful when you need it.

STEAK & WEDGE SALAD

This steakhouse favorite is great for lunch or dinner, or add an egg to it for brunch

There are many types of lettuces available in today's supermarket, but iceberg is the lettuce of choice for this salad. Iceberg gets its name from its crisp and cool character and great crunch.

Iceberg lettuce was for many years the only lettuce on the market, and the new crops of baby greens and others have caused some people to poo-poo the virtues of this lettuce. Don't believe the hype. Iceberg has that incredible crunch and milk flavor that make it ideal for this salad and as a sandwich topping or a base for seafood salads or even some stir-fries. Look for firm and heavy heads with no visible brown on the stem. *Yield: 1 big salad*

Ingredients

¹/₂ head iceberg lettuce

Salt and pepper to taste

1 medium ripe beefsteak tomato, cut into thick rounds

¹/₂ small red onion, cut into slivers

1 tablespoon red wine vinegar

3 tablespoons extra-virgin olive oil

¹/₂ teaspoon Dijon mustard

1 garlic clove ground into a paste with a little salt

1 6-ounce piece flank steak, grilled to medium and rested for 5 minutes before slicing

3 ounces crumbled blue cheese

Steak and Wedge Salad

- Cut the lettuce into four wedges and arrange on a large plate. Season each wedge with salt and pepper. Top each wedge on one side with a slice of tomato and onion slices.

- Combine the vinegar, oil, mustard, and garlic paste with a little salt and pepper.

- Place in a small jar and shake to make the dressing.

- Slice the steak thinly across the grain and drape over the wedges.

- Sprinkle blue cheese all over and drizzle with dressing.

Lobster or Crab and Wedge Salad: Although classically made with sliced steak, you could kick up the elegance factor of this dish by using a real luxurious item like lobster. Simply steam or boil a lobster (7 minutes per pound), cool in ice water, and then pick out the meat. Slice the tail and drape the meat over the salad as you would the steak.

This recipe calls for "resting the meat," but many folks do not understand why this is done. After meat is cooked, the juices are moving around in the piece of meat. If you cut into it without resting, the juices will spill out onto the plate. If you rest the meat the juices settle back into the fibers of the meat, yielding a juicer product.

Salads as Main Meals

Going against the Grain

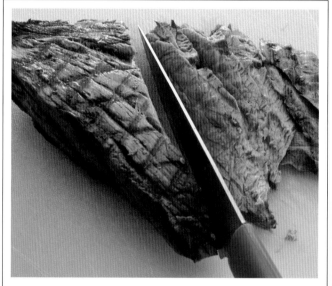

- Serving a salad as a main meal is an excellent way to have your vegetables and main course at the same time. These meals are particularly great in warmer months.

- Try supersizing the amount of greens from a normal salad and add a protein of your choice.

- "Flavor bombs" such as blue cheese, bacon, smoked ham, avocado, and Parmesan cheese are all great to add to an entree salad.

- Most meat has a visible grain, which is the direction that the fibers of the meat run.

- Flank steak, brisket, and skirt steak are a few cuts of beef that have a very visible grain structure.

- It is critical to slice meat against the grain. When you cut against the grain, you effectively shorten the meat fibers, resulting in more tender slices.

- If you cut with the grain, you will be chewing long and tough fibers of meat.

ENTREE SALADS

BALSAMIC CHARRED RADICCHIO

Charring radicchio and sprinkling it with vinegar yields an amazing and complex blend of flavors

Radicchio is a lettuce-like vegetable that has been widely cultivated in Italy for hundreds of years. The most common radicchio available in the United States is the Chioggia variety, which is round and about 6 to 8 inches in diameter. It is a deep purplish-red color with stark white ribs and veins running through it.

There is also a Treviso variety, which is long and resembles a Belgian endive. This long version is less visible in the market, but is starting to show up here and there. Radicchio is commonly used as a colorful lettuce added to other greens to provide color. It is also separated into "cups" and the leaves filled with sauces as a garnish. *Yield: 1 salad*

Ingredients

1 head radicchio cut into four wedges through the core

2 tablespoons extra-virgin olive oil

Salt and pepper to taste

2 tablespoons balsamic vinegar

1 ounce prosciutto, thinly sliced

3 ounces goat cheese

4 basil leaves

Balsamic Charred Radicchio

- Cut the radicchio through the core so the leaves will not fall apart when grilling. Toss with the oil and season with salt and pepper; grill over high heat until well charred on all sides. Toss with vinegar and set aside.

- Arrange the prosciutto to cover the bottom of a serving plate. Top with the radicchio wedges.

- Crumble the goat cheese over the salad and tear the basil leaves over the top.

- Drizzle with a little more olive oil and vinegar.

ZOOM

Radicchio is a member if the chicory family. The roots of chicory plants have been used as a coffee supplement for many years. The roots are roasted and ground and mixed with coffee. There is also research showing that radicchio may play a role in reducing intestinal parasites. It seems that when livestock are fed radicchio, the incidence of worms and other parasites decreases dramatically.

• • • • RECIPE VARIATION • • • •

Substitute Out the Radicchio: Almost any member of the chicory family can be substituted for the radicchio in this dish. Belgian endive would be a great choice, as it is very dense and works well on the grill. Another nonchicory option is to use small hearts of romaine lettuce and briefly grill them. Do not put as deep a char on them as you would the radicchio, however.

Use Mother Nature

- Cutting the radicchio through the core, making sure the leaves remain attached to the core, is a great trick.

- This also works when grilling fennel, onions, endive, and anything else where the core can hold the bulk of the vegetable together.

- If you eliminate the core, you can skewer the radicchio leaves on a stick and then season and grill like a kabob.

- If vegetables are very small or baby, you can grill them intact without cutting at all.

Almost Burn It

- Don't be afraid to put a very deep char on the radicchio. It should almost look burned.

- Charring is like caramelizing, as it burns the sugars in vegetables and brings out the sweetness.

- Items with an inherent bitterness benefit greatly from charring, as the caramelizing sugars offset the bitterness.

- You will be surprised how dark you can grill a vegetable and it will still have great flavor.

ENTREE SALADS

163

CLASSIC WARM SPINACH SALAD

This is a great wintertime salad; try a firmer blue cheese such as buttermilk blue

Tossing greens with a hot or warm dressing is a nice change for the standard cold plate of greens. It is important to have all your ingredients ready once you start tossing with a hot dressing, as the greens will start to wilt once the vinaigrette hits them. Sturdy greens fare better than delicate greens for these types of applications.

When choosing spinach, look for curly spinach as opposed to the baby or flat-leaf spinach that seems to dominate the market these days. These flat-leaf spinaches have a few pitfalls. First, they do not have the deep true spinach flavor and are somewhat bland. Second, the flat spinach will wilt very quickly if tossed in a hot dressing. *Yield: 1 salad*

Ingredients

2 strips raw bacon, diced

1 tablespoon extra-virgin olive oil

1/2 cup thinly sliced white onion

1 cup thinly sliced white mushrooms

1 garlic clove, sliced thin

2 tablespoons sherry vinegar

4 cups washed curly leaf spinach

Salt and pepper to taste

1/4 cup crumbled blue cheese

1 hard-boiled egg, chopped

Classic Warm Spinach Salad

- Place the bacon and oil in a small skillet and cook slowly until the bacon is crispy. Remove the bacon from the pan; leave the fat.

- In the same pan add the onion, mushrooms, and garlic and cook over medium heat for 3 to 4 minutes.

- Add the vinegar and turn off the heat. Toss the warm dressing with the spinach leaves and season with salt and pepper. Place in a large bowl.

- Top with cheese, hard-boiled eggs, and reserved bacon.

• • • • RECIPE VARIATIONS • • • •

Baconless Salad: Although the bacon in the salad provides an essential flavor component, there are those who will not want to put bacon in their salad. A nice substitute would be to double the amount of oil to make up for the rendered bacon fat and to add a small clove of minced garlic to the oil while sautéing the vegetables. The garlic will add a depth of flavor.

Poached Egg Salad: Classically, this salad was served with a warm poached egg on top instead of the hard-boiled eggs in this recipe. This is a wonderful variation, as the runny warm yolk of the egg blends with the dressing and forms an incredible creamy "sauce" for the salad. If you have the patience, make a poached egg and drop it on top of the salad.

Some Like It Hot

- Hot vinaigrettes are a simple concept. The basic rule is that you use about a third the amount of vinegar to oil.

- Be sure the oil and any aromatic ingredients are cooked thoroughly before adding the vinegar.

- Once the vinegar is added to the pan, turn off the heat, as the vinegar will reduce and become more sour.

- Lemon juice, lime juice, verjuice, and very dry wine can be used in place of vinegar.

Toss It Up

- When tossing salads either in warm or traditional dressings, it is important not to overdress the salad.

- The dressing should just coat all the ingredients and not pool in the bowl.

- Usually the bulk of calories in a salad are from the dressing. So it makes sense to ease off a bit.

- Creamy dressings are sometimes too thick to evenly coat. Try thinning with a tablespoon of water.

THAI SHRIMP & WATERCRESS SALAD

Both crisp and refreshing, this salad makes a wonderful summer lunch; use high-quality shrimp

Watercress is a horribly underutilized vegetable in the United States. Many people see it in the market but have no idea what to do with it. Watercress has very bulky stems and small leaves, and that combination is confusing to most. The fact is, the stems are tender and can and should be eaten.

Watercress can be eaten raw as a salad and cooked as a vegetable. One of the most famous uses for watercress is as soup. Traditionally it is mixed into a light potato soup and pureed into a velvety green potage that can be eaten hot or cold. Its unique peppery flavor is wonderful. Seek out watercress and experiment. *Yield: 1 salad*

Ingredients

8 16-20 count white shrimp, peeled and deveined

1 teaspoon Thai fish sauce

1 teaspoon soy sauce

1 teaspoon sugar

1 teaspoon lime juice

1 clove garlic, crushed

1 teaspoon sriracha chili sauce

2 tablespoons coconut milk

1 teaspoon vegetable oil

3 cups watercress, washed and cut into 2-inch lengths with stems

1/4 cup matchstick carrots

1/2 cup matchstick jicama

1/4 cup thinly sliced white onion

6 grape tomatoes, halved

Thai Shrimp and Watercress Salad

- Combine the shrimp with the fish sauce, soy sauce, sugar, lime juice, garlic, sriracha, and coconut milk. Place in a skillet with the vegetable oil and cook over low heat just until the shrimp are cooked through.

- Remove the shrimp. Cool the liquid in the fridge for 5 minutes.

- Toss the liquid with the watercress and remaining vegetables.

- Arrange the salad on a plate and arrange the shrimp over the top of the salad.

Watercress is actually grown in water. It is found in small, cold spring-fed creeks and mountain streams. Many people forage for wild watercress in the springtime, especially on the East Coast. Watercress is also reputed to contain some anti-cancer compounds and is especially effective on some lung cancers. It is also shown to have positive effects on the thyroid gland.

• • • • RECIPE VARIATION • • • •

Simple Watercress Salad: This salad has many ingredients and a strikingly Asian flavor. If you are interested in trying watercress but do not want to spend the time with all the other ingredients, try this: Toss the watercress with a simple dressing of three parts olive oil to one part good vinegar and a little crushed garlic. Season with salt and pepper and enjoy.

Is It a Vein?

- Deveining shrimp is a common practice, especially when wild shrimp are used.

- You will notice a black line running along the top of the shrimp. This "vein" is actually the simple digestive tract of the shrimp.

- Remove it by making a shallow cut along the shrimp and gently pulling the vein out with the tip of a small knife.

- Cultivated or farmed shrimp usually do not have a visible vein, as the farms stop feeding the shrimp two or three days before harvesting.

Shrimp Basics

- Much depends on the species of shrimp. Texture and flavor are directly tied to species. The texture of the "white" shrimp in this recipe is nice and firm.

- When cooking in liquid, it is important to cook gently, as it is easy for the shrimp to become tough.

- Tiger shrimp are freshwater shrimp and tend to be mushy when cooked.

- A great way to check the cooking time of shrimp is to take one out of the pan, cut a small piece off, and taste it.

CLASSIC POTATO LEEK SOUP

A classic for good reason, this soup has countless variations, and you should try them all

The potato is such a humble ingredient and yet can yield the most luxurious products. Potato soup is ultimately satisfying, and, when made properly, it is incredibly rich and comforting. The most famous incarnation of this soup is the cold version called vichyssoise. The legend is that King Louis XV of France was extremely paranoid about being poisoned.

Once his potato soup passed from food taster to food taster and then finally to him, it was cold. It seemed as though he liked this cold soup, and thus vichyssoise was born. The soup in this recipe is a classic unadorned version of this soup, which is perfect in its simplicity. Idaho potatoes work best, as opposed to waxy new potatoes. *Yield: 2 entree-size bowls*

Ingredients

1¹/₂ cups leeks, white part only, diced and washed

¹/₂ stick butter

3 cups peeled, diced potatoes

5 cups chicken stock

1 sprig fresh thyme

1 bay leaf

Salt and pepper to taste

¹/₂ cup heavy cream

4 fresh chives

Classic Potato Leek Soup

- Place the leeks and butter into a large pot. Cook slowly over low heat for about 5 minutes or until the leeks have softened. Do not brown.

- Add the potatoes, stock, thyme, bay leaf, and salt and pepper and bring to a boil.

- Reduce to a slow simmer and cook very gently, uncovered for 25 minutes.

- Remove the thyme and bay leaf and puree with an immersion blender until very smooth. Add the cream and stir well.

- Garnish with chives.

Adding Flavorful Greens: This soup screams for variation. Besides being able to garnish this soup with all manner of items such as bacon bits, cheese, sour cream, sautéed mushrooms, and even pieces of sausage or ham, it is wonderful to puree additional items into the soup. Try adding 1 cup of arugula and pureeing directly into the soup.

YELLOW ● LIGHT

Leeks are notoriously sandy and dirty. If you do not clean the leeks properly, all your effort will be in vain. The trick is to trim and cut the leeks into small pieces, then place in a very large bowl or sink full of water and agitate. Pull the leeks out of the water; do not pour into a colander, as you will pour the sand back over them.

Sweating vs. Sautéing

- Slowly cooking leeks in butter without browning is called sweating. It is a very important step in this and most other soups.

- The leeks act as a baseline flavor and complement the potatoes without overpowering them.

- Sweating is designed to bring out and develop the flavors of aromatics in a gentle way.

- Sautéing is cooking over higher heat and adding color to the vegetables by slightly caramelizing them, resulting in a deeper flavor.

Cream It!

- Adding cream to a soup at the end of the process is called creaming. It adds richness to a dish.

- If cream is added too early to a dish and it boils for too long, it can break and ruin the soup.

- Milk does not act the same as cream. Milk changes the color of the soup, but does not add the required richness.

- Half-and-half can be substituted for cream in most cases.

SOUPS & STEWS

VEGETARIAN LENTIL SOUP

Lentils are a small member of the legume family; there are many on the market today

Lentils are a very important food staple in many parts of the world. In India, where there is a huge vegetarian population, lentils form a vast bulk of the diet. Referred to as daal, they are cooked into thick, highly seasoned stews.

The lentil contains 25 percent protein, which is one of the highest in the vegetable world. Although many think the lentil is a small bean, it is actually a seed of a family of plant called pulses. Lentils need to be sorted before cooking to be sure no small pebbles made it into the package. Unlike beans, lentils do not need to be soaked before cooking and cook fairly quickly. Lentils are very popular for soups. *Yield: 2 large bowls*

Ingredients

¹/₂ cup balsamic vinegar

3 tablespoons vegetable oil

¹/₂ cup white onion, diced

¹/₄ cup thinly sliced celery

¹/₄ cup carrots, diced

1 garlic clove, minced

¹/₂ teaspoon dry thyme leaves

1 bay leaf

1 tablespoon tomato paste

Salt and pepper to taste

¹/₂ pound lentils

1 quart vegetable stock or water

1 tablespoon finely chopped Italian parsley

Vegetarian Lentil Soup

- Simmer the vinegar in a pan and reduce until 1 tablespoon remains. Set aside.

- Heat oil in a large pan over medium heat. Add onion, celery, carrots, garlic, thyme, and bay leaf and sauté until vegetables soften; add tomato paste and season with salt and pepper.

- Add the lentils and stock and bring to a boil. Immediately turn down to a gentle simmer and cook for 30 minutes, uncovered. Season with salt and pepper.

- Place soup in a bowl, toss in parsley, and drizzle with vinegar reduction.

If you want to make this same soup but spend a little less time and energy, employ a slow cooker or Crock-Pot. Omit the balsamic vinegar and oil and simply place all the ingredients into the slow cooker and set on medium. Go to a couple of classes and when you return, the soup will be ready. The slow cooker can be a real time-saver, especially with preparing soups and stews.

Balsamic vinegar is a true artisan food product. Only made in the town of Modena in Italy, balsamic vinegar comes in different grades based on age. As the vinegar ages, it becomes thicker and sweeter and more complex. Reducing the vinegar to a syrup mimics the old aged vinegars that can cost hundreds of dollars a bottle. The syrup will have a great texture and flavor.

The Seduction of Reduction

- Many sauces employ the technique of reduction. Simply put, it is slowly boiling down to thicken.

- When reducing, it is important to cook gently and skim off any scum that may rise to the top.

- Some items may become overly bitter or sour when reduced too much. Taste frequently.

- Another simple reduction that makes a great soup drizzle is ruby port wine. Simply reduce to a syrup consistency.

Aromatics Rule

- Sweating these vegetables and herbs together is a very important step in making this soup.

- The aromatic ingredients give up their essential oils into the fat in which they are sweated and intensify.

- There is a noticeable flavor decline in a soup that is made without sweating the aromatics.

- The simplest soups and stews almost always start with just sweating an onion. It is a basic culinary building block.

SOUPS & STEWS

171

ROTISSERIE CHICKEN "STOUP"

Not a stew and not a soup, this thick and hearty dish is a "stoup"

This "stoup" is inspired from a Pennsylvania Dutch dish known as chicken potpie. Interestingly enough, what the Pennsylvania Dutch call potpie has nothing to do with the piecrust filled with chicken, peas, and carrots, but a hearty, noodle-based soup with chicken, carrots, and often potatoes. It is made with thick noodles that are often large and uneven in shape. The soup is so thick that it is joked that you could walk on it. In many Mennonite and Amish communities, they have potpie dinners as fundraisers, and people come in large numbers to enjoy hearty bowls of potpie. This version has a nice shortcut method and uses leftover rotisserie chicken, which gives the stoup a little more flavor. *Yield: 2 large bowls*

Ingredients

4 tablespoons vegetable oil

$^1/_2$ cup diced onions

$^1/_2$ cup diced carrots

$^1/_4$ cup diced celery

1 bay leaf

1 teaspoon dry dill weed, plus some for garnish

2 cups pulled rotisserie chicken meat

5 cups chicken broth

1 potato, thinly sliced

1 cup dry wide egg noodles

Salt and pepper to taste

Rotisserie Chicken "Stoup"

- Heat the oil in a pot large enough to hold all the ingredients. Sauté the vegetables, bay leaf, and dill for 5 minutes.

- Add the chicken meat and broth; bring to a boil.

- Add the potato; cook for 10 minutes. Add the noodles and cook for another 10 minutes. Season with salt and pepper.

- Ladle into large shallow bowls and garnish with a little more dried dill.

The Pennsylvania Dutch do not actually have any Dutch heritage at all. They were all German immigrants, and in the German language *Deutsche* is the word for "German." Their American native neighbors soon changed it to Dutch. They have a distinct cuisine marked with hearty dishes and many noodle and potato dishes based on German recipes. They are also famous for shoofly pie.

• • • • RECIPE VARIATION • • • •

Spicy Chicken Stoup: This dish has very basic flavors of chicken, vegetables, and noodles, but it can be spiced up quite a bit and changed into an Indian-inspired dish. In order to make a curried chicken stew with noodles, add 2 tablespoons curry powder while sweating the vegetables. You can then garnish the soup with a pile of fresh cilantro leaves.

You Say Potato

- The potatoes provide the stoup with an extra level of heartiness, and the starch helps to thicken the broth.

- Slice the potatoes quite thinly, as it is nice if they "melt" into the stoup just a little bit and make the broth a little thicker.

- A mandoline is a great tool for slicing the potatoes thinly if you are making a large batch.

- Potatoes brown quickly after being cut, so place them in cold water to keep them from oxidizing.

Noodlelicious

- Egg noodles are typically used in this dish because of their hearty nature and wide shape.

- Amish-style noodles are slightly thicker than store bought egg noodles.

- It is easy to make home-made noodles, but the process is time-consuming. True Amish noodles are rolled with a pin on a floured board.

- Look for no-yolk egg noodles, which are made with only the whites, if you are looking to reduce your cholesterol.

DOMINICAN SHRIMP ASOPAO

This is a thick and hearty soup, often referred to as a burgoo or bog in the Deep South

Asopao is one of those hearty one-pot meals that warm the heart. Very popular in the Dominican Republic and Puerto Rico, there are as many versions of asopao as there are households. Some cooks use chicken, beef, or pork and make a meaty version, but more often than not some type of seafood is used. One of the best is made with octopus and is stewed for hours to soften the mighty shellfish.

Asopao is basically a soupy rice dish loaded with flavor and garnish. It is ideal to make if you have some leftover rice from, say, a Chinese take-out meal, but of course is totally worth making from scratch. Use your imagination and just keep the soupy rice concept front and center. *Yield: 2 hearty bowls*

Ingredients

8 16-20 white shrimp, peeled, deveined, and diced; shells reserved

1 quart chicken stock

1 cup water

1 cup finely diced white onions

$^1/_2$ cup finely diced carrots

2 cloves garlic, minced

1 teaspoon dried oregano

$^1/_2$ teaspoon cumin

$^1/_4$ cup extra-virgin olive oil

2 tablespoons tomato paste

1 cup long grain rice

Hot sauce to taste

Salt and pepper to taste

$^1/_4$ cup cilantro leaves

$^1/_2$ lime

Dominican Shrimp Asopao

- Boil the shrimp shells with the chicken stock and water hard for 10 minutes. Set aside.

- Sauté the onions, carrots, garlic, oregano, and cumin in the oil for 5 minutes. Add the tomato paste and stir well. Add the rice and coat with the fat and tomato paste. Add the reserved shrimp broth and simmer gently for 30 minutes.

- Add the shrimp and turn off the heat. Adjust seasoning with hot sauce and salt and pepper. Stir in the cilantro and ladle into bowls. Squeeze lime over soup.

Chicken Asopao: Another popular version of this soup is made with chicken. Make the dish in the same way but omit the shrimp. Use a whole chicken and poach it in water until very soft. Pick the meat off the bone and use the resulting broth to cook the rice. When the soup is finished, toss the picked chicken meat back into the soup and garnish with cilantro and lime.

San Juan Asopao: To make this stew, sauté ¼ cup each of onions and peppers, add 1 teaspoon of oregano, 3 cloves of crushed garlic, and 1 cup of diced tomatoes in oil. Add 1 14-ounce can drained pigeon peas with ¾ cup of chicken broth and cook until tender. Add rice and cook for 10 minutes. Garnish each serving with small pimento-stuffed olives and cilantro. It also makes a great side dish.

Fortifying Broth

Coating Rice

- Adding the shrimp shells to the broth and boiling them imparts a great seafood flavor to the broth to perfume the rice.

- Always save shrimp and shellfish shells and store in the freezer. When you accumulate a bunch, make a broth.

- Meat scraps should also be saved. They can be browned and used to fortify meat broths.

- Roasting vegetables with some tomato paste adds another level of flavor to broths.

- Many rice dishes call for coating the rice in fat, flavorings, or both. This serves a few purposes.

- When cooking dishes like risotto, coating the rice in the fat allows the grains to stay separate when cooked.

- Coating rice in tomato paste and/or spices allows for the seasoning to adhere to the individual grains.

- When making classic rice pilaf, it is important to evenly coat all the grains in butter and sautéed onions. This helps the rice stay fluffy.

SOUPS & STEWS

CHUNKY CHOCOLATE CHILI

No ground beef and no beans are what make this chili authentic and challenging

There is a lot of chili lore out there, particularly when it comes to the origins of the dish. Some say that it was invented in Texas prisons, the many spices camouflaging the stench of rotting meat. Others point to Mexico and its many rich and deeply flavored stews, particularly the many mole dishes. And there are those in Cincinnati who claim chili has cinnamon in it and needs to be served over a pile of spaghetti. Whatever the true origins are, true chili—cook-off chili that is—must adhere to a few rules. Perhaps the most surprising to many is that it contain no beans. If you enter a chili cook-off and there are beans in your chili, you will be disqualified, no matter how yummy your pot of chili is. *Yield: 4 big bowls of chili*

Ingredients

- ¹/₂ cup vegetable oil
- 2 cups diced white onion
- 1 cup diced red bell pepper
- 1 jalapeño pepper, seeded and minced
- 5 cloves garlic, minced
- 2 tablespoons dark chili powder
- 2 tablespoons smoked paprika
- 2 tablespoons ground cumin
- 1 tablespoon ground coriander seed
- ¹/₄ teaspoon ground cardamom
- 1 cup canned diced tomatoes, drained
- 2 packets instant gravy mix
- 1 bottle dark beer
- 1 quart chicken stock
- 2 tablespoons Worcestershire sauce
- 2 pounds beef chuck, diced into ¹/₂-inch pieces
- Salt and pepper to taste
- ¹/₄ cup semisweet chocolate chips

Chunky Chocolate Chili

- In the oil, sauté the onion, peppers, and garlic for 5 minutes. Add the dry spices and cook for 3 minutes.

- Mix together the tomatoes, gravy mix, and beer and add to the pot. Add the stock and Worcestershire sauce.

- Add the beef; bring to a boil. The beef should be covered by 1 inch of liquid; add water if needed. Turn down to a gentle simmer and cook partially covered, for 2 hours.

- Adjust salt and pepper. Turn off heat and add chocolate.

Chili certainly has its origins in Mexico, and so does the surprise ingredient in this version: chocolate. The flavors of chocolate and chili peppers are natural together and are expressed most notably in mole sauce. This chili capitalizes on the relationship. Some cooks even add a pinch of chili powder to their chocolate cakes and desserts for an unusual and surprising twist.

• • • • RECIPE VARIATION • • • •

Turkey Chili: This chili can be made with turkey with excellent results. As with the beef in this chili, it is recommended that you not use ground turkey, but raw diced turkey. The meat from the thighs is ideal, as they will not dry out when cooked for long periods of time. It will take a bit of time to dice the turkey thighs, but you will be thrilled with the results.

Choosing Beef for Stewing

- It is very important to choose the proper cuts of beef that will be cooked long and slow.

- Cuts from the loin are generally not well suited for stewing; they will become dry and tough.

- Ideal cuts to stew are from the leg or shoulder. Chuck, bottom round, and brisket are excellent for stewing.

- Some interesting alternate cuts that are great for stewing are oxtails (really cow tails) and shank, which is cut from the shin. These cuts have bones but make excellent stews.

Sweet and Savory

- Adding chocolate to this chili creates a complex blend of sweet and savory, a common flavor balance in global cooking.

- In Chinese cooking there is always a balance of sweet, sour, salty, and bitter, as many savory recipes call for a touch of sugar.

- Most curries have a sweet component. In India it is coconut milk and dried fruits; in Southeast Asia it is usually palm sugar.

- The German pot roast sauerbraten uses gingersnap cookies to thicken the sour gravy, adding a sweet touch.

KILLER CURRIED LAMB STEW

Slow cooking softens the strong flavor of curry, and the fruit adds a distinctive sweetness

Curries are a complex breed of dishes. There are red curries, yellow curries, and green curries. There are Indian curries, Thai curries, and Japanese curries. The common thread is a blend of a large number of spices, herbs, and seasonings and a slow, complex cooking method. Curries are wonderfully warming, and lamb is ideally suited for the currying process.

Lamb has a stronger flavor than beef, pork, or chicken, and the curry is strong enough to stand up to and complement the flavor of the lamb. Always use stewing meat cuts and do not waste your money on a rack of lamb to turn into a dry stew. Goat meat can be substituted for lamb in this dish, if you can find it. *Yield: 2 big bowls*

Ingredients

1 pound lamb stew meat, cut into 2-inch cubes

$1/2$ cup vegetable oil, divided

Salt and pepper to taste

1 cup diced white onions

1 cup $1/4$-inch carrot rounds

1 tablespoon fresh grated ginger

1 tablespoon fresh chopped garlic

3 tablespoons Madras curry powder

1 cup canned diced tomatoes, drained

1 packet instant gravy mix

$1/4$ cup golden raisins

8 dried apricots, halved

6 cups chicken broth

6 small new potatoes, quartered

1 cup small cauliflower florets

$1/4$ cup cilantro leaves

Killer Curried Lamb Stew

- Toss lamb with 3 tablespoons oil and salt and pepper; brown in a very hot pot in batches. Set aside.

- Add remaining oil to the pot with the onions, carrots, ginger, garlic, and curry powder. Cook for 3 minutes. In a separate bowl, mix the tomatoes and gravy mix and add to pot.

- Add raisins, apricots, lamb, and broth; simmer gently for 1 hour.

- Add the potatoes and cauliflower and cook for 20 minutes. Adjust salt and pepper and stir in cilantro.

• • • • RECIPE VARIATION • • • •

No-Lamb Stew: There are two types of people in this world: those who like Neil Diamond and those who don't. The same goes for lamb. For those in the no-lamb camp, you can easily substitute chicken, beef, or pork in this curry. Be sure you use boneless skinless chicken thighs, pork shoulder, or beef bottom round or chuck if making the switch. Cook as directed in the recipe.

MAKE IT EASY

This dish is a great candidate for the slow cooker, which might make it easier to cook around your class schedule. Sauté the vegetables and curry powder just as in the recipe. Then add this mixture to the slow cooker. You will not need to sear the meat for the slow-cooker version. Simply add the remaining ingredients and cook on low for about 6 hours. You will need to skim off fat while cooking.

Searing the Meat

- Browning the lamb for this stew will add a dimension of flavor to this curry that is noticeable.

- The browning also allows for some of the fat to melt away before it goes into the pot so you have to skim less off at the end.

- Adding a little flour to the meat before browning will allow for a crisper crust and deeper color.

- You can brown large batches of meat under the broiler to save time.

Ancient Flavors

- People in India have been making curries for well over a thousand years; they have a rich history.

- The Indian spice trade fueled the world's new hunger for spices that Indians had been using for centuries.

- Fruit and sweet spices are added to curries to subdue the hot and spicy flavors.

- Intense aromatics such as ginger and garlic are also essential to this very old cuisine.

SOUPS & STEWS

CLASSIC CUBANO PRESS

One of the world's great sandwiches, the Cubano combines familiar flavors to create a masterpiece

Take a trip to Little Havana in Miami and you will be inundated with the sights, smells, and sounds of lively Cuban cuisine. Black beans and rice, octopus stew, and plates of ripe and green fried plantains adorn the tables in sidewalk cafes. Music plays, and excellent café con leche is sipped from cups while neighbors chat and gossip. But during lunch there is one item that you will see handed over counters again and again: the Cubano. This serious sandwich combines the natural partners of roasted fresh pork and ham with Swiss cheese and dill pickles and melds them all together in the heavy, foil-covered sandwich presses of Miami's lunch spots. Now you can make a version at home. *Yield: 1 sandwich*

Ingredients

1 12-inch soft sub roll

2 tablespoons mayonnaise

1 tablespoon yellow mustard

2 slices deli Swiss cheese

¼ pound thinly sliced smoked ham

¼ pound thinly sliced roasted pork

1 medium dill pickle, sliced very thin

Classic Cubano Press

- Split roll in half completely. Spread mayo on one side, mustard on the other. Tear cheese slices in half and coat each side of bread with cheese.

- Layer meats and pickle on the sandwich and close the sandwich.

- Press in a sandwich press until piping hot. If you do not have a press, preheat oven to 375°F and spray each outer side of bread with cooking spray.

- Place sandwich between two cookie sheets and press hard to compress. Bake 15 minutes.

• • • • RECIPE VARIATIONS • • • •

Cubano with Roast Turkey Breast: Sometimes you want to make this sandwich but don't have the time or patience to make the roasted pork. A reasonable substitute is roast turkey breast. Turkey has a similar texture to pork and a mild flavor. Simply replace the pork with turkey and assemble the sandwich with the ham and other ingredients. Just don't tell anyone in Miami!

Tampa-Style Cubano: In the southern parts of Florida, tomatoes, lettuce, and mayonnaise are added to this sandwich, while in Tampa, only yellow mustard is used. There are also versions that include thin slices of spicy chorizo sausage layered between the meats. The most interesting variation is the use of Genoa salami.

The Job Pickles Do

- The slices of pickles in this sandwich seem simple but perform a complex culinary role.

- The acidity of the vinegar in the pickles creates an excellent foil to the rich meats and cheese in the sandwich.

- In France, tiny pickles called cornichons are often served with sandwiches and sliced meats to create the same balance.

- You can add almost any pickled vegetable to this sandwich in place of standard pickles.

Necessity Is the Mother

- If you don't have a sandwich press, the cookie-sheet method is an excellent way to achieve the same results.

- This method is great for a party. You can make several sandwiches at once.

- Be sure to spray the bread. If you are feeling adventurous, a little melted butter with garlic is excellent.

- Don't be afraid to press the sandwich flat. Some shops pride themselves on having the flattest sandwiches.

PANINI DI PROSCIUTTO

The creamy mozzarella and salty complex prosciutto are perfect together

Prosciutto di Parma is widely called the "king of hams." Its method of production has remained unchanged for hundreds of years. Legs from specially raised and fed pigs are trimmed and rubbed in coarse salt. Then they are turned and pressed for about two months to squeeze out any excess blood. Then the hams are hung in a dark, cool, well-ventilated space for at least nine months and up to two years. The hams take on a silky texture and complex nutty flavor that is prized by gourmands. Seek out the real deal when making this sandwich. Although expensive, a little goes a long way, and it makes a big difference in this sandwich. *Yield: 1 sandwich*

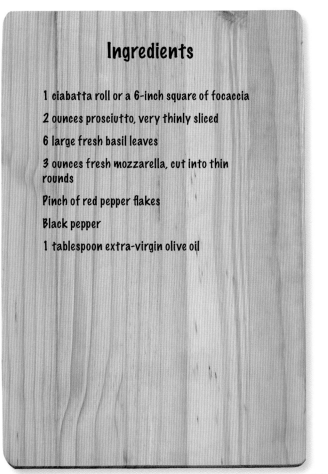

Ingredients

1 ciabatta roll or a 6-inch square of focaccia

2 ounces prosciutto, very thinly sliced

6 large fresh basil leaves

3 ounces fresh mozzarella, cut into thin rounds

Pinch of red pepper flakes

Black pepper

1 tablespoon extra-virgin olive oil

Panini di Prosciutto

- Split the bread in half all the way through.

- Gently drape the prosciutto on the bottom of the bread, being careful to separate the thin slices and not place them down in one slab. Top with basil leaves.

- Top with mozzarella slices and sprinkle with red and black pepper. Drizzle with olive oil.

- Cover with the top bread slice and press in a panini press or use the cookie-sheet method (see page 181) in the oven until gooey.

ZOOM

In some parts of Italy, especially in the northeast corner, prosciutto is often smoked. This ham is usually referred to as speck and is an incredible substitute for the traditional prosciutto, if you can find it. If you have prosciutto or speck sliced for you at a deli, make sure the store trims off the very tough skin before slicing. Some inexperienced slicers forget this important step.

ZOOM

In Italy there is another incredibly popular ham known as prosciutto cotto, which translates laterally to "cooked ham." Do not be confused if you see this at the market. This ham is completely different. It is not dry cured, but wet-steamed, and is a fully cooked ham, much like a Polish or boiled ham. In Italy it is often the first solid food given to babies when they graduate from baby food.

Dry-Cured Ham 101

- Prosciutto is a dry-cured ham, meaning it is never cooked and is hung to dry after salting.

- Because of the texture of these hams, it is essential that they are sliced very thin or they will be too tough.

- It is important to gently drape or "feather" the slices. If you just pack them on top of each other, the meat will be tougher.

- Other examples of dry-cured hams include serrano, speck, and even American Smithfield ham.

Thanks, George

- The sandwich press has made it from the shops of Italy into our kitchens in no time.

- Be sure you keep your press clean and lightly spray with cooking spray between each use.

- Some thinner sandwiches will require a hotter press, while thicker sandwiches should be cooked longer on lower heat.

- Always unplug this sucker after each use to save electricity and prevent any (rare) sudden flare-ups.

ROASTED TOMATO & FONTINA

Fontina cheese has a wonderful silky quality when melted, and the roasted tomatoes are divine

Tomatoes are a relatively new food for the Western world. They are a member of the nightshade family of plants, which are mostly poisonous, and Americans and Europeans initially believed that eating tomatoes would be deadly. The tomatoes were planted as ornamental plants, and it took more than a hundred years before an intrepid soul proved to the

world that tomatoes were not only edible but delicious. The tomato was so quickly adopted into Italian and Spanish cuisines that it is hard to believe that these cultures have not been making tomato dishes for thousands of years. The roasted tomatoes in this dish are incredible. They can be simply tossed with pasta, or just eaten on bread. *Yield: 1 sandwich*

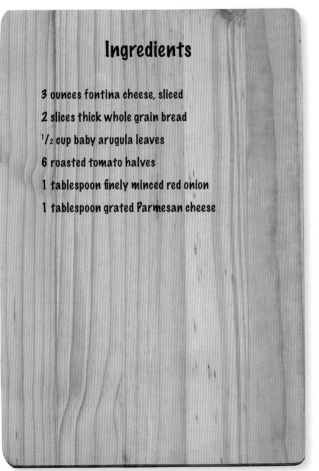

Ingredients

3 ounces fontina cheese, sliced

2 slices thick whole grain bread

1/2 cup baby arugula leaves

6 roasted tomato halves

1 tablespoon finely minced red onion

1 tablespoon grated Parmesan cheese

Roasted Tomato and Fontina

- Place the fontina on both sides of the bread.

- Top the bottom slice with the arugula leaves and nestle the roasted tomatoes into the leaves.

- Sprinkle with the minced red onion and Parmesan cheese.

- Top with the remaining cheese-covered bread and press in a panini press or use the cookie-sheet method (see page 181) until cheese melts.

MAKE IT EASY

Fontina has a smooth, semisoft texture, which allows it to melt into a very creamy texture. Fontina cheese may be hard to find in some markets. When looking for a substitute, look for cheeses that are firm but soft enough to press into with a finger. Look for Edam, Gouda (not aged Gouda), Bel Paese, or Appenzell if you can find it. This sandwich is great with almost any cheese

ZOOM

These roasted tomatoes are a take on the Italian tradition of sun drying tomatoes. Sun-dried tomatoes are usually salted and then set to dry on mats in the sun until they are very dry and almost leathery. These roasted tomatoes retain a good amount of juice but do not have the overly strong flavor of sun-dried tomatoes that many people object to. These tomatoes can be stored in the fridge.

Roasting the Tomatoes

- Cut six plum tomatoes in half and toss with enough extra-virgin olive oil just to coat.

- Season with salt, pepper, a pinch of sugar, a dash of red pepper flakes, and 1 teaspoon fresh thyme leaves.

- Place on a rack over a cookie sheet and roast at 275°F for 6 hours. Cool and store in an airtight container.

Choosing Tomatoes to Roast

- Once you make these roasted tomatoes, you will certainly get many requests for more.

- Look for very firm and meaty plum tomatoes. Buy one and cut into it, making sure it is thick.

- You can make these sandwiches with beefsteak tomatoes, but they will require a bit more cooking time, as they are juicier.

- Yellow plum tomatoes will work just as well and make a nice color contrast if mixed with reds.

GRILLED EGGPLANT & RICOTTA

A take on eggplant rollatini, this sandwich captures all the flavors of this Italian favorite

Eggplant is another member of the nightshade family, but unlike the tomato, has been eaten for centuries. It is believed that the first eggplants came from India and then spread to China and the Mediterranean before jumping the pond with Italian immigrants.

There are so many recipes and uses for eggplant, and cooks are constantly coming up with more. In Arabic countries, cooks make baba ghanoush by roasting whole eggplants over coals and then mixing with garlic and olive oil. The mash is eaten as a dip with warm pita bread. In Thailand, cooks use tiny round eggplants in curries and soups. *Yield: 1 sandwich*

Ingredients

1 medium eggplant, peeled and cut into $1/4$-inch slices lengthwise

1 medium beefsteak tomato, cut into $1/2$-inch-thick slices

Salt and pepper to taste

Olive oil cooking spray

$1/2$ cup part-skim ricotta cheese

1 teaspoon freshly minced garlic

1 tablespoon freshly minced Italian parsley

Pinch of red pepper flakes

1 tablespoon freshly grated Parmesan cheese

Pinch of dried oregano

1 8-inch crusty sub roll, split

$1/2$ cup baby spinach leaves

Grilled Eggplant and Ricotta

- Preheat a grill or grill pan. Lay out the eggplant and tomato slices and season each side with salt and pepper and spray with the olive oil cooking spray. Grill until tender, about 2 minutes per side. Keep warm.

- Mix together the ricotta, garlic, parsley, red pepper, Parmesan, and oregano. Spread onto the bottom of the roll.

- Top with the baby spinach leaves and then the tomato, followed by the eggplant.

- Top with the other half of the roll.

ZOOM

People often ask why the eggplant has this peculiar name. Some folks say that the creamy texture when cooked resembles scrambled eggs. A much more likely reason is that there is a very popular variety of eggplant that has pure white skin. These eggplants are on the small side, and it is said that fields of them look like fields of plants growing eggs. Most eggplants today have purple skin.

YELLOW LIGHT

Some eggplants are loaded with seeds and can be a bit bitter. To diminish this flavor, slice the eggplant and then sprinkle lightly with salt. Allow the eggplant slices to sit for 20 minutes and then blot away the liquid that rises to the surface with paper towels. This will slightly reduce the bitter flavor as well as allow less oil to soak into the eggplant during grilling or frying.

Grilling Veggies

- Grilled veggies have become one of the most popular vegetarian entree and sandwich options.

- Be sure your grill is hot and that it is clean and rubbed with a film of oil. This will prevent foods from sticking.

- Toss the veggies in just enough olive oil to coat them and season them with salt and pepper.

- Grill immediately and leave some space between the veggies so you have room to turn them.

The Magic of Ricotta

- Ricotta means "recooked" in Italian. It is made by re-fermenting and cooking the whey left over from other cheeses.

- It is slightly chunky but still creamy and is used in lasagna and other stuffed pastas, such as ravioli.

- Ricotta can also be salted and aged. This ricotta salata is grated over salads and pastas.

- Ricotta drizzled with honey, served with some good bread and coffee, makes a nice breakfast.

TURKEY, APPLE, & BRIE-WICH

This sandwich is a winner; the creamy Brie and apples elevate the simple turkey sandwich

Brie is one of the great cheeses of France. It is a cow's milk cheese and can be made with whole or partially skimmed milk. It can range from 30 percent to almost 90 percent fat content and is creamy and rich. The white moldy rind on the outside of the cheese is supposed to be eaten, not peeled off as many do. The rind has an almost mushroom flavor, and this

cheese is sometimes studded with mushrooms in one of its variations. Brie will continue to ripen as it ages and become more runny and pungent as it does. Young Brie is better for this sandwich, as the heat will melt the cheese, and a runny cheese would simply ooze out. *Yield: 1 sandwich*

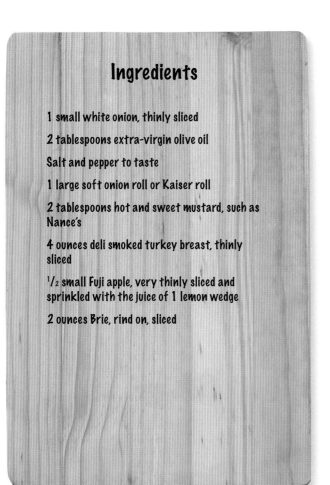

Ingredients

1 small white onion, thinly sliced

2 tablespoons extra-virgin olive oil

Salt and pepper to taste

1 large soft onion roll or Kaiser roll

2 tablespoons hot and sweet mustard, such as Nance's

4 ounces deli smoked turkey breast, thinly sliced

$\frac{1}{2}$ small Fuji apple, very thinly sliced and sprinkled with the juice of 1 lemon wedge

2 ounces Brie, rind on, sliced

Turkey, Apple, and Brie-wich

- Sauté the onion in oil with a bit of salt and pepper until deeply caramelized. Set aside.

- Slice the roll in half and spread mustard on each side. Top the bottom half with the smoked turkey.

- Arrange the apple slices on the turkey and then the caramelized onions.

- Top with Brie and the top of the roll.

- Place in a preheated 350°F oven for 6 minutes.

188

ZOOM

As Brie ripens not only does it get softer and more pungent, but the rind begins to take on a faint smell of ammonia. This is natural, and you should not be alarmed. However, if the ammonia smell becomes overwhelming, you should discard the cheese. This reaction only happens when the cheese is very soft and runny, and most Brie you find in the supermarket is young and firm.

• • • • RECIPE VARIATION • • • •

Fruit Substitutions: A nice variation with this sandwich is to cook the apples a bit before adding to the sandwich. You could sauté slices of apples with the onion, or you could even grill slices of apples. Substituting pears for apples is also wonderful on this sandwich. You can sauté or grill the pear slices as you would apple. Fruit and Brie are a match made in Heaven.

Sweet as Honey

Fruit and Cheese

- Onions have the most sugar of any vegetable and are very sweet when cooked long and slow.

- To truly caramelize onions, they must first be cooked over medium heat for at least 20 minutes.

- If the pan gets a bit dry and the onions appear to start to burn, add a few tablespoons of water and scrape the bottom of the pan.

- Onions will loose about 80 percent of their volume when caramelized.

- The combination of fruit and cheese is a classic, and there are many ways to enjoy it.

- Try a simple combination of grapes served with blue cheese and make sure to get a bite of each simultaneously.

- An interesting tradition in upstate New York is to melt a slice of cheddar cheese over a piece of apple pie.

- Grilling a half a peach and then filling the cavity with Gorgonzola makes an amazing summer appetizer.

189

THANKSGIVING ON A ROLL
This sandwich is best made the Friday after Turkey Day, but try making it anytime

Thanksgiving is a festival of the harvest and its bounties. It is not clear when the first true Thanksgiving dinner was served and rumors range from New England to Florida. Turkey is usually the main item, but some families prefer a fresh ham. In some parts of Maryland, pork and sauerkraut, cooked together for hours, is the main course, reflecting the German heritage of the area. This sandwich assumes you have made a turkey and have some leftover stuffing, cranberry, and gravy on hand, and that you have slept well, are hungry again, and the game is about to start. Be sure you have some great bread for this sandwich, and bring plenty of napkins, as it can get messy! *Yield: 1 mongo sandwich*

Ingredients

4 ounces leftover cooked turkey, both white and dark meat

$^1/_4$ cup leftover gravy

1 egg

1 cup leftover stuffing

1 tablespoon butter

2 thick slices country-style white bread

2 tablespoons mayonnaise

$^1/_4$ cup whole-berry cranberry sauce or relish

Thanksgiving on a Roll

- Combine the turkey and gravy and gently warm. Set aside.

- Beat the egg and mix well with the stuffing. Form into a patty about the size of the bread and fry in the butter on both sides until piping hot in the center.

- Lightly toast the bread and spread with mayo. Top with the stuffing patty, then the turkey, then the cranberry sauce, and finally the other slice of bread.

- Eat with plenty of napkins and maybe some extra gravy to dip.

ZOOM

If you are still nursing that food hangover from last night's dinner, you do not have to go to the trouble to fry the patty of stuffing. Simply reheat the leftover stuffing any way you like and put it on the bread with the other ingredients. The main focus is that there is some kind of stuffing on the sandwich; otherwise, it just isn't the same.

•••••••••• RED ● LIGHT ••••••••••

Mixing cubes of bread with aromatic vegetables and stuffing it inside a bird is an extremely old technique. If you cook your stuffing in the turkey, as opposed to in a separate pan, it is very important to make sure that your turkey comes to 165°F and that the center of the stuffing reaches that same safe temperature. Many people get sick each holiday, as the turkey's juices have seeped into the stuffing and are not heated thoroughly.

Killer Patties

- These stuffing patties are so good that some families serve stuffing like this for Thanksgiving.

- You can take an extra step and bread the patties with flour, egg, and bread crumbs and then fry for a more decadent crunch.

- This same technique works well with corn bread stuffing as well as with traditional bread stuffing.

- If the mixture seems too wet, add a few bread crumbs to dry the mixture.

Jelly, Sauce, or Relish?

- There are many variations of cranberry sauce that are enjoyed during Thanksgiving.

- Jellied cranberry sauce is sold in cans, and many folks like to cut both sides off the can, slide the cranberry out, and slice it.

- Cranberry sauce is usually made with whole berries cooked with sugar, orange juice, and spices.

- Cranberry relish is usually made from chopped cranberries and is a little less saucy than cranberry sauce.

BUDGET STEAK & MUSHROOMS

Flatiron steak is an excellent value for quality; ask your butcher to order it

There are so many types of steaks available in the market that, unless you have some real knowledge, it can be difficult to understand what is what. Almost without fail, price is a good indicator of which steaks will be the most tender. Cuts from the loin, such as T-bone, porterhouse, filet mignon (tenderloin), New York strip, rib eye, and Delmonico steaks, are all

excellent but expensive steaks. There are a few "value" steaks on the market these days, which are worth seeking out. One is hanger steak, which is also called the butcher's tender, and the other is what we use here—flatiron steak. This steak is the second-most tender cut of beef after the tenderloin. *Yield: 1 serving*

Ingredients

2 tablespoons vegetable oil, divided

1 8- to 10-ounce flatiron steak

Salt and pepper to taste

1 cup assorted sliced mushrooms

1 shallot, minced

1 garlic clove, minced

$1/4$ cup dry red wine

1 teaspoon butter

$1/4$ cup chicken broth

1 teaspoon minced fresh parsley

Budget Steak and Mushrooms

- In a heavy skillet, heat 1 teaspoon oil until barely smoking. Season the steak with salt and pepper and brown well on both sides. Set aside.

- Add the remaining oil to the pan, then the mushrooms, shallot, and garlic. Sauté until the liquid from

the mushrooms' release evaporates. Add the wine.

- Boil until the pan is just about dry. Add the butter, broth, and parsley.

- Return the steak to the pan. Cook until desired doneness. Serve mushroom sauce on top.

The general rule of thumb with beef is this: If it comes from the shoulder, it is tough. This is generally true, but the flatiron steak is an exception. These steaks come from the infraspinatus muscle, and it takes a skilled butcher to remove and fabricate these steaks. The economy has spurred the meat industry to rethink the way they cut parts of the animal in order to find more specialty cuts.

• • • • RECIPE VARIATION • • • •

Hanger Steak and Mushrooms: The other value cut mentioned here, the hanger steak, is also a great option. The big difference in using the hanger steak is that it must be sliced before serving, much like a flank steak. The hanger steak has an extremely visible grain, as well as a large tendon that runs right down the middle of the cut.

Pan Searing

- Pan searing meat is a very effective way to add flavor to a simple steak or chop.

- It is important to have a heavy pan that is very hot. For many steaks with a high-fat content, you may not need to add any oil to the pan.

- If the cut of meat is very thick, it can be seared and then slipped into the oven to continue cooking.

- This technique works equally well for poultry and fish.

Pan Sauces

- Pan sauces are quick and incredibly flavorful. It is important to have all your ingredients on hand.

- The basic ingredients needed are chopped shallots, wine, broth, and butter. All manner of garnishes can be added.

- When the meat is removed from the pan, shallots are added, and the wine is used to deglaze the pan, releasing the crystallized juices from the pan into the sauce.

- Finally broth and butter are added and the mixture is reduced slightly so it will coat the meat.

193

RUM-GLAZED PORK CHOP

Pan searing and oven roasting are the key techniques for success with this dish

Pork chops are a dinnertime favorite all over the world. There is nothing better than a perfectly cooked, juicy chop. You can make this dish when you're feeling particularly homesick.

This recipe uses the classic combination of fruit with pork. Before pork was raised on such a grand scale and fed a steady diet of grain, there were domesticated pigs and wild boars.

Both of these meats had a much stronger flavor compared to today's mild white-fleshed pork. Very often, fruit was paired with pork in order to contrast the strong meat flavor. Pork and apples are still a classic combination—and not just pork chops and applesauce. There is a reason you always see a roast pig with an apple in its mouth. *Yield: 1 serving*

KNACK COLLEGE COOKBOOK

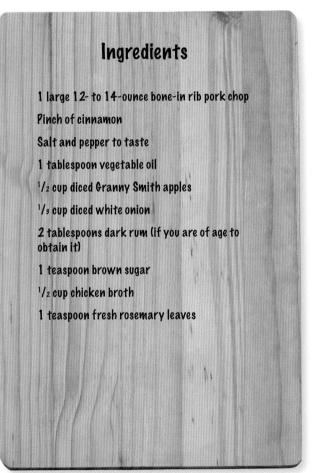

Ingredients

1 large 12- to 14-ounce bone-in rib pork chop

Pinch of cinnamon

Salt and pepper to taste

1 tablespoon vegetable oil

$^1/_2$ cup diced Granny Smith apples

$^1/_3$ cup diced white onion

2 tablespoons dark rum (if you are of age to obtain it)

1 teaspoon brown sugar

$^1/_2$ cup chicken broth

1 teaspoon fresh rosemary leaves

Rum-Glazed Pork Chop

- Season the pork chop with the cinnamon, salt, and pepper. Heat the oil in a heavy skillet to barely smoking. Brown the meat well on one side.

- Flip the meat and add the apples and onions.

- Add the rum, sugar, broth, and rosemary. Place the entire pan in a preheated 400°F oven and cook for 5 to 6 minutes. Remove the meat from the pan and rest on a plate.

- Add the meat and any juices back to the pan and glaze by tossing with the sauce. Serve.

· · · · RECIPE VARIATION · · · ·

Seasonal Variations: Since fruit and pork are such a natural marriage, it is nice to change this dish up with the seasons. In fall, apples and pears are great. In winter, try citrus fruits and juices. In spring, seedless grapes are a good choice, and in summer, peaches and nectarines are amazing with a pork chop. Fruit and pork are a natural; play around and impress some friends.

YELLOW ● LIGHT

Many people are paranoid about eating pork that is remotely pink or juicy because of fear of food-borne illness. However, the disease of trichinosis is almost never found in pork these days. Trichinosis was caused by pigs being fed garbage (this is now illegal) and is almost unheard of today. Pork that is slightly pink and juicy is so much more flavorful than the dry, overcooked pork chops Grandma made.

Sauce Garnishes

- This simple pan sauce uses apples and onions, but there are countless nonfruit variations.

- Mushrooms are always a classic. Just make the sauce the same way and add 1 cup raw sliced mushrooms when you would add the apples.

- You can also add very tart items to pan sauces. Capers and olives are excellent.

- Almost anything can be a sauce garnish. This is a great way to clean out the produce drawer.

Rest Easy

- When meat cooks, the juices are moving around the fibers of the meat. If the meat is cut prematurely, the juices will run out.

- Resting the meat actually allows the juices to pull back into the meat.

- There will always be some juices that escape, and they should always be saved or added back to the sauce.

- You can rest a large roast or turkey loosely covered with foil for over 30 minutes with no heat loss.

ROASTED CHICKEN WITH VEGGIES

A perfectly roasted chicken is a sight to behold, so buy a big chicken for leftovers

Chicken is one of the most popular foods, and for good reason. Chicken is relatively inexpensive, easy to prepare, readily available, and tasty. Roasting a whole chicken is easier than you think—especially these days with the little pop-up thermometers telling you when it is done. When choosing a chicken, always read the label and look at the expiration date, making sure that it has not expired. Look for chickens with clean whitish or yellowish skin with no visible bruises or blood on the surface. The chicken should smell good and have no tacky or slimy feeling to the skin. Always remove the giblets before roasting. *Yield: At least 2 servings*

Ingredients

1 large roasting chicken with pop-up thermometer

1 bunch fresh thyme

1 lemon, halved

2 tablespoons soft butter

Salt and pepper to taste

1 10-ounce package large whole white mushrooms

1 cup baby carrots

4 stalks celery, cut into 2- inch-long pieces

1 cup large diced turnip

1 fennel bulb, trimmed and cut into quarters through the core

1 large onion, cut into wedges through the core

2 cups chicken broth

Roasted Chicken with Veggies

- Preheat oven to 375°F. Wash and dry chicken. Place thyme and lemon in cavity. Place giblets except liver in the roasting pan.

- Rub chicken with butter and season well with salt and pepper. Place the veggies in the roasting pan and put the chicken on top of the veggies and giblets. They will act as a rack.

- Add the broth and roast until thermometer pops. Remove chicken from pan and rest for 10 minutes. Strain veggies from liquid and defat. Serve with the veggies and defatted juice.

• • • • RECIPE VARIATION • • • •

Spicy Chicken with Veggies: This chicken is roasted with a simple salt and pepper seasoning and some fresh herbs. The recipe is very basic. If you want a more aggressive flavor to the skin, you can make a dry spice rub and season the outside of the skin. One killer rub is equal parts onion powder, garlic powder, paprika, dry mustard, black pepper, salt, and ground sage.

YELLOW ● LIGHT

Chicken can contain salmonella. Clean and sanitize all surfaces that come into contact with the raw poultry. Be sure that when cooking the chicken, the deepest part of the thigh registers at least 165°F. The pop-up thermometers are good, but can fail, so make sure that the juices from the thigh run clear when the chicken is pricked.

Not the Rack!

- It's a good idea to elevate the chicken so it does not stew in a mess of juices on the bottom of the pan.

- You can buy a roasting rack and place it in the bottom of the roasting pan, or you can make your own.

- A "rack" of vegetables and giblets does a great job of keeping the chicken elevated and adding flavor to the sauce.

- You can also roll up "logs" of aluminum foil and use them as a rack.

Lose the Fat

- Chicken has quite a bit of fat and, when cooked, will give off its fat into the cooking juices.

- Defatting the juices is an important step to achieving a sauce that is not greasy.

- You can simply skim the fat off the top of the juices with a spoon or ladle or use a fat-separating measuring cup.

- You can also cool the juice down; the fat will congeal on the top in a solid mass, making it very easy to remove.

SESAME-CRUSTED SOY SALMON

This recipe is so easy yet looks like you spent all day on it

Salmon is a popular fish on today's tables and restaurant menus. It is very flavorful and loaded with nutrients, including omega-3 fatty acids. Atlantic salmon is the species that is typically farmed; these fish are incredible animals. They have the ability to spawn multiple times in their lives and are very powerful. Pacific salmon are typically caught wild and can only spawn once and then die. Most salmon found in the market are farm-raised Atlantic salmon. Wild Pacific salmon are very expensive and less available in the market, but are superior in flavor and texture. If you can find and afford wild salmon, by all means grab it. *Yield: 2 portions*

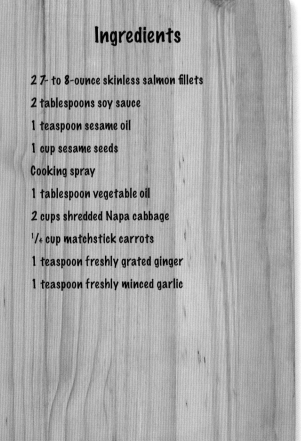

Ingredients

2 7- to 8-ounce skinless salmon fillets

2 tablespoons soy sauce

1 teaspoon sesame oil

1 cup sesame seeds

Cooking spray

1 tablespoon vegetable oil

2 cups shredded Napa cabbage

$1/4$ cup matchstick carrots

1 teaspoon freshly grated ginger

1 teaspoon freshly minced garlic

Sesame-Crusted Soy Salmon

- Preheat oven to 400°F. Marinate the salmon in the soy sauce and sesame oil for 20 minutes. Reserve marinade.

- Lay the seeds on a cutting board and press the top of the fillets into the seeds. Place the fillets in a small skillet coated with cooking spray.

- Spray the top of the seeds with cooking spray and place in the oven. Roast for 10 minutes. Remove from pan.

- In the same pan add oil, veggies, ginger, garlic, and reserved marinade. Sauté for 2 minutes.

Potato-Crusted Salmon: Crusting salmon is a popular technique and is only limited by your imagination. A really neat trick is to use a potato crust. Brush the salmon with 1 tablespoon Dijon mustard and then press about ¾ cup freshly shredded raw potatoes on top. Quickly place the potato side down in a hot pan filled with ¼ inch of oil, then place in a 400°F oven for 7 to 8 minutes. Gently turn over and serve.

Asian Persuasion Salmon: Some people do not eat seeds for various reasons. You can make this same dish without the seeds. Instead of roasting the salmon, marinate the same way and then sauté in a hot pan with 2 tablespoons peanut or canola oil. Cook for 3 to 4 minutes on each side. The soy will form a nice glaze.

Other Simple Crusts

- The sesame seeds that form this crust are one of the simplest ways to crust a piece of fish.

- Another quick crust is to brush the fish with mayonnaise and top with seasoned bread crumbs. Spray with cooking spray and roast as in the recipe.

- You can also top the fish with a layer of shredded Parmesan cheese and then roast.

- A simple crust of bread crumbs, moistened with eggs and horseradish, makes a very sophisticated crust.

Simple Slaws

- This vegetable medley is similar to a slaw, with the cabbage component playing a major role.

- Another quick slaw can be made by shredding fennel very finely and adding a little minced onion and shredded carrot.

- Jicama makes an excellent quick slaw. Simply shred and toss with lime juice and olive oil. Serve with the fish.

- Of course cabbage is the go-to slaw vegetable. Try different cabbages such as savoy, red, Chinese, and white.

199

GINGER SHRIMP STIR-FRY
This is a great way to learn stir-frying, and a cast-iron skillet is an acceptable wok substitute

Stir-frying is an amazing technique. The invention of the wok was brilliant, and it is one of the most versatile pieces of cookware ever. The wok can steam, deep-fry, smoke, braise, and even bake, if an expert is at the helm. Stir-frying allows you to cook foods very quickly in a small amount of oil while keeping the vegetables crunchy and vitamins intact. If you use a

wok, you really need high heat underneath it; otherwise, go for a cast-iron pan and do not overcrowd it. The key is to not lose heat in the pan as the food items cook, ensuring the nice sear on the meats and veggies that give stir-fried foods their signature slightly smoky flavor. *Yield: 2 servings*

Ingredients

12 16–20 peeled and deveined white shrimp

2 tablespoons soy sauce

1 tablespoon sesame oil

1 teaspoon dry sherry

3 tablespoons peanut oil, divided

1 teaspoon freshly minced garlic

1 teaspoon freshly minced ginger

2 scallions, minced

1/2 cup thinly sliced onion

1/2 cup thinly sliced on the bias celery

1/2 cup julienned snow peas

1/2 cup julienned red bell pepper

1/2 cup chicken stock

2 tablespoons cornstarch dissolved in 2 tablespoons cold water

Ginger Shrimp Stir-Fry

- Marinate the shrimp in the soy sauce, sesame oil, and sherry for 20 minutes.

- Heat 2 tablespoons peanut oil in a wok to barely smoking. Add the shrimp and stir-fry 1 minute. Reserve the marinade.

- Add the remaining oil and the garlic, ginger, and scallions. Cook 1 minute; add the remaining vegetables. Cook 3 minutes; add the shrimp back.

- Add the stock and any leftover marinade. Bring to a boil.

- Thicken with the cornstarch.

Varying on Proteins: One of the great things about stir-frying is that you can use almost any ingredients. If you do not like shrimp, use ¾ pound beef, chicken, or pork—any type of protein will do. Simply cut the meat into thin strips and marinate the same way you would the shrimp. Cook the dish the exact same way with any of the proteins you choose.

Szechuan Spin: Many people are in love with the cuisine of the Szechuan province of China, which is marked by the copious use of hot chili and garlic. If you want to put a Szechuan spin on any stir-fry, simply do the following: Double or even triple the amount of garlic in the recipe and add 1 teaspoon per person of hot Chinese chili paste.

Stages

- Almost all stir-fries follow the same basic steps or stages.

- First, the meat is seared and briefly cooked. It is taken out of the wok and put aside.

- Next the vegetables are stir-fried, and flavorings such as chili or black bean sauce are added.

- The sauce components are then added and the meat comes back into the wok. The sauce is thickened—and that's it.

Don't Overcook It

- Removing the shrimp and then adding them back to the stir-fry is an essential step.

- This is so the shrimp can get a nice sear on them but not overcook. Holding them to the side while the veggies cook is the best way to achieve this.

- Otherwise you would have to make the entire stir-fry and then add raw shrimp to it. The flavors would not be as good.

- Practice this technique and you will find stir-frying quite easy and fun.

SUMMER SPAGHETTI WITH TUNA

Be creative and see what's in the fridge for this great warm-weather pasta dish

Spaghetti is one of those comfort foods. Almost everyone loves long strands of noodles dressed with a sauce. There is something childlike and silly about slurping up those long noodles that inadvertently makes us remember that famous scene from Disney's *Lady and the Tramp*. This dish eschews the long-cooked sauces and allows you to make this dish with one pot. Although some purists will tell you they never serve Parmesan cheese with sauces that have seafood in them, the cheese here adds a nice depth of flavor and helps make the pasta a bit creamier in the way it blends with the olive oil. This is a classic "uncooked" pasta sauce and is wonderful. *Yield: 2 servings*

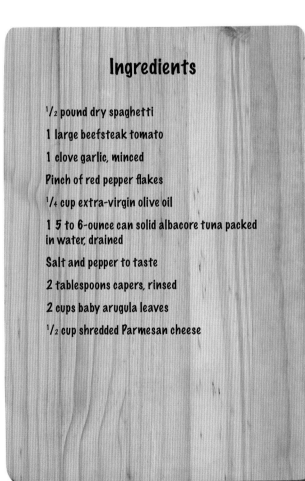

Ingredients

¹/₂ pound dry spaghetti

1 large beefsteak tomato

1 clove garlic, minced

Pinch of red pepper flakes

¹/₄ cup extra-virgin olive oil

1 5 to 6-ounce can solid albacore tuna packed in water, drained

Salt and pepper to taste

2 tablespoons capers, rinsed

2 cups baby arugula leaves

¹/₂ cup shredded Parmesan cheese

Summer Spaghetti with Tuna

- Bring a pot of salted water to a boil; drop the pasta in.

- Dice the tomato very fine and place in a bowl. Add the garlic, red pepper flakes, olive oil, tuna, and salt and pepper. Let sit 5 minutes.

- Add the capers and arugula leaves and toss well. Season with salt and pepper.

- When the pasta is done, drain and add to the tomato mixture. Toss well. Add the Parmesan and toss again.

Salsa Cruda: One of the most famous uncooked pasta sauces is called *salsa cruda*, which literally translates to "raw sauce." This is a sauce of 2 cups raw chopped ripe tomatoes, 2 cloves crushed garlic, $\frac{1}{3}$ cup olive oil, and $\frac{1}{4}$ cup chiffonade basil. You simply place these ingredients in a bowl and toss with hot pasta. The heat of the pasta slightly cooks the sauce and warms it enough to release the flavors of the garlic and basil.

Raw Sauces: Boil the water and drop in the pasta. While the pasta cooks, place the following in a large mixing bowl: 3 smashed anchovy fillets, 1 clove garlic paste, 2 cups baby spinach, $\frac{1}{2}$ cup extra-virgin olive oil, $\frac{1}{2}$ cup shredded Parmesan cheese, and some salt and pepper. Drop the hot pasta into the bowl, toss, and serve.

Details, Details

- In a simple uncooked dish like this, the small details are really important, such as pre-marinating the tomatoes.

- When using capers it is a good idea to rinse them of their salty brine before adding them to the dish.

- Be sure your arugula is washed, dried, and free of any bruises or wilted leaves before adding to the pasta.

- Use "real" Parmesan cheese in this dish instead of the grated green-canned stuff; the flavor is much more complex.

My Friend, Al Dente

- You know Al? I went to high school with him. Along with Sal Monella and Patty O'Furniture.

- But seriously, folks, cooking pasta to the al dente or "to the tooth" stage is critical for really enjoying pasta.

- Be sure you cook pasta in plenty of boiling salted water.

- When checking the pasta, pull out one strand and bite into it. Look carefully into the center. If there is a visible white center, the pasta needs a bit more time.

HERB-ROASTED BABY POTATOES
These simple and delicious potatoes are equally good cold the next day in a salad

Potatoes may be the most cherished of all side dishes. They are pure culinary comfort. Dense and full of carbohydrate yumminess, the potato is incredibly versatile and nourishing.

From the Andes Mountains in South America, the potato spread widely across the globe. There are potato dishes ingrained throughout Europe, the Americas, the Middle East, and even India. In fact, Indian cuisine has embraced the potato so much that it would be hard to imagine Indian food without it. Potato dishes can be creamy, crunchy, and anywhere in between. They have an incredible ability to soak up and transform all manner of sauces and gravies, and they taste great hot or at room temperature. *Yield: 4 servings*

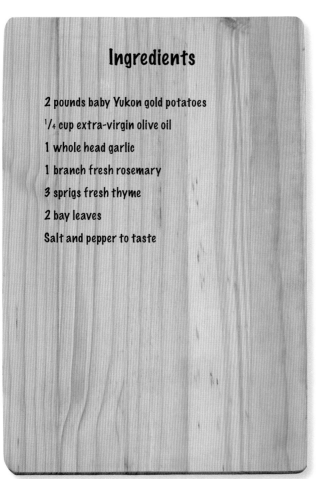

Ingredients

2 pounds baby Yukon gold potatoes

1/4 cup extra-virgin olive oil

1 whole head garlic

1 branch fresh rosemary

3 sprigs fresh thyme

2 bay leaves

Salt and pepper to taste

Herb-Roasted Baby Potatoes

- Preheat oven to 400°F. Cut potatoes in half. Place in a bowl and toss the potatoes with the oil.

- Break apart the garlic head into cloves. Do not peel. Add to the bowl. When cooked, you can push the roasted garlic out of the skins.

- Toss the herbs, still intact on the sprigs, and bay leaves in the bowl. Add salt and pepper and toss well.

- Place the potatoes, well spaced, on a cookie sheet or heavy skillet and place in the oven. Roast for 25 minutes or until tender.

• • • • RECIPE VARIATION • • • •

Potato Dish Riffs: These roasted potatoes are made in a very classic style with rosemary and garlic. Use this recipe as a baseline recipe and feel free to "riff" on it. One great riff on this dish is the simple addition of Parmesan cheese. When making this dish, follow the recipe as written and then, 10 minutes before the potatoes are done, sprinkle them with Parmesan.

ZOOM

Yukon gold potatoes are a relative of the yellow Finn potato and were initially cultivated in Canada and released to the market in 1981. The flesh is unusually deep yellow in color, and the potatoes have a truly creamy texture when cooked. They are also nice because the texture of the flesh is good when baked or used in mashed potatoes. Other potatoes, like red bliss, tend to be more waxy.

Roasting Potatoes 101

- The basic technique for roasting potatoes is the same whether the potatoes are big or small.

- Be sure to preheat the oven to 400°F and place the rack you will be using in the center of the oven.

- Cut the potatoes at the last minute so they don't oxidize, or turn brown.

- Be sure the potatoes are coated with fat. Oil, bacon fat, butter, and duck fat (the best!) are all good choices.

- Space well, so the potatoes do not steam.

Magical Roasted Garlic

- The whole cloves of garlic, which roast along side these potatoes, are a real treat. However, there are other ways to make roasted garlic.

- Rub a whole head of garlic with oil, wrap with foil, and roast at 350°F for 1 hour.

- You can also cover whole peeled cloves with oil and gently poach in a small pan until the garlic is completely soft.

- The bonus with the oil method is the tasty garlic oil that you can roast the potatoes in.

KILLER SIDES

EASY SICILIAN SAUTÉED SPINACH

This dish is familiar and yet different enough to wow a group at dinner

Having leafy greens as a side dish is an excellent way to "health up" a meal, especially if the main item is very rich or a huge slab of meat. Having leafy greens takes some of the guilt out of the meal.

Experiment with some unfamiliar greens besides spinach. Some greens, like collard greens, require a long and slow cooking time. Others seem to wilt and cook in seconds, like arugula. Spinach seems to fall in between, especially true curly spinach and not the faux flat-leaf spinach, which falls apart easily and has very little flavor. Seek out curly spinach and pull any large stems or ribs out of the leaves before cooking. *Yield: 2–4 servings*

Ingredients

2 10-ounce bags curly leaf spinach

2 cups water

1 teaspoon salt

3 tablespoons extra-virgin olive oil

1 teaspoon fresh minced garlic

2 tablespoons pine nuts

Pinch of red pepper flakes

3 tablespoons golden raisins

Salt and pepper to taste

Easy Sicilian Sautéed Spinach

- Pull any large stems out of the spinach and place the spinach in a bowl. Boil the water with salt and pour over spinach. Mix well. Strain and press well to remove excess water.

- In a sauté pan, heat the olive oil over medium heat and add garlic, pine nuts

- and pepper flakes. Cook for 30 seconds.

- Add the spinach, and raisins, and sauté slowly for about 5 minutes, until the water is evaporated.

- Adjust salt and pepper.

ZOOM

Many vegetable dishes in the southern part of Italy use a combination of raisins and pine nuts, often with a dash of vinegar. This sweet and sour/savory combination is not, in fact, Italian in origin, but a culinary shadow of the occupation of Sicily and Sardinia by Arab conquerors, who for centuries used this combination to flavor everything from vegetables to meats.

• • • • RECIPE VARIATION • • • •

Onion Substitution: If this mixture of raisins and nuts seems too bizarre for you, please try this wonderful variation. Before sautéing the spinach, sauté $1/2$ cup thinly sliced onion and the garlic in olive oil. Brown slightly and then add the spinach. Cook as directed in the recipe. The onion adds a sweet, savory, and familiar flavor to the spinach.

Blanch Away

- Blanching is the technique of very briefly cooking in boiling water. It is often used as a parboiling technique.

- Blanching spinach makes it much easier to get all the greens in the pan, as opposed to wrestling with a big pile of leaves.

- Another common use for blanching is precooking green vegetables before sautéing, which preserves the vegetables' green color.

- Tomatoes are also quickly blanched in order to loosen their skins before peeling.

Watery Spinach Is Bad

- Blanching spinach undoubtedly adds water, which needs to be eliminated before serving.

- The first step, of course, is to squeeze as much water out of the greens as possible.

- The second step is to make sure that you cook the spinach long enough to evaporate all the water in the pan.

- If too much water remains, the plate will be full of green water, which is not very appealing.

207

AMAZING SCALLOPED POTATOES

Like a classic French gratin without the fuss, these potatoes are always a crowd-pleaser

Having these potatoes at a dinner party is an instant guarantee of getting requests for the recipe. Variations of this dish are served throughout Europe, particularly in France. In the United States, this dish is called scalloped potatoes, and in France it is called au gratin. One of the most famous incarnations of this is Gratin Dauphinoise, which uses Gruyère cheese in the mix. The beauty of this gratin is that it is ridiculously simple and uses only a few ingredients. You don't need eggs or cheese, and yet these potatoes are redolent with flavor, which it grabs from the garlic and rosemary. This dish is more than worth the effort. *Yield: 3–4 servings*

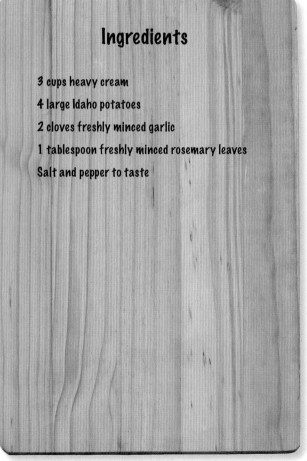

Ingredients

3 cups heavy cream

4 large Idaho potatoes

2 cloves freshly minced garlic

1 tablespoon freshly minced rosemary leaves

Salt and pepper to taste

Amazing Scalloped Potatoes

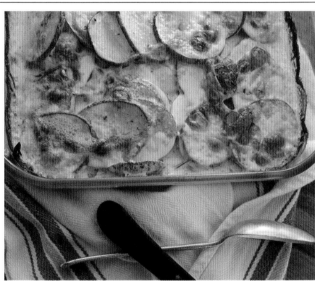

- Preheat oven to 425°F. Pour cream into a bowl. Peel the potatoes and slice into thin rounds; add to the cream. Add the garlic and rosemary.

- Season well with salt and pepper, as the potatoes will soak up much of the salt.

- Spoon the potatoes into a shallow baking dish and pour in enough of the cream to just cover the tops of the potatoes.

- Bake for 45 minutes, remove from the oven, and rest for ten minutes to allow cream to soak in.

Cheese Scalloped Potatoes: Of course, cheese is a great addition to this dish. In this recipe, add $1/2$ cup grated Gruyère or Comté cheese directly to the dish and mix it into the potato and cream mixture. Then top the gratin with a healthy amount of freshly grated Parmesan cheese. Cook as described in the recipe. The top will get ultrabrown and crisp.

Horseradish Creamed Spuds: This is a great variation, especially if you are serving a big haunch of roasted beef or some great steaks. Simply add 2 tablespoons prepared horseradish to the cream and cook as directed in the recipe. Don't add too much; it will curdle the cream.

Just Enough to Coat

- This step in the recipe may be the most important. Too much cream and the potatoes will be soupy, too little and they will be dry.

- Add just enough cream to come just to the top of the potatoes without covering them completely.

- Press down with your hands a bit to moisten the tops of the potatoes.

- You can slightly baste the top of the potatoes with some of the hot cream from the baking pan during the cooking.

Assemble with Care

- As noted, the amount of cream you add to the potatoes is important.

- The potatoes themselves should be between 2 and 3 inches thick.

- Before pouring the cream over the potatoes, taste it to make sure there is enough salt and pepper in the mix.

- You can also make these potatoes the exact same way, but put them in individual baking dishes or even muffin tins to make single portions.

NUTTY, FRUITY WILD RICE
This makes a wonderful side dish for roasted poultry; try it for Thanksgiving

Wild rice is actually not rice at all. It is related to true rice, but is a wild grass native to the northern part of the United States. It grows in shallow lakes and slow-moving streams near the Great Lakes and can be one of four different species. Native Americans harvested this rice by beating the grass with sticks while paddling a canoe through the shallow waters where the rice grows. The rice is simply cooked in water until the grains swell and "pop" at the tips. The flavor of this rice is nutty, and the texture is firm. It is an excellent source of dietary fiber and contains many essential vitamins and minerals. It is particularly nice during Thanksgiving because of its Native American provenance. *Yield: 4 servings*

Ingredients

¹/₄ cup toasted pecan pieces

¹/₄ cup toasted pine nuts

4 tablespoons butter, divided

¹/₂ cup finely diced white onion

¹/₂ cup finely diced celery

2 cloves minced garlic

¹/₂ teaspoon dried thyme

2 cups wild rice

3 cups chicken broth

¹/₂ cup dried cranberries

¹/₄ cup diced dried apricots

¹/₄ cup fresh chopped parsley

Salt and pepper to taste

Nutty, Fruity Wild Rice

- Toast the nuts by placing them on a cookie sheet and baking at 350°F for 5 minutes. Reserve.

- Heat half the butter in a pot and sauté the onion, celery, garlic, and thyme for 4 minutes. Add the rice and stir well.

- Add the broth and bring to a boil. Immediately turn down to a low simmer and cover the pot. Cook at the lowest setting for 45 minutes.

- Turn off the heat and fold in the dried fruit, nuts, and parsley. Add remaining butter, salt, and pepper.

ZOOM

• • • • RECIPE VARIATION • • • •

White and Wild: For a while, all the rage in boxed rice was the long-grain-and-wild-rice combination. Everyone was doing it, and many still are. For this version, cook 1 cup plain white rice separately from wild rice and combine when both are done. Remove nuts and fruits from recipe and add $1/2$ cup finely chopped scallions and 1 teaspoon dried "rubbed" sage leaves.

There is one type of wild rice that is grown in Asia. Its roots commonly get infected with a sort of fungus called a "smut." This smut swells the roots and stops the plant from flowering. It also turns the root into a tasty vegetable, which is commonly eaten in China. The United States currently prohibits wild rice imports from China for fear of the disease spreading to American crops.

Multipurpose Grain

- At the step when the rice is stirred with the sweated vegetables you have many options.

- You can continue with the recipe as written and make some yummy wild rice.

- Or you can add double the amount of broth and omit the fruit and nuts. You will be blessed with a wild rice soup.

- You can also complete the wild rice recipe and then cool. If you mix it with 4 cups toasted bread cubes and 4 eggs, you can serve this as a stuffing.

Other Garnishes

- Dried fruits and nuts are a classic garnish for wild rice, but there are other interesting and delicious possibilities.

- Try adding a pile of sliced mushrooms in with the veggies when you are sautéing them.

- Roasted or boiled chestnuts are a luxurious and sophisticated garnish for wild rice.

- Gently folding raw shucked oysters into the rice at the very end is a very traditional combination.

THE REAL-DEAL RISOTTO

You may have made Cheaters' Risotto as an underclassman, but this is worth the effort

Making risotto is an excellent skill to learn, as there are not too many other foods as satisfying as a perfectly cooked creamy risotto. The little things make a big difference when making risotto, as there are only a few ingredients, and all of them are fairly simple. The broth can be store-bought chicken broth, but if you can make homemade fortified broth, you will have an even better risotto. The rice needs to be the correct rice. If all you have is a box of plain white rice do not attempt risotto. The varieties of rice used to make risotto include Arborio, Vialone Nano, and Carnaroli. Use real Parmigiana Reggiano, as it will make a difference. *Yield: 4–5 servings*

Ingredients

2 tablespoons butter, divided

1 tablespoon extra-virgin olive oil

$1/2$ cup minced red onion

2 cloves garlic, minced

1 cup Arborio rice

$1/2$ cup dry white wine, or 1 teaspoon white vinegar

4 cups simmering chicken broth

$1/2$ cup grated Parmigiana Reggiano cheese

$1/4$ cup freshly chopped parsley

Salt and pepper to taste

The Real-Deal Risotto

- Heat 1 tablespoon butter and all the oil in a high-sided sauté pan. Sauté the onion and garlic for about 3 minutes; do not brown.

- Add the rice and stir. Continue cooking and stirring for 2 minutes.

- Add the wine and reduce to dry.

- Add a third of the broth. Continue stirring frequently and add broth in thirds as each batch dries. When al dente, turn off heat. Add the remaining butter, Parmigiana Reggiano, parsley, and salt and pepper.

• • • • RECIPE VARIATIONS • • • •

Porcini Mushroom Risotto: There are an infinite number of risotto variations. One popular risotto uses porcino mushrooms. Take about ³/₄ cup porcino mushrooms and soak in hot water for an hour. Remove them from the water and then strain water through a coffee filter to remove any sand. Add the mushroom liquid to broth and add mushrooms to the rice after the wine.

Leftover Risotto: Make enough risotto to have some leftovers. The next day, when the rice is cold, add 1 egg per 2 cups risotto and 3 tablespoons flour. Form the risotto into 3-inch-round cakes and press in some seasoned bread crumbs. Fry them in olive oil and butter until crisp and hot in the middle. Serve as a side dish or make tiny ones as appetizers for a party.

Not Just for Drinking

- Adding wine (or vinegar) to this risotto is an important step, as it adds a small amount of acidity that balances the flavors of the dish.

- Wine is a very important culinary ingredient, and the rule is to never cook with a wine you would not drink.

- Do not use supermarket cooking wine. This is low-grade wine with tons of salt added to it.

- A nice touch is to use wine from the country of the food you are cooking. For example, use an Italian white for risotto.

Dreamy and Creamy

- The starch in the risotto rice is what allows the risotto to make its own sauce. The finished consistency is very important.

- The finished rice should have a visible amount of creamy liquid surrounding the rice.

- It is okay for the rice to be wetter than you think it should be, as it will continue to soak up the liquid very rapidly.

- Do not sacrifice texture for creaminess; the rice should be al dente. Do not overcook it.

KILLER SIDES

213

TOMATO & MOZZ PANZANELLA

Bread salad is a new concept for many people, but you will become an instant fan

Panzanella is a popular dish in the northern region of Italy, especially Tuscany. It is sometimes referred to as pan molle. This recipe calls for toasting the bread cubes in the oven. In Italy, the bread is cut and then allowed to go stale instead of toasting. This produces a slightly different texture than the toasted bread, and if you have the patience, you should try this traditional method. You can also toast the bread in a generous amount of olive oil flavored with a little garlic for a richer and more robust flavor and texture. This is certainly not traditional, but since when do copious amounts of olive oil and garlic make anything worse? *Yield: 3–4 servings*

Ingredients

4 cups 1- to 2-inch cubed European-style country bread

2 cups diced ripe beefsteak tomatoes

1/4 cup minced red onion

1 clove garlic, ground into a paste with a little salt

1/2 pound fresh mozzarella, cut into 1-inch dices

3/4 cup extra-virgin olive oil

4 tablespoons red wine vinegar

Salt and pepper to taste

15–20 leaves fresh basil

1/2 cup finely grated Parmesan cheese

Pinch of red pepper flakes

Tomato and Mozz Panzanella

- Place the bread on a cookie sheet and toast in a 300°F oven for 10 minutes. Cool at room temperature for 5 minutes.

- Add the tomato, onion, garlic, mozzarella, oil, vinegar, and salt and pepper; stir well. Let sit for 5 minutes.

- Lay the basil leaves on top of one another and shred into very thin strips with a knife. Add to the bowl.

- Toss in the cheese and red pepper and serve.

Bright and Pungent Panzanella: A very nice variation is to add a few acidic components to the dish to brighten the flavor. To this recipe add: $1/4$ cup rinsed capers; $1/4$ cup chopped black, brined olives; the zest of $1/2$ a lemon; and $1/4$ cup very finely minced celery. This more acidic and astringent version is particularly good as a side dish for grilled or roasted fish or shellfish.

Winter Panzanella: If you want to make this panzanella but it is the dead of winter and tomatoes are out of season, have no fear. You can make a more deeply flavored wintery version of this salad by adding grilled or roasted veggies. Try adding roasted cubes of eggplant, butternut squash, and some roasted onions to the dish for a nice change.

The Cult of Basil

Not Too Dry or Too Wet

- Basil is one of those herbs that people are crazy about. It has a unique inherent sweetness.

- Basil is a classic component to a proper pizza and marries well with tomatoes. Some people feel these two should always be together.

- Basil is a member of the mint family, and in the most southern part of Italy, mint is used just as basil is.

- Dry basil is not a good substitute for this salad. Use dried only in long-cooked items like sauces.

- Bread salads run the risk of becoming too soggy or too dry; it is critical to get the texture right.

- It is important for the bread to be very dry, as residual moisture in the bread can throw your recipe off.

- Add the wet ingredients gradually; stir and taste and wait a few minutes before adding more.

- If you are using fresh tomatoes, the tomatoes will purge quite a bit of water once they come in contact with salt.

KILLER SIDES

BETTER-THAN-DELIVERY PIZZA
Save yourself some money and calories and make this pizza

This may be the ultimate comfort food. There are very few people who do not love pizza, and there are even fewer who do not have strong feelings on what makes a great pie. In Chicago, pizza is deep dish; in New York, the crusts are thin and the slices folded when eaten.

One town that is also well-known for pizza is New Haven, Connecticut. New Haven is known for what the locals call apizza. It has an ultrathin crust made in a superhot coal-fired oven. This pizza is sublime. So, if you ever find yourself on Interstate 95, passing through this shoreline city, stop in at Sally's, Pepe's, or, if you really know your stuff, Modern Pizza for a slice or two. *Yield: 1 medium pie*

Ingredients

1 1/2 cups canned crushed tomatoes

1 clove garlic, ground into a paste with a little salt

1 teaspoon dried oregano

Pinch of red pepper

Salt to taste

4 tablespoons extra-virgin olive oil, divided

1 medium fresh pizza dough from your favorite pizzeria at room temperature. (cold dough is hard to work with)

Flour to work with

8 ounces fresh mozzarella, diced small

1/2 cup grated Parmesan

8 basil leaves

Better-than-Delivery Pizza

- Place pizza stone or large seasoned cast-iron skillet into the oven. Preheat oven to 500°F.

- Mix together the tomatoes, garlic, oregano, red pepper, salt, and half the oil.

- Flour your hands and stretch the dough. You can use a rolling pin if you have not yet perfected your skill. Place on the stone or in the pan.

- Immediately top with the sauce, cheeses, and remaining oil. Bake until the top is bubbling. Remove and rest for 2 minutes. Tear basil over the top.

MAKE IT EASY

Working with fresh dough is pretty daunting for most folks and may require some practice. You should make sure the dough is at room temperature and have plenty of flour on your hands and work space to keep the dough from sticking. Also, completely preheat the oven before you start doing anything, as you need to move quickly once you start handling the dough.

• • • • RECIPE VARIATION • • • •

The New Haven White Clam Pie: To make this pie, omit the tomato sauce and drain a 6-ounce can baby clams. Mix the clams with $1/2$ cup grated Parmesan; $1/3$ cup extra-virgin olive oil; 3 cloves garlic, smashed; $1/2$ teaspoon dried thyme; the grated zest of 1 lemon; and the diced mozzarella and red pepper flakes. Simply spread over the crust and cook as directed in the recipe.

Working with the Dough

- Relax, take a deep breath, and flour up. Don't worry; you don't have to spin the dough to make a great pizza.

- One trick is to just grab an edge of the dough and allow gravity to pull and stretch it.

- While doing this, simply rotate the dough in your hands and it will stretch.

- You can always use a rolling pin, but learning how to stretch is more fun.

Use Caution

- Pizza is volcanically hot when it is removed from the oven; be careful or you will be peeling the roof of your mouth off!

- Allow the pizza to rest for about 2 minutes before cutting; the cheese will settle a bit and not slide off.

- Sliding the pizza onto a large cutting board and placing the board on the table is a nice technique.

- Invest in a rolling pizza cutter; it is easier than a knife for cutting pizza.

MIND-BLOWING GRILLED WINGS

Patience and a grill are the only special tools required to make these mind-blowing wings

Wings are one of the most popular take-out foods. They also seem to show up quite frequently on happy hour menus, and most pizzerias now serve some sort of wings. They're great for late-night studying sessions or after outings with friends. The thing that makes wings so yummy is the great ratio of meat to skin, as every bite gets a little bit of both. Frying is the most popular method of cooking wings, and for good reason. The skin becomes supercrisp, and the meat stays moist and juicy. These wings are grilled, and if done right, are just as mouthwatering as the fried variety. Look for jumbo wings, as they do a little better on the grill. *Yield: Depends how hungry you are!*

Ingredients

2 pounds jumbo chicken wings

6 cloves garlic

$1/4$ cup loosely packed basil leaves

$1/4$ cup loosely packed cilantro leaves

$1/4$ cup loosely packed oregano leaves

3 scallions, minced

2 tablespoons brown sugar

2 teaspoons ground cumin

1 tablespoon salt

1 teaspoon red pepper flakes

1 teaspoon black pepper

$1/2$ cup vegetable oil

3 tablespoons red wine vinegar

Water as needed

Mind-Blowing Grilled Wings

- Cut the tips off the wings and slightly cut into the joint. Place in a bowl.

- Place the rest of the ingredients into a blender and blend well into a fine puree. Use a little water if the blender is not pureeing easily.

- Marinate the wings in this mixture for at least 3 hours or overnight.

- Grill the wings very slowly over medium-low heat, turning frequently for about 30 minutes, ensuring a well-charred finish on the wings.

Add the Heat: Many people equate wings with spicy heat. If you consider yourself a heat devotee, here is a nice recipe: Replace the basil and oregano leaves with 1 whole fresh jalapeño pepper, seeds and all. For some reason, jalapeño peppers with rounded and blunt ends seem to be less hot than peppers with sharp, pointy ends.

If you do not have a grill or do not want to spend the time with all that turning on the grill, there is a broiler option. Preheat your broiler on high and raise the rack in the oven to the highest position. Place the wings on a rack over a cookie sheet and broil on one side until very deeply charred, turn over and broil the other side.

Blender Beauty

- The blender makes short work of pureeing these ingredients for the marinade.

- Blenders work particularly well for marinades that have a fair amount of liquid, as well as fresh herb leaves, in them.

- If your blender is not spinning the marinade effectively, add water, a little at a time, until it moves freely.

- Blenders are better at pureeing than food processors are. But you can use a food processor in a pinch if you do not have a blender.

Patience Makes Perfect

- Grilling these wings imparts that one-of-a-kind smoky flavor that comes about when bits of marinade and fat drip and burn.

- Turn the wings during the grilling process to ensure that every square inch of the wings is well charred.

- These take some time to be done right, so bring a frosty beverage and some friends with you to the grill.

- These puppies are screaming hot when they come off the grill; wait a minute before chomping down.

OVEN-FRIED CHICKEN TENDERS
Save the fat and maximize the flavor with these great tenders

Chicken tenders are small muscles that run directly under the breasts of the bird. Do not confuse tenders with nuggets, which are sometimes made with ground bits of chicken from who knows where on the bird. The technique of oven frying is an excellent way to save on both mess and fat.

Be sure you have all your breading ingredients ready and set up in three separate pans next to each other before you start, or you will have a mess on your hands. It is also recommended that you keep a wet hand and a dry hand when breading food, unless you want all your fingers to be breaded just like your chicken tenders. *Yield: 2 servings as an entree, 4 as an appetizer*

Ingredients

2 cups all-purpose flour

Salt and pepper to taste

1 tablespoon garlic powder

1 tablespoon Old Bay seasoning

1 teaspoon dried oregano leaves

$1/2$ teaspoon cayenne pepper

3 cups plain bread crumbs

$1/2$ cup finely grated Parmesan cheese

4 eggs beaten with 2 tablespoons water

12 raw chicken tenders

Cooking spray

Marinara sauce, ranch dressing, and barbecue sauce to dip

Oven-Fried Chicken Tenders

- Preheat oven to 375°F. In a shallow container, season the flour with salt and pepper. Add the dried herbs and spices.

- In another container, mix the bread crumbs and cheese. Mix the eggs and water in a third container.

- Dredge tenders in the flour, shaking off excess, and then dip them into the egg. Finally, dip them into the bread crumbs.

- Place on a cookie sheet, well spaced, and spray with cooking spray to coat with a foam of spray. Bake for 12 minutes.

Spicy Tenders: What's really cool about breading your own stuff is that you can doctor up the breading mixture. Add flavorings such as dried herbs and spices to both the flour and bread crumbs, and you can even add some liquid flavorings to the egg. To make a spicy tender, add 1 teaspoon cayenne to flour and 2 teaspoons chipotle powder to bread crumbs.

Breading foods requires a fair amount of flour and bread crumbs, and the instinct not to let food go to waste is a strong one. Do not make the mistake of keeping the leftover bread crumbs, eggs, or flour, however, as they have all been in contact with raw chicken. There is one cool option, though, and that is to mix them all together and fry them in a little butter. This is an old school cook's treat.

Proper Breading Technique

- There are many opinions about which order to dip foods for breading, but there is really only one way that works.

- The first dip into the flour acts as the "glue" that allows the egg to stick next. Always shake off the excess.

- The dip into the eggs allows the next item (in this case bread crumbs) to stick.

- The dip into the bread crumbs should be thorough, and the crumbs should be patted and pressed into the chicken. Shake off the excess.

Trick with Spray

- This technique of heavily spraying the chicken with a "foam" of cooking spray is essential to your success.

- This foam completely covers the chicken yet contains much less fat than conventional frying.

- It is that fat that allows the heat from the oven to evenly surround the chicken and give you that crispy coat.

- You can purchase cooking sprays that are 100 percent olive oil, butter flavored, or canola oil.

TAKE-OUT REVISITED

BLUE CHEESE–STUFFED BURGERS

You can use any cheese you like, but blue really accentuates the beefiness of burgers

Mmmm . . . burgers. Perhaps no food is more American. The hamburger has a long and storied history. Many agree that the first hamburger restaurant was and still is located in that pizza-centric town of New Haven, Connecticut. Louis' Lunch is still in business in New Haven, although it has been relocated from its original address. Vertical cast-iron broilers cook the hamburgers, just as they have been for more than a century. The burgers are served on white toast with tomato, cheese sauce, or both. No ketchup, mustard, or "special sauce" in this joint. After you have digested your New Haven pizza, head over to Louis' Lunch for a burger.

Yield: 2 righteous burgers

Ingredients

1 pound 80/20 ground beef

1 tablespoon garlic powder

1 teaspoon salt

2 teaspoons black pepper

4 tablespoons blue cheese

2 large burger buns

2 tablespoons mayonnaise

2 tablespoons Dijon mustard

1 cup arugula leaves

4 slices beefsteak tomato

Blue Cheese–Stuffed Burgers

- Very gently mix together the beef, garlic powder, and salt and pepper. Divide into two equal balls.

- Begin forming the burgers and in the center of each burger place 2 tablespoons of the blue cheese. Seal the burgers well.

- Grill the burgers over medium heat. Test by inserting a thin knife into the center. If the knife is hot, they are done.

- Spread the mayo on one side of the buns and the mustard on the other. Build the burgers with the arugula and tomatoes.

Garlic Burgers: Stuffing burgers with cheese is a nice way to up the ooze factor and provide the burger with an internal flavor bomb. There are other goodies you can stuff into the middle of the burger. Try mixing 2 tablespoons soft butter with a crushed garlic clove and a little lemon juice. Freeze the butter and stuff inside the burger. It sort of bastes the burger from the inside out.

YELLOW ● LIGHT

Ground beef can contain one of the most dangerous pathogens in food: *E. coli*. This bacteria lives in the intestinal tract of cattle and is transferred to ground beef by poor butchering and cross-contamination at the plant. Grinding your own chuck is probably the safest way to enjoy undercooked ground beef. Seek out butcher shops that grind their own meat, as it is infinitely safer than mass-produced burgers.

Pocket Rocket

- Getting the cheese to stay in the burger during the cooking process is important.

- To avoid a blowout, be sure the pocket you form is in the dead center of the burger.

- Try to firmly pack the meat around the cheese and be sure there are no wide gaps in the meat.

- Cook, turn, and flip gently to avoid breaking the burger during the cooking process.

- Even with these precautions, you might lose the cheese to the grill.

Take Your Temperature

- It is important to understand the proper temperatures for cooking anything, especially ground beef.

- It is always a good idea to invest in an instant-read stemmed food thermometer. These are readily available in retail stores.

- To recap: 120°F is rare, 130°F is medium rare, 145°F is medium, and 160°F is cooked to well done, and this final temperature will kill *E. coli*.

- Inserting a paring knife in the center of the burger is a great trick, but it's not foolproof.

TAKE-OUT REVISITED

LEFTOVERS INTO LO MEIN

Chinese takeout is notoriously greasy and calorie laden; this is a great home version

Lo mein translates from Chinese to "stirred noodles." In China, lo mein noodles are more brothy and typically served in soups as well as stir-fried with meats, vegetables, and sauces. These noodles are very popular in the United States, probably because they are spaghetti-like and easy to eat with a fork.

This recipe uses spaghetti, but true lo mein noodles are readily available at Asian supermarkets and are worth seeking out. They are typically sold fresh in bags and can be frozen for later use. When making this dish at home, try to get your pan really hot to achieve the "sear" that a hot wok is so famous for producing. *Yield: 2 servings*

Ingredients

3 tablespoons peanut oil

1/2 cup thinly sliced onion

1/2 cup julienned carrots

2 scallions, minced

1 teaspoon minced garlic

1 teaspoon minced fresh ginger

1/2 pound cooked and cooled spaghetti

1/4 cup chopped water chestnuts

8 canned baby corn, halved lengthwise

1 cup chopped or shredded leftover meat, fish, shellfish, chicken, or tofu

3 tablespoons soy sauce

1 tablespoon sugar

1 cup chicken broth

2 tablespoons cornstarch dissolved in 2 tablespoons cold water

1 teaspoon sesame oil

Leftovers into Lo Mein

- Heat the oil in a wok or large skillet to almost smoking. Add the onions, carrots, scallions, garlic, and ginger. Stir-fry 30 seconds.

- Add the spaghetti, water chestnuts, corn, and protein and allow to sit undisturbed for 1 minute. Stir well, then add the soy sauce, sugar, and broth.

- Boil hard for 2 minutes, tossing occasionally

- Carefully stir in the cornstarch slurry. Immediately turn off the heat and stir in the sesame oil.

Chow Funny: In China there is a popular noodle used in this type of recipe, called chow fun. These are very wide and thick noodles and are usually stir-fried in a very hot wok. Try substituting the widest egg noodles you can find for the spaghetti in this dish to make a pseudo version of chow fun. Use the same amount of cooked egg noodles as spaghetti.

ZOOM

In China (and most of Asia), the length of noodles is significant. As a matter of fact, the longer the noodle, the better, as the length of noodles are symbolic of the length of life. There are some noodle masters in Asia who are capable of making a noodle hundreds of feet long, and some big bowls of noodles are actually one long noodle piled into a bowl.

Wok and Roll

- One of the reasons a true wok works so well is that it sits inside a hole with flames underneath.

- This provides heat up the sides of the wok and not just on the bottom.

- Most home cooks can sit a wok only on top of the burner, and this will never provide the same type of heat.

- A cast-iron pan works as a reasonable substitute because of its great heat retention.

Making Sauce with Cornstarch

- The Chinese have adapted the use of cornstarch in the past two hundred years. Before then they used tapioca starch.

- To get an effective thickening agent, it is important to make your thickening slurry with equal parts cornstarch and cold water.

- One way to make the slurry by eye is to make sure the finished slurry looks like whipping cream, not like skim milk.

- Always add slurry very gradually to boiling liquid, as it thickens instantly.

HOME-STYLE ASIAN NOODLE SOUP

Nothing is more comforting than a bowl of noodles; you'll need chopsticks and a spoon

In Asia, noodle soups are a religion. Long noodles are added to flavorful broths and all manner of garnishes, from fried bread to frogs' legs, are added, depending on the mood of the diner. Entire restaurants are devoted to noodle soups, and some to one soup in particular. The Canton province in China has the famous wonton soup, which always has thin

long noodles and often roasted meats such as pork or duck.

In Japan, ramen reigns supreme, with braised pork belly and a soft cooked egg added to the soup. Vietnam has the incredible beef pho perfumed with Thai basil and star anise. This recipe is a nice attempt at replicating this type of soup at home. You need chopsticks and a spoon. *Yield: 1 bowl*

Ingredients

3 cups chicken broth

1 tablespoon soy sauce

1 splash fish sauce

1 sliced "coin" fresh ginger

1 scallion, halved

1 teaspoon sugar

6 shitake mushroom caps, halved

4 frozen Chinese dumplings, cooked

Salt to taste

4 ounces cooked chicken meat, shredded

1 cup cooked angel-hair pasta, cooled

2 tablespoons cilantro leaves

Home-Style Asian Noodle Soup

- Simmer together the broth, soy sauce, fish sauce, ginger, scallion, sugar, and mushrooms for 10 minutes. Discard the ginger and scallion.

- Add the dumplings and simmer for 3 minutes more. Check for salt and add if necessary.

- Place the chicken meat and pasta in serving bowls and bring the broth to a vigorous boil.

- Pour the broth over the noodles and chicken and garnish with cilantro leaves.

Egg Drop Soup: Some people's idea of Chinese soup is one thing: egg drop soup. You can easily add egg drops to any soup (it does not have to be Chinese). For this soup, add it right before you pour the broth over the noodles and chicken that are in the bowl. Gently stir 1 beaten egg into the boiling broth and thicken with 2 tablespoons cornstarch slurry.

Hot and Sour Soup: The other classic take-out soup, of course, is hot and sour soup. It is pretty easy to turn this soup into a hot and sour version. First, for a true flavor, replace the chicken with diced firm tofu. Second, when the soup is in its final boiling stage, add 2 tablespoons rice vinegar and 1 tablespoon hot Chinese chili paste. Of course, you can ease off a bit on the paste if it is too hot.

Incredible Ginger

- Ginger is an excellent culinary ingredient and has been used in Asia for thousands of years.

- Look for ginger with smooth and shiny skin that is free of wrinkles. A large piece of ginger is called a "hand."

- There are many claims, some proven scientifically, of ginger's medicinal powers.

- Boiling a 2-inch piece of smashed ginger with a ¼ cup brown sugar and 2 cups water until reduced to 1 cup is a folk remedy for colds and flu.

Finishing Touch

- When making this soup it is critical that the broth is boiling when it is poured over the ingredients in the bowl.

- This is an especially effective method when making this soup for a large group.

- Cilantro is a great garnish, but so are minced scallions and basil leaves. A few drops of sesame oil are nice, too.

- Serve with hot sauce on the side for those who like to dip the noodles in some heat.

GET YOUR GEAR ON

RESOURCES

Outfitting your dorm room, apartment kitchen, kitchenette, or camper, for that matter, is essential to being a successful cook. There are many equipment resources available these days, including Web sites, retail stores, restaurant supply houses, garage sales, and mom's attic. Get creative, but only get what you need; avoid "gimmicky" gadgets and try to buy the best that you can afford. Another trick is to find factory seconds, which are products that have cosmetic blemishes but do not have any functional deficiencies. Remember, great cooking gear will last a lifetime. Here is a list of suppliers where you can find some exceptional gear:

Great shopping Web sites:

www.bowerykitchens.com: A great retail store in New York City with a Web site. Buy professional-quality cookware. It's like having a real restaurant supply house online.

www.chefdepot.net: A great Website with professional and hon cooking equipment. It even has a "sportsman's corner" for hunte with meat grinders, jerky kits, and large butcher blocks.

www.chefsresource.com: Solid deals on enamel cookware, all cl pans, and even some gourmet food items.

www.cooking.com: This site has everything from cookware to coc ing DVDs and resources for kids' cooking as well as great deals closeouts.

www.cookware.com: A great source for an easy to navigate site wi tons of stuff including lines of items from Paula Deen and Rachael R

www.italiancookingsupply.com: A fantastic web site for specialty It ian items such as espresso pots.

www.overstock.com: A cool Web site which offers great deals cookware including factory seconds and refurbished items as well new in-the-box.

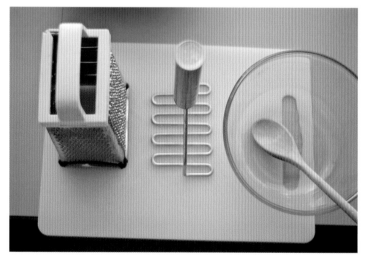

Sur la Table: Super-cool retail stores that not only have great gear, but offer cooking classes taught by real pros.

Target: A wide selection of reasonably priced gadgets, small appliances, and tableware make this a fun store to visit.

Williams-Sonoma: High-end, not cheap, but what they carry will last you a lifetime. Great for special items and holiday shopping.

Retail stores worth visiting:

Bed, Bath & Beyond: They have got it all. Knives, cookware, storage solutions, and almost anything you could think of to outfit your kitchen at any price point.

JC Penney: You might just think of sheets and towels, but the Penney has quite a selection of cookware at good prices.

Sears: The old standby still has loads of small wares as well as small and large appliances.

HOTLINES & MANUFACTURERS

It is amazing how much information is available for free just by calling manufacturers of foods and equipment. The beauty of these hotlines is that the information they give out is almost always time-tested and true. If you have a question about a product you bought at the store, check the package; there is probably a toll free number on the box, bag, or pouch that you can call to have your questions answered promptly and accurately.

Food hotlines:

Butterball Turkey Talk-Line, 1 800 288 8372: This hotline is available all year, but Thanksgiving is the busiest time for the line.

Kraft Foods, 1 800 323 0768: From mac and cheese to fondue, these peeps can help you.

Land O' Lakes, 1 800 328 4155: Questions about butter, sour cream, or recipes containing them.

USDA Meat and Poultry Hotline, 1 888 674 6854: This is a great hotlin to call especially with questions regarding cooking temperatures fc meats and poultry and food safety questions in general.

Tyson Foods Hotline, 1 800 233 6332: Info about meats, poultry, an seafood. Freezing, thawing, and cooking tips.

Equipment manufacturers:

All-Clad Metalcrafters, www.all-clad.com: This company may be th best maker of pots and pans out there.

Cuisinart, www.cuisinart.com: This maker of gear and gadgets ca help you with the equipment as well as explain uses to you an recipes.

Dexter-Russel, www.dexter-russel.com: A great source for American made products and affordable knives and cutlery.

Le Creuset, www.lecreuset.co.uk: Absolutley the finest cast iron/enamel cookware on the planet.

OXO tools, www.oxo.com: Great hand tools and gadgets for the home cook. Really good stuff.

Global knives, www.global-knife.com: These excellent Japanese knives are among the best and most reasonably priced.

Kitchenaid, www.kitchenaid.com: The maker of the famous mixer has tons of useful info about this and many other gear they make.

BOOKS & MAGAZINES

RESOURCES

In this world of digital media, please don't forget what our cooking ancestors have been using for hundreds of years: the ancient media of print. From the earliest works printed in Rome, to your Mom's collection of dog eared favorites, to the trendy magazines available at your local bookstore/coffee house, there is nothing like feeling some paper between your fingers while you read and get hungry. The array of cookbooks out there is mind-numbing and deciding which to choose can be difficult. Books with lots of great photos are pretty to look at but may not offer the best recipes or recipes that actually work. Consult the great cooks you know in your life and ask them which books they refer to regularly to help you make your choices. The world of culinary magazines has grown exponentially over the years and there are many to choose from. Go to a good magazine shop and browse a bunch of them and see which format and style you feel most comfortable with, or which make you hungry! Here are some great choices.

Books for people who actually cook:

The Chez Panisse Café Cookbook by Alice Waters: From the queen of the local and organic movement. Waters had no idea that when she opened her small restaurant in Berkeley, California, she would change the food world.

On Food and Cooking by Harold McGee: A bit technical, but an amazing source of information regarding the science and chemistry behind cooking. A must-read for the science geek/cook.

Lidia's Family Table by Lidia Bastianich: Incredible "everyday" Italian foods made simple. Superb techniques and recipes for the beginner and the advanced cook. This lady can cook her you-know-what off!

The Silver Palate Cookbook by Sheila Lukins and Julie Rosso: This is one of the all-time best selling cookbooks, and for good reason. Based on recipes from one of New York's first gourmet shops, this book is full of great recipes that work every time.

Food & Wine: Great magazine with lots of good vino info as well as travel and lifestyle.

Saveur: Fantastic magazine with great recipes, info, history, and photographs. The team at Saveur does great research and it shows.

Cool magazines to keep you interested:

Cooking Light: A really great magazine for healthy cooking and living with surprisingly delicious recipes. Even offers a helpful "Cooking 101" section.

Cook's Illustrated: One of the best all-around recipe/cooking guides there is. This magazine is a bit pricey as there are no advertisements in it. But it is full of no-nonsense info, product reviews, and killer recipes that work every time.

WEB SITES

The Internet is a boon for those interested in food and cooking. From shopping to recipes, restaurant reviews and blogs, the Web is chock full of incredible information for the aspiring as well as advanced cook. It is important to remember that just because it is written on a Web site, it does not mean the information is true or even remotely accurate. Just as your professors do not allow you to use Wikipedia as a source for your papers, you should take Internet info with a grain of salt and do your homework before relying on a recipe or article to hinge an important dinner or event on. Here are some great Web sites with a plethora of info.

Recipe resources:

www.allrecipes.com: A great comprehensive Web site with user reviews on zillions of recipes.

www.epicurious.com: Super site with recipes, blogs, community bulletin boards, and more.

www.foodclassics.com: A smart site with links to blogs, shopping sites, and a newsletter.

www.ichef.com: A site chock full of recipes smartly categorized. Also includes cooking videos.

www.recipezaar.com: Almost half a million free recipes in 45 categories.

www.recipesource.com: Cleverly sorted by ethnicity and dish type categories. Simple and easy to use site.

www.simplyrecipes.com: A comprehensive site with great dessert resources.

Great blogs:

www.behindtheburner.com: This is a cool site, which gets culinary pros to spill the beans on tips and tricks of the trade. Like sneaking a peek into the back of your favorite joint.

www.poorgirlgourmet.blogspot.com: Her tag line is "low-budget, high quality." This is perfect for the student on a budget.

www.seriouseats.com: Great articles, restaurant reviews, recipes, and current info on the food world. Fun to read.

Don't forget to look through www.youtube.com for all manner of free cooking demos and recipes from grandmothers to professional chefs. Have fun surfing!

METRIC CONVERSION TABLES

Approximate U.S. Metric Equivalents

Liquid Ingredients

U.S. MEASURES	METRIC	U.S. MEASURES	METRIC
¼ TSP.	1.23 ML	2 TBSP.	29.57 ML
½ TSP.	2.36 ML	3 TBSP.	44.36 ML
¾ TSP.	3.70 ML	¼ CUP	59.15 ML
1 TSP.	4.93 ML	½ CUP	118.30 ML
1¼ TSP.	6.16 ML	1 CUP	236.59 ML
1½ TSP.	7.39 ML	2 CUPS OR 1 PT.	473.18 ML
1¾ TSP.	8.63 ML	3 CUPS	709.77 ML
2 TSP.	9.86 ML	4 CUPS OR 1 QT.	946.36 ML
1 TBSP.	14.79 ML	4 QTS. OR 1 GAL.	3.79 L

Dry Ingredients

U.S. MEASURES	METRIC	U.S. MEASURES		METRIC
¹⁄₁₆ OZ.	2 (1.8) G	2⁴⁄₅ OZ.		80 G
⅛ OZ.	3½ (3.5) G	3 OZ.		85 (84.9) G
¼ OZ.	7 (7.1) G	3½ OZ.		100 G
½ OZ.	15 (14.2) G	4 OZ.		115 (113.2) G
¾ OZ.	21 (21.3) G	4½ OZ.		125 G
⅞ OZ.	25 G	5¼ OZ.		150 G
1 OZ.	30 (28.3) G	8⅞ OZ.		250 G
1¾ OZ.	50 G	16 OZ.	1 LB.	454 G
2 OZ.	60 (56.6) G	17³⁄₅ OZ.	1 LIVRE	500 G

COMPLEMENTARY RECIPES

This book talks a lot about making "intelligent shortcuts" and using the convenience of the supermarket and premade items. This is all great stuff, but the truth remains that some basic items are important to understand and master, especially after you have moved on and have a real kitchen to work with. Once you have tasted certain dishes and items made with classic techniques, you will understand. Although you may not make these items in your college life, please reference these recipes when you have some time and want to explore some basic recipes and techniques.

Basic Chicken Stock:

Nothing makes a better homemade soup than real chicken stock. Store bought broths and stocks are a good substitute, but please try this simple, but slightly time-consuming recipe when you have the desire. You will see the light. Make extra and freeze the rest for future soups! Yield: 1 gallon

Ingredients:

7 pounds of chicken bones, large pieces of skin and fat removed

$1/2$ pound rough cut onions

$1/4$ pound rough cut leeks

$1/4$ pound rough cut celery

$1/4$ pound rough cut carrots

2 bay leaves

10 sprigs fresh thyme

20 black peppercorns

3 cloves garlic

2 tablespoons salt

6 quarts cold water

Method:

- Rinse the bones in cold water and place in a pot large enough to hold all the ingredients.

- Add the remaining ingredients and bring to a boil.

- Immediately reduce to a very gentle simmer and cook for five hours. It is important to skim any scum and fat that rises to the surface throughout the process.

- Strain the stock and discard the bones and aromatics. Cool the broth as quickly as possible and store in airtight containers in the fridge or in the freezer until needed.

Homemade Mayonnaise:

It is important to note the use of raw egg in this dish, as there are health issues associated with the consumption of raw eggs. This is really an excellent sauce, and you will be amazed by how different it is from the store bought stuff. Yield: 3 cups

Ingredients:

1 egg yolk

1 teaspoon white wine vinegar

1/2 teaspoon dry mustard

1/2 teaspoon lemon juice

1 teaspoon room temperature water

2 cups canola oil

1 splash Tabasco sauce

Salt and pepper to taste

Method:

- Place the egg yolk, vinegar, mustard, lemon juice, and water in the bowl and whisk until foamy (about one minute).

- Very slowly add the oil in a thin stream while continuously whisking until all the oil is incorporated and the mixture is thickened.

- Season with the Tabasco, and salt and pepper. Keep very cold and use within twenty-four hours.

Marinara Sauce:

There are so many tomato or marinara sauces available in the market these days that it seems only Italian grandmothers still make theirs at home. They do this because it is worth it. The following recipe contains a bit of pork, and it can be omitted for a still-wonderful sauce. Simply omit the pork and cut the cooking time in half. This can be frozen for months and lasts for two weeks in the fridge. Yield: 2 quarts

Ingredients:

1/4 cup extra virgin olive oil

1/2 pound pork neck bones

1 cup finely diced white onion

4 cloves minced garlic

1/4 cup chopped Italian parsley

Pinch of red pepper flakes

4 28-ounce cans of filetto di pomodoro (available at Italian markets) or whole San Marzano tomatoes gently crushed in your hand

8 basil leaves

2 teaspoons kosher salt

1 teaspoon freshly ground black pepper

Method:

- Heat the oil in a pot large enough to hold all of the ingredients over medium high heat.

- Add the pork bones and brown for about five minutes.

- Add the onion, garlic, parsley, and red pepper and cook, stirring occasionally for another five minutes.

- Add the remaining ingredients and bring to a boil.

- Immediately reduce to a gentle simmer and cook, partially covered, for 1 hour.

- Remove the pork bones. Some folks like to puree this sauce and others like it as-is, slightly chunky. If you like a smooth sauce, place immersion blender in the pot and blend until smooth.

- Cool and store in airtight containers.

GLOSSARY

Good lingo for you to know:

Acidulated water: Water that has some lemon juice or vinegar (acid) added to it in order to use as a batch to keep foods such as cut apples from browning.

Al forno: Italian for "cooked or baked in the oven."

Al dente: Italian for "to the tooth" often referred to in pasta cooking.

Baste: To spoon fats and meat juices over meats while they are roasting in the oven to promote browning.

Blanch: To plunge foods (usually vegetables) into boiling water very briefly and then to stop the process by plunging into ice water.

Broth: A flavored liquid made from boiling meats and vegetables in water. Used in soup and sauce making.

Caper: The small pickled unopened flower bud of a Mediterranean bush. Used mostly in sauces and condiments.

Chiffonade: Translates from French into "made of rags"; a way to finely cut food (mostly leaves such as basil) into very fine strands.

Deglaze: Adding liquid to a pan after meats have been sautéed in order to use in the complementing sauce.

Devein: Removing the "vein" which is really the digestive tract of shrimp.

Extract: Concentrated flavorings derived from foods usually by distillation or evaporation. Often used in baking.

Fiber (dietary): Also referred to as "roughage" which comes from plants and legumes and aids in digestion.

Folding: The method of gently adding a light and airy product (such as whipped cream) into a heavier product (such as custard).

Garum: An ancient Roman flavoring made from fermented fish. was used like salt.

Ginger coin: Slices of ginger root cut across the grain to make "coins"

Glaze: Coating foods with a glossy and shiny coating, often with some sugary component.

Herbs: The fragrant parts of plants used in cooking.

Hoisin sauce: A thick soy-based sauce used as a condiment and cooking ingredient in Chinese and Asian foods.

Induction cooking: A method of transferring heat by electromagnetic energy. A relatively new cooking method.

Jicama: A root vegetable often used in Mexican cooking. Mostly eaten raw, it tastes like a potato crossed with an apple.

Jus: Usually refers to the juices derived from roasting meats.

Knead: A technique of working with dough in order to develop its consistency.

Langustino: The Spanish word for shrimp or prawn.

Latke: A traditional Jewish potato pancake often fried in chicken fat during Chanukah.

Marinate: The process of seasoning meats, vegetables, or fish in a highly seasoned liquid.

Mayonnaise: A thick and creamy sauce made from egg yolks and oil and whipped together to form an emulsion.

Olive oil: The oil derived from pressing ripe olives and separating the oil from the liquid. The first cold pressing is referred to as extra virgin.

Pan drippings: The juices and fat left in a pan after meats have been roasted. Often used to make gravies.

Par boil: To boil foods briefly in order to quicken cooking time. Often done for dense foods such as carrots.

Pickle: A food that has been preserved in a seasoned brine of vinegar and salt. Often done with vegetables such as cucumbers.

Quinoa: A grain that was used by the Incas and called "the mother grain." It is incredibly nutritious and is considered a complete protein.

Reduce: To boil a liquid or sauce until it becomes thickened.

Roast: To cook foods (usually meats) in the oven. Roasting is considered a dry heat method of cooking. The term can also be applied to a large piece of meat.

Saffron: The world's most expensive spice derived from the stigmas of a crocus which is grown in Spain and Iran.

Sear: To brown meat in a very hot pan or under a broiler.

Toss: To turn foods over until they are well mixed as in a salad.

Vegan: A person who eats no animal foods or products made from animals. Some will not even eat honey as it is produced by bees.

Verjuice: An acidic, sour liquid made from unripened grapes and/or other fruits. Mostly used in salad dressing.

INDEX

243